T0199559

Democratic Governance and New Technology

This volume argues that new information and communication technologies (ICTs) play an important role in the process of restructuring and redefining basic relations within the political systems of Western democracies. It demonstrates that ICTs will therefore be central to new models of democracy.

The authors create an innovative theoretical framework to explore their argument. They begin with four models of democracy: consumer, demo-elitist, neo-republican and cyber. They then analyse a number of technologically mediated innovations in political practices (TMIPPs) in relation to these. Case studies highlight such TMIPPs as:

- the use of websites by political parties
- the development of electronic ID cards
- the use of closed-circuit television
- the emergence of virtual communities

Each case highlights relationships within the political system, such as governance and public services, local government and democracy, political parties and the information society and citizens and the state. In this way the development of ICTs is shown to impact upon core concepts of political science, including democracy and legitimacy.

Democratic Governance and New Technology brings together recent debates on electronic democracy and on crises of democracy and legitimation, thus offering a comprehensive reassessment of issues currently at the heart of political science.

Jens Hoff is an Associate Professor in the Department of Political Science, University of Copenhagen, Denmark.
Ivan Horrocks is a Lecturer in Management at the Scarman Centre, University of Leicester, UK.
Pieter Tops is a Professor in Public Administration at Tilburg University, the Netherlands.

Routledge/ECPR Studies in European Political Science

Formerly edited by Hans Keman, Vrije University, the Netherlands; now edited by Jan W. van Deth, University of Mannheim, Germany, on behalf of the European Consortium for Political Research

The Routledge/ECPR Studies in European Political Science series is published in association with the European Consortium for Political Research – the leading organisation concerned with the growth and development of political science in Europe. The series presents high-quality edited volumes on topics at the leading edge of current interest in political science and related fields, with contributions from European scholars and others who have presented work at ECPR workshops or research groups.

Democratic Governance and New Technology

Technologically mediated innovations in political practice in Western Europe

**Edited by Jens Hoff,
Ivan Horrocks and Pieter Tops**

Routledge
Taylor & Francis Group

LONDON AND NEW YORK

First published 2000
by Routledge
2 Park Square, Milton Park, Abingdon, Oxon, OX14 4RN

Simultaneously published in the USA and Canada
by Routledge
270 Madison Ave, New York NY 10016

Transferred to Digital Printing 2005

Routledge is an imprint of the Taylor & Francis Group

Editorial material selection © 2000 Jens Hoff, Ivan Horrocks and Pieter Tops

Individual chapters © 2000 the individual contributors

Typeset in Baskerville by Stephen Wright-Bouvier
of the Rainwater Consultancy, Faringdon, Oxfordshire

British Library Cataloguing in Publication Data
A catalogue record for this book is available
from the British Library

Library of Congress Cataloging in Publication Data
Democratic governance and new technology : technologically mediated
    innovations in political practice in Western Europe / edited by Ivan
    Horrocks, Jens Hoff, and Pieter Tops.
         p.   cm.
    Includes bibliographical references and index.
        1. Democracy. 2. Communication—Political aspects.
    3. Information society—Political aspects.   4. Information
    technology—Political aspects.   I. Horrocks, Ivan, 1955– .
    II. Hoff, Jens.   III. Tops, P. W., 1956– .
    JC421.D46384   1999
    320.94′ 0285—dc21   99–20556
                                                                              CIP

ISBN 0-415-18922-5

Contents

Illustrations

Figures

Tables

Contributors

Victor Bekkers is associate professor of public administration at Tilburg University. In 1997 and 1998 he was awarded a two-year post-doctoral fellowship of the Dutch Organization of Scientific Research (NWO), which enabled him to study the influence of ICTs on the boundaries of government organisations. One of the issues addressed in this study regarded ICTs and public service delivery.

Christine Bellamy is Professor of Public Administration at Nottingham Trent University. She has published widely on the development and use of new technology in public administration, and the relationship between new technology and democracy. She is the joint author of *Government in the Information Age* (Open University Press, 1998).

Marcel Boogers is Assistant Professor of Public Administration at Tilburg University, where he is affiliated with the Center for Law, Public Administration and Informatization. His research interests include local government, intergovernmental relations and the relationships between citizens and the government. He is currently involved in a research programme on ICT mediated patterns of governance and institutional change.

Wim van de Donk (1962) is Associate Professor of Public Administration. He holds a Masters Degree in political science and administrative sciences from Nijmegen University (1987, cum laude) and a PhD from Tilburg University (1997 cum laude). He is working at Tilburg University in the Centre for Law, Public Administration and Informatization of the Schoordijk Institute. He has published widely about the meaning of informatization for politics, democracy, law, policy-making and public administration. For his dissertation ('De Arena in Schema') he has won an annual award (G. A. Van Poelje jaarprijs) of the Dutch Association of Public Administration.

   Together with Prof. John Taylor he chairs the permanent study group on informatization in public administration of the European Group for Public Administration. He is a member of the Editorial Board of *Information Infrastructure and Policy*, the International Journal of Public Administration and Information, Communication and Society. He was and is (as project-manager) involved in many research projects in the field of informatization for Dutch ministries and did also work for the government of Galicia (Spain) and the Council of Europe. From 1990–1993 he was working in the Cabinet of the Minister of Justice and acting as an advisory member of a ministerial committee on the reorganization of the Dutch Health Care system.

He (co)edited books on expert systems in public administration (together with Snellen and Baquiast) informatization and democracy (with Snellen en Tops) and a 'handbook' on *Public Administration in an Information Age* (together with Snellen). He is also working in the field of the policies and politics of data protection, and co-edited (with Charles Raab and Colin Bennett) a special issue regarding these subjects of the *International Review of Administrative Sciences*. Recently he also was directing a research project aimed at a broad reassessment of the pilotage in the dutch sea-harbours, an assessment that made clear that ICTs have a profound impact on existing systems, positions, practices, opinions and beliefs. Together with colleagues from research groups in Irvine (California), Kassel (Germany), Nottingham/Glasgow (Scotland) he organizes international conferences and research projects. Statal and civil or voluntary organizations. See for recent research projects his home page at http://cwis.kub.nl frw/people/wimdonk/index.htm).

Jens Hoff is an associate professor at the Institute of Political Science, University of Copenhagen, where he teaches and does research in informatics and public administration. Between 1996 and 1998 he was director of the Centre for Research on Public Organization and Management in Copenhagen, and he is now the chairman of COST Action A14 on 'Government and Democracy in the Information Age'. He is the editor and co-author of a number of books on public administration, democracy and information technology and has published in numerous Danish and international journals.

Ivan Horrocks is a lecturer at the Scarman Centre for Public Order, University of Leicester.

Karl Löfgren is a Ph.D. student at the Institute of Political Science, Copenhagen University, and Centre for Research on Public Organisation and Management, Copenhagen Business School. He graduated in 1995 (public administration and Society, Science and Technology) from Roskilde University and University of East London, UK. His Ph.D. project includes the relationship between Information and Communication Technologies (ICTs) and democracy with a certain focus on political parties in Denmark and Sweden. (e-mail:kl.cos@cbs.dk)

Jacob Rosenkrands (MA in Political Science) has worked as a freelance journalist writing about ICT, for among others the Danish Board of Technology and the daily newspaper *Politiken*. He is now employed by the Danish Broadcasting Corporation (Danmarks Radio), and engaged in COST Action A14.

Kees Schalken is a Ph.D. student of Public Administration at Tilburg University, the Netherlands. He studied Legal Administration at Tilburg University, graduated in 1993 and specialised in local government. Since March 1993 he has worked as a research assistant at the Center for Law, Public Administration and Informatization, Tilburg University. His Ph.D. research concerns the effect of ICT on democracy. He is doing research on government involvement in on-line virtual communities and community networks such as FreeNets and Digital Cities.

Colin Smith BA (Hons) Politics & Modern History (Strathclyde), MSc Information and Administrative Management (Glasgow Caledonian). Currently lecturer in Business Information Management, Department of Business Administration, Glasgow Caledonian University, City Campus. His contribution draws on current Ph.D. research into the use of information and communications technologies by British political parties. He is a member of the Centre for the Study of Telematics and Governance (CSTAG), Glasgow Caledonian University.

Pieter Tops is professor of public administration at the Centre for Law, Public Administration and Informatization at Tilburg University in the Netherlands. His publications cover a range of subjects related to democracy, (local) politics and management and information and communication technology.

Gerrit Voerman is Director of the Documentation Centre for Dutch Political Parties at the University of Groningen. He has published widely on Dutch political parties. As a researcher he is interested in the development of political parties and the implications of ICTs in this respect. He is preparing a doctoral thesis on the relationship between the Dutch Communist Party and the Communist International in the interwar period.

C. William R. Webster is a researcher at the Centre for the Study of Telematics and Governance (CSTAG), Glasgow Caledonian University. He is currently completing a doctorate on the policy processes surrounding the uptake of Closed Circuit Television (CCTV) surveillance cameras in public places across the UK and has a number of publications in this area. His other research interests include developments in the delivery of electronic public services and citizenship, governance in the information age, electronic democracy and the relevance of telecommunications policy and regulation to these innovations. He is a member of the European Group of Public Administration (EGPA) Permanent Study Group on Informatization in Public Administration and the European Union Co-operation in the Field of Science and Technological Research (COST) Action 14, 'Government and Democracy in the Information Age' (GaDIA) research programme, e-mail: w.webster@gcal.ac.uk

Stavros Zouridis is a researcher at the Centre for Law, Public Administration and Informatization, Tilburg University. His research interests include information technology and the organisation of public administration, local democracy and the implications of information and communication technologies and the electronic highway for the openness of government and privacy.

Preface

This book can trace its origins back to September 1996. An application to the European Consortium for Political Research (ECPR) to convene a research planning group meeting, under the rubric 'Governance and Democracy in the Information Age' (or GaDIA as it became known) had been successful. As a result, a group of seven people from various European countries met in Heidelberg to discuss the possibility of establishing an on-going collaborative research programme to explore the relationship between new forms of information and communication technologies and the practices and processes of governance and democracy. Our initial objective was more specific, however. Amongst the members of the group there was widespread agreement that new technologies were playing an important – but largely unrecognised – role in the processes of restructuring and redefinition (or de-centring and re-centring to use the terms we originally chose) of relations within the polities of Western. European countries. We hope that this book goes some way to providing evidence and analysis to support this claim and thus meets the first objective of the GaDIA group.

Our second objective was to try to establish a permanent network of researchers within the EU countries who could continue to develop collaborative and comparative research in this field. Initially this idea got nowhere, until one of the editors of this book had the foresight to submit the research proposal prepared post-Heidelberg to the Danish Social Science Research Council for possible support of one kind or another. The outcome has taken our ideas beyond the confines of one country and led to the adoption of the proposal by Directorate General XII of the European Commission under the COST (Cooperation in the field of Scientific and Technical Research) Social Sciences Actions. The COST A14 Action, as GaDIA has now become, commenced in April 1998 and will run for a period of five years. It is already evident that this will lead to the fulfilment of the second objective of the original GaDIA group – the development of a broad-based, pan-European, network of researchers committed to developing collaborative and comparative research in the field of new information and communication technologies and governance and democracy.

Having provided something of the background to this book it remains for us to take this opportunity to acknowledge the role others have played in bringing this project to fruition. First, we should like to thank those friends and colleagues who made up the rest of the 'original' GaDIA group, namely John Taylor, Gerd-Michael Hellstern, Sara Eriksen and Christine Bellamy. It follows that we should also thank the ECPR for making the planning session possible in the first place.

Second, we would like to acknowledge the role of our respective institutions – Nottingham Trent University (and more recently the Scarman Centre, University of Leicester), Copenhagen Business School and the Department of Political Science, University of Copenhagen, and the Centre for Law, Informatization and Public Administration, University of Tilburg – in supporting our work on this book, and continuing to support our involvement with the A14 (GaDIA) programme.

Finally, we should acknowledge that without the support of the Danish Social Science Research Council and, subsequently, DG XII and the COST programme, this book, and the realisation of the European-wide research network which is now emerging, would almost certainly never have come to fruition.

Jens Hoff
Ivan Horrocks
Pieter Tops

Abbreviations

BBS	bulletin board systems
CCTV	closed circuit television
CIEC	Citizens' Internet Empowerment Coalition
CIS	computerised information systems
CMC	computer-mediated communication
FAQ	frequently asked questions
FOC	fear of crime
ICT	information and communication technology
IS	information systems
KWS	Keynesian welfare state
PEN	public electronic network
SCOT	social construction of technology
STS	science, technology, society
TMIPP	technologically mediated innovations in political practices

Introduction

New technology and the 'crises' of democracy

Jens Hoff, Ivan Horrocks and Pieter Tops

The focus of this book is the relationship between new forms of information and communication technology (ICT) and the current restructuring and redefinition of many of the fundamental relations within the political systems of the Western European countries. The basic claim in the book, and our main reason for writing it, is that ICT plays an important role in this process of restructuring and redefining. This role is not fully acknowledged by citizens, politicians, or most researchers (often because they are simply unaware of ICT-related developments) and definitely not analysed in any thorough or systematic fashion. What we want to do here, therefore, are basically two things: first, bring forward evidence indicating that ICT actually plays the role we claim; second, demonstrate that ICT therefore becomes part and parcel of different new 'visions' or models of democracy.

In discussing this topic we are informed by two debates which are often linked only superficially. The first is the debate on 'electronic democracy';[1] a topic which is currently enjoying a boom in popularity as evidenced by the attention given in books,[2] journals,[3] the mainstream mass media,[4] and of course on the Internet.[5] The second is the body of literature devoted to discussing the so-called 'crises of democracy' – literature which has, under such different headings as 'legitimation crises', 'ungovernability' and 'governance', attempted to detail and analyse the problems of political steering and democracy in Western countries during the last three decades.

Comment on each of these two debates is necessary in order to demonstrate our position in relation to each, and to illustrate the manner in which we attempt to bring these two debates together.

THE ELECTRONIC DEMOCRACY DEBATE

The debate on electronic democracy has historically been a lively one, and has increased in intensity in recent years especially on the Internet. While there is every reason to congratulate the many participants in these debates on their success in raising important democratic issues, intervening in policy debates, organising political actions and so on, the debate has, nevertheless, been flawed in at least three respects. First, it has focused too greatly on the technology itself at the expense of other aspects of democracy. Second, it has until quite recently been highly Americano–centric, which gives the debate a certain narrowness and brings into question its value outside the USA. Third, and again until relatively recently, much of the debate has been based on rather loose or normative speculation on future developments and thus lacked a solid empirical foundation on which to base comment and analysis.[6]

The overwhelming focus on technology, particularly the interactive and asynchronous features of the Internet, is particularly surprising given the existence of a number of works from the 1970s and 1980s which expose the limitations and problems associated with such a view. In particular, Arterton's (1987) evaluation of a number of experimental teledemocracy projects undertaken in the 1980s concluded that:

> the largest differences in the nature, the role, and the effectiveness of political participation were rooted not in technological capacity but in the models of participation that project initiators carried in their head. Essentially, what I had taken to be an examination of the capabilities of different technologies proved to be an exercise in evaluating a number of institutional arrangements or contexts in which citizens participate politically.
>
> (Arterton 1987: 26)

This view closely echoed that of Laudon (1977) and the subsequent work of Abrahamson et al. (1988). However, many participants in this debate still seem beset by a certain technological determinism, as expressed in ideas about the inherent democratic character or qualities of ICT and especially the Internet. Grossman, for example, has stated that 'the question is not whether the transformation to instant public feedback through electronics is good or bad, or politically desirable or undesirable. Like a force of nature, it is simply the way our political system is heading' (Grossman 1995: 154).

Even if this is a correct prognosis of the future of our political systems, it is our conviction that this kind of technological determinism constitutes a particularly bad point of departure for analysis. Thus, it excludes the possibility that human agency can make a difference in relation to the design and use of new technology. By so doing it reduces our awareness of the range of possible uses of ICT – as a perusal of contemporary IT/organisation studies research illustrates only too well (Knights and Murray 1994; Orlikowski and Baroudi 1991; Scarborough and Corbett 1992). Below we therefore present our view on new technology, which is inspired in particular by the so-called 'social construction of technology' literature (see e.g. Bijker 1995) but adds an institutional dimension to this approach. For this reason also we substitute electronic democracy – as a concept denoting the complex relationship between computer technology and political processes – with the concept 'technologically mediated innovations in political practices' – or TMIPPs as we shall refer to them from this point on. As we intend to demonstrate, it is by adopting this concept that we hope to avoid the determinism inherent in the concept of electronic democracy.

Much of the debate concerning electronic democracy, and the Internet in particular, has, and continues to focus on the American political system and its democratic problems. It is thus tainted heavily by the strong anti-establishment or anti-state tradition in the USA, and both right-wing groups as well as grass-roots movements, citizen initiatives, etc. seem to have found a common vehicle for their organising and criticising efforts in the Internet. As the primary aim of both of these groups is to bring 'government back to the people', they have consequently formulated visions for a 'cyberdemocracy'. However, their strategies are, not surprisingly, very different. Thus, on the one hand, conservatives and libertarians stress the importance of a free market and unfettered capitalism.[7] While, on the other hand, liberal and communitarian citizen initiatives stress community values and self-empowerment.[8] Both groups have, however, formulated visions for a direct, electronic democracy in which there is little, if any, role for elected representatives and Congress. An important part of this particular debate on electronic democracy therefore focuses on the pros and cons of direct versus representative democracy. To us, this seems a somewhat narrow discussion, which neglects most of the subtleties and actual problems involved in discussing democratic steering.[9] Finally, it is also important to note that the domination of the electronic democracy debate by American academics and commentators means that it focuses largely on the special characteristics of the US political system; i.e. the strong separation of powers and the complicated relations between the different administrative levels in the federal structure. Both of these features make the US political system quite unique, meaning that there is reason to question the relevance for Europe of many of the American experiences and ideas concerning electronic democracy.

THE 'CRISES OF DEMOCRACY' DEBATE

The 'crises of democracy' debate has run through different stages in the post-war period. In the 1970s and the early 1980s the debate was dominated by the systems-oriented theories of Jürgen Habermas and Claus Offe.[10] The main thrust in these works is that the clash between, or mix of, the rationalities of the market, democracy and bureaucracy, necessitated by the accumulation problems in late capitalism, produced both problems of steering ('steering pathologies') for the state, as well as a more or less manifest 'legitimation deficit', or a 'legitimation crisis'.[11]

Both the concepts of 'steering crisis' and 'legitimation crisis' have haunted the debate on democratic steering since then. However, towards the end of the 1970s the debate took a neo-liberal turn. The focus was now mainly on the steering problems of the Western welfare states, and the problem was formulated as either an 'overload' problem (i.e. citizens, organisations and firms demanding 'too much' of the state, see Crozier et al. 1975), or as a question of 'ungovernability' mainly caused by the budget maximising behaviour of state agencies and bureaucrats (Niskanen 1971). However, in those welfare states with strong Social Democratic parties there remained some discussion about the 'legitimation crisis'; a 'crisis' which was now primarily regarded as being caused by a diminishing solidarity with the welfare state due to the undermining of the principle of equality, and corresponding increase in incidents of tax evasion, the 'black economy', 'sponging' of welfare benefits and so on (Rold Andersen 1984).

Towards the end of the 1980s the crises of democracy debate took yet another turn. As criticism and refinement of the neo-corporatist literature continued (Schmitter 1982) different analyses demonstrated how the state was becoming fragmented and/or poly-centred, and how many policies were formulated in networks including a range of both public and private actors (see e.g. Marin and Mayntz 1991). The term 'policy networks' which had been devised and employed to characterise such developments now gradually seemed to be supplanted by the term 'governance' as the dominant concept (Kooiman 1993; Rhodes 1997; Stoker 1998). However, the term 'governance', or 'democratic governance', also seemed to indicate a shift away from a top-down oriented means of perceiving political steering, towards an understanding of steering as also consisting of horizontal relationships (heterarcy), and as something in which the creation of capabilities and identities of different actors plays a major role (March and Olsen 1995).

The advent and recognition of a governance mode of steering has seriously brought into question the once dominant model of democratic steering – the electoral chain of command or the constitutional model – both as a normative frame of reference and as an analytical tool (see Fig. 1). This development has made many contemporary researchers, politicians and concerned citizens uneasy commuters between adherence to the 'constitutional model' and other more 'realistic' (i.e. governance) models.

The way in which we see the debates concerning electronic democracy and crises of democracy converging is through the first question which springs to mind when one is concerned about the uses of ICT in the political world:

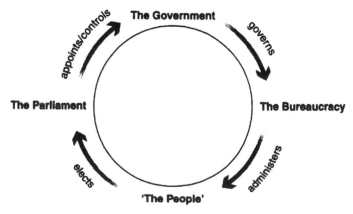

Figure 1 The electoral chain of command or the constitutional model

whether the types of ICTs that we now see being used and introduced in politics and in the political–administrative systems in Western Europe are meant to restore or reinvent 'the electoral chain of command' or whether they are part of new political practices pointing towards the development of new models of democracy? This is our fundamental research question. Furthermore, posing it in this way is important if we are to explore the relationship between governance, democracy and new technology. For example, what types of TMIPPs are being developed in different European countries? Do we see national variations, and why? Do these developments lead to greater national variations in democratic practices or to greater uniformity? Which political actors support or oppose which TMIPPs? And how do these actors formulate the relationship between ICT and other aspects of democracy, such as citizens' rights or the role of parliament?

THEORY AND METHODOLOGY

In attempting to address these questions we employ a series of exemplary case studies, chosen specifically to illustrate the role which different TMIPPs play in different relations within the political–administrative systems in three Western European countries: the United Kingdom, the Netherlands and Denmark. In the European context these countries are normally thought of as being in the forefront concerning the introduction and use of ICT. In order to be able to draw democratically and politically relevant conclusions from these case studies – which deal with different countries and different sets of relationships within the polity – we have constructed an analytical framework loose enough to allow the specificity of each case to emerge, yet tight enough to allow comparison.

Our analytical strategy has been to construct a number of models of democracy on the basis of a review of contemporary literature on the crises of democracy and changes in political and administrative processes, as well as the literature on electronic democracy. We are using the term 'model' here to denote the building of a set of 'theoretical constructs designed to reveal the chief elements of democratic form(s) and (their) underlying structure or relations' (Held 1987: 6). On the basis of our review we have devised four models of democracy. These models can all be seen as 'emergent' models of democracy in which ICT plays a role. Also, they can all be compared with or contrasted to the 'electoral chain of command', and seen as different ways of renewing democratic steering relations.

These four models of democracy seem to be fighting to gain hegemony in the current processes of restructuring and redefinition of Western democracy. Each of the models seems to combine – more or less explicitly – ideas on uses of ICT with certain conception(s) of citizenship embodying certain political values and certain ideas on political steering/democratic governance that also embody certain democratic procedural norms. In so doing they lead to certain understandings of the use of ICT in the 'political' world, which typically results in the aforementioned technologically mediated innovations in political practices (TMIPPs) (see Fig. 2). Our reference to a struggle for hegemony indicates that we see these models as (conflicting) existing or developing discourses which contain both practices and strategies adopted and/or pursued by certain actors or coalitions of actors in their attempt to dominate democratic development.

This analytical scheme – four emerging models of democracy for the information age perceived as discourses, practices and strategies – makes it possible for us to undertake a thorough assessment of the political and democratic roles which different TMIPPs seem to be playing at the moment. More specifically, using the concept of 'model' makes it possible for us to analyse how different ICTs in daily practice are related to (articulated with) certain democratic elements, and the way in which these relations are stabilised. In addition, it also makes it possible for us to analyse whether a specific country seems to be moving towards a certain model, and whether differences between countries are becoming more or less significant. Thus, by treating the models as discourses the authors of the different case studies have been forced to focus on the way in which the relationships between ICTs, conceptions of citizenship and democratic governance are articulated. This highlights the 'blind spots' that exist in much of the literature on electronic democracy concerning the conceptions of citizenship and governance that are really implied in this literature.[12] Treating the models as strategies makes it possible to discuss which actors participate in the struggle for any one model to become dominant. In addition, it makes it possible to analyse how the various actors, whether from the commercial or public sector or civil society, engage in this struggle, make alliances, shift their standpoints, and so on.

In Chapter 2 we set out our four different models in much greater detail, specifying the relationship between dominant ICTs, conceptions of citizenship and ideas on democratic governance in each of the models. Our theoretical approach and standpoint is – as we explain and elaborate in Chapter 1 – eclectic, combining elements of theories of democracy, citizenship, governance and technology. We are normative in the sense that our main preoccupation is a concern for democracy, and the threats and possibilities confronting it through the development of an ever-increasing number of TMIPPs. Our four models of democracy therefore act as our basic standard for evaluating these developments. However, we try not to be prescriptive, suggesting that no one model is necessarily 'better' or preferable to any other. Nevertheless, it is clear that we cannot fully live up to this kind of objectivity and have personal preferences for models which stress the necessity of empowering citizens, and which stimulate their possibilities of becoming publicly spirited persons willing and able to participate in public life and to take on the responsibilities that such engagement inevitably involves.

Our methodology is constructivist as our focus is on how (political) uses of ICT become a part of the restructuring and redefinition of a number of relations within the political systems of various countries. Thus, we use a number of case studies to analyse the restructuring/redefinition of the most

	Consumer	*Demo-elitist*	*Neo-republican*	*Cyberdemocratic*
View on citizenship	(neo-liberal)	(pluralist) liberal	Republican/ social democratic	Communitarian/radical democratic
Dominant democratic value	Freedom of choice	Effectiveness	Deliberation and participation	Community, acceptance of diversity
Political nexus	'moment of truth' (producer/consumer relation)	Expert discourse	Public sphere, media	Electronic discussion (Internet)
Central form of political participation	Choice of public services (exit)	Consensus creation, lobbying	Public debate, associations	Virtual debate, virtual and real actions
Main political intermediary	Service declarations, consumption data	Negotiation and campaign institutions	Meetings, hearings (real and virtual)	Electronic networks, electronic communities
Dominant procedural norm	Development of capabilities (rights)	Development of adaptive political system	Development of identities, development of adaptive political system	Development of identities, development of capabilities (competences)
Typical ICT application	These will emerge from the case studies, see Figure 6, Chapter 11			
Dominant political issues	[Ditto above]			
Dominant democratic ambiguities	[Ditto above]			

Figure 2 Emerging models of democracy for the information age (1): main features

important relations within these systems: the relation between citizens and their political representatives (political parties and organisations), between citizens and administration and among citizens themselves when they meet (in reality and virtuality) to solve problems of common concern.[13] These case studies enable comparisons between countries within each relation, and thus generalisations at a certain level. However, arriving at such generalisations (conclusions) is only part of our aim. Our ambition also involves the construction of an exploratory research design meant to generate a number of hypotheses which can constitute the basis of a new, genuinely comparative research project.[14]

Notes

1 As others have noted (cf. Hagen 1998) the term 'electronic democracy' is very impre-
cise, if by the term one wants to discuss the complex relationship between computer
technology and political processes. Thus, it can also refer, for example, to the use of
an electronic microphone or television. The term 'digital democracy' would be more
precise in terms of what most of the debate concerns (see Percy-Smith 1995). Terms
such as cyberdemocracy (Ogden 1994; Poster 1995; Tsagarousianou et al. 1998),
virtual democracy, information age democracy (Snider 1994) and teledemocracy (e.g.
Becker 1981; Arterton 1987) have also been used. However, the term 'electronic
democracy' seems to be the most widely used and understood, and we shall therefore
use it here, at least initially, when referring generally to relations between computer
technology and political processes. However, as we make clear in this chapter, we
would like to substitute it with the term 'technologically-mediated-innovations-in-
political-practices' or TMIPPs.

2 See e.g. Tsagarousianou et al. 1998; Bellamy and Taylor 1998; Calabrese and Borchert
1996; Friedland 1996; van de Donk et al. 1995.

3 Journals such as *Media, Culture and Society* and *Communications Quarterly*, and periodicals
such as *Wired* and *The Futurist* have had numerous contributions discussing different
aspects of electronic democracy.

4 Since early 1996 features on democracy and new technology have been regularly
aired on a wide range of programmes dealing with new technology on BBC 2 and
Channel 4 in Britain. In addition all the broadsheet newspapers (e.g. *The Guardian,
Independent, Financial Times*, etc.) have featured similar articles.

5 Electronic democracy is being discussed and practised in numerous locations on the
Internet. Among the more well established and well known are Minnesota E–democracy
(http://freenet.msp.mn.us/govt/e–democracy/), Vote Smart Web (http://www.vote-
smart.org), The Well (http://www.well.com), Electronic Frontier Foundation (http:/
www.eff.org) and Global Democracy Network (http://www.gdn.org). While these older
sites are typically American, newer European sites have been established, and are gradually becoming well known. See e.g. UK Citizens Online Democracy (http://www.
democracy.org.uk) or De Digitale Stad (http://www.dds.nl/)

6 See e.g. Bimber 1998; van de Donk et al. 1995; and Tsagarousianou et al. 1998. This
book can also be seen as an attempt at closing this gap.

7 These groups are championed by the Progress and Freedom Foundation (PFF), whose
Magna Carta for the Knowledge Age was the first attempt to create a political theory
of cyberspace. Its authors include Alvin Toffler, James Keyworth, a former Reagan
technology adviser, Esther Dyson and George Gilder. The PFF is close to Newt
Gingrich (Hagen 1998; Bredekamp 1996).

8 An exponent for these groups is Howard Rheingold, who has formulated a
community-oriented version of cyberdemocracy (The Virtual Community). He is
associated with the above-mentioned Bulletin Board System The Well. His ideas are
widely shared by others; see e.g. Poster 1995; Doheny-Farina 1996.

9 An example of the issues we think important to bring into such discussion can be
found in Horrocks and Bellamy 1997.

10 Habermas's book *Legitimationsprobleme im Spätkapitalismus* was first published in 1973,
and also Offe published various works in the 1970s, a collection of which is presented
in John Keane's (ed.): *Contradictions of the Welfare State* (1984).

11 This idea is developed in much greater detail in Habermas's monumental work:
Theorie des Kommunikativen Handelns, where he puts forward his ideas on the colonialisa-
tion of the life-world by the systems-world (1981: Band 2: 447 ff).

12 Hagen (1998), who is one of the few researchers who have worked with models of
electronic democracy in a way which is somewhat familiar with ours, operates with
three models: teledemocracy, cyberdemocracy and electronic democratisation. These

models have some similarities with what we call the neo-republican, the cyberdemocracy and the constitutional model. However, he has no models which correspond to the models we refer to as demo-elitist and consumer democracy. These are the models that are most disappointing from a participatory democratic standpoint and it is symptomatic of much of the literature that these are the ones that remain unexplored in the elaboration of models of democracy for the information age based solely on discussions of electronic democracy.

13 The role of governments will not be discussed in this book. This is a clear shortcoming in our attempt to cover all important relations within the political system. We will try to overcome this deficiency in our next round of studies. For contributions dealing with this aspect, see e.g. Frantzich 1982 and Hoschka, Butscher and Streitz 1992.

14 Such work is now underway through the setting up of a number of work groups under the COST Action A14 *(Government and Democracy in the Information Age)*. However, these work groups will also consider or work on the basis of other theoretical frameworks.

References

Abrahamson, J. B., Arterton, F. C. and Orren, G. R. (1988) *The Electronic Commonwealth: The Impact of New Technologies upon Democratic Politics*, New York: Basic Books.

Arterton, F. C. (1987) *Teledemocracy: Can Technology Protect Democracy?*, London: Sage Publications.

Becker, T. (1981) *The Futurist* December.

Bellamy, C. and Taylor, J. A. (1998) *Governing in the Information Age*, Buckingham: Open University Press.

Bijker, W. E. (1995) *Of Bicycles, Bakelites and Bulbs: Towards a Theory of Sociotechnical Change*, Cambridge, Mass.: The MIT Press.

Bimber, B. (1998) 'Towards an empirical map of political participation on the Internet', paper presented at the 1998 annual meeting of the American Political Science Association, Boston, USA, September 3–6.

Bredekamp, H. (1996) 'Cyberspace, ein Geisterreich', in *FAZ 3.2., Bilder und Zeiten.*

Calabrese, A. and Borchert, M. (1996) 'Prospects for electronic democracy in the United States: rethinking communication and social policy', *Media, Culture and Society* 18 (2): 249–268.

Crozier, M. et al. (eds) (1975) *The Crises of Democracy*, New York: New York University Press.

Doheny-Farina, S. (1996) *The Wired Neighbourhood*, New Haven and London: Yale University Press.

Frantzich, S. E. (1982) *Computers in Congress: The Politics of Information*, Beverly Hills, Calif.: Sage Publications.

Friedland, L. A. (1996) 'Electronic democracy and the new citizenship', *Media, Culture and Society* 18 (2): 185–212.

Grossman, L. K. (1995) *The Electronic Republic: Reshaping Democracy in the Information Age*, New York: Viking (20th Century Fund).

Habermas, J. (1973) *Legitimationsprobleme im Spätkapitalismus*, Frankfurt am Main: Suhrkamp Verlag.

——(1981) *Theorie des Kommunikativen Handelns*, Frankfurt am Main: Suhrkamp Verlag.

Hagen, M. (1998) 'A typology of electronic democracy', Internet paper downloaded from http://www.uni-giessen.de/fb03/vinci/labore/netz/hag–en.htm. A longer version with the title 'A road to electronic democracy? Politische Theorie, Politik und der Information Superhighway in den USA' is found in Hans J. Kleinsteuber (ed.) *Der 'Information Superhighway'*, Opladen: Westdeutscher Verlag, pp. 63–85.

Held, D. (1987) *Models of Democracy*, Cambridge: Polity Press.

Horrocks, I. and Bellamy, C. (1997) 'Telematics and community governance: issues for policy and practice', *International Journal of Public Sector Management* 10 (5): 377–387.

Hoschka, P., Butscher, B. and Streitz, N. (1992) 'telecooperation and telepresence: technical challenges of a government distributed between Bonn and Berlin', *Informatization and the Public Sector* 2 (4): 269–299.

Keane, J. (ed.)(1984) *Contradictions of the Welfare State* [Claus Offe], London: Hutchinson.

Knights, D. and Murray, F. (1994) *Managers Divided: Organisation Politics and Information Technology Management*, Chichester: John Wiley & Sons.

Kooiman, J. (ed.)(1993) *Modern Governance*, London: Sage.

Laudon, K. (1977) *Communications Technology and Democratic Participation*, New York: Praeger.

March, J. G. and Olsen, J. P. (1995) *Democratic Governance*, New York: The Free Press.

Marin, B. and Mayntz, R. (eds)(1991) *Policy Networks: Empirical Evidence and Theoretical Considerations*, Frankfurt an Main: Campus Verlag.

Niskanen, W. A., Jr. (1971) *Bureaucracy and Representative Government*, Chicago and New York: Aldine-Atherton.

Ogden, M. R. (1994) 'Politics in a parallel universe: is there a future for cyberdemocracy?', *Futures* 26 (7): 713–729.

Orlikowski, W. J. and Baroudi, J. J. (1991) 'Studying information technology in organizations: research approaches and assumptions', *Information Systems Research* 2(1): 1–28.

Percy-Smith, J. (1995) *Digital Democracy: Information and Communication Technologies In Local Politics*, London: Commission for Local Democracy.

Poster, M. (1995) 'Cyberdemocracy: Internet and the public sphere', MS., University of California, Irvine, downloaded from http://www.hnet.uci.edu/mposter/writings/democ.html.

Rhodes, R. A. W. (1997) *Understanding Governance*, Buckingham: Open University Press.

Rold Andersen, B. (1984) *Kan vi bevare velfærdsstaten?*, København: AKF Forlag.

Scarborough, H. and Corbett, J. M. (1992) *Technology and Organization: Power, Meaning and Design*, London: Routledge.

Schmitter, P. C. (1982) 'Interest intermediation and regime governability in contemporary Western Europe and North America', in S. Berger (ed.) *Organizing Interests in Western Europe*, Cambridge: Cambridge University Press.

Snider, J. H. (1994) 'Democracy on-line: tomorrow's electronic electorate', *The Futurist* September/October: 15–19.

Stoker, G. (1998) 'Local governance', *International Social Science Journal* 155 (March): 17–28.

Tsagarousianou, R., Tambini, D. and Bryan, C. (eds) (1998) *Cyberdemocracy – Technology, Cities and Civic Networks*, London: Routledge.

van de Donk, W. B. H. J. et al. (eds) (1995) *Orwell in Athens: A Perspective on Informatization and Democracy*, Amsterdam: IOS Press.

Part I
The nature of the problem

1 Technology and social change

The path between technological determinism, social constructivism and new institutionalism

Jens Hoff

At the present stage in the development of theories dealing with technology in general and ICT in particular it may seem like a waste of time to once again take up the issue of technological determinism, and to properly criticise and refute the notion. However, as we noted above, the idea of technological artefacts[1] or technological systems with a certain rationality and a certain telos – a built-in future which will inevitably unfold itself across time and space – continues to have a strong attraction. This, we will argue, is for obvious reasons. Thus, we have all in our daily lives experienced how certain technological artefacts dictate our behaviour – how a car, an electricity system, a piece of software allows, enables, forbids or constrains us in doing certain things. For most people these artefacts represent 'facts' or 'reality'; something we have to live with and can do little about.[2] And as technology 'develops' we adapt, because there seems little else to do. These every-day observations of how technology seems to 'determine' our behaviour easily leads to the attribution of agency to the technological artefacts themselves. This attribution is the basis of technological determinism, and it is a way of perceiving technology which is quite compatible with the heritage of the Enlightenment, and which is therefore deeply rooted in Western culture.[3] This deep-rootedness means that technological determinism as a mode of perceiving the role of technology in society is difficult to do away with; probably more so than its critics expect. Furthermore, the showdown with technological determinism is impeded by three factors. First, more 'advanced' theories for understanding the role of technology in society, for example the 'social construction of technology' (SCOT) theory, seem to have a difficult time being acknowledged by hardware/software developers and vendors, the community of politicians and other decision-makers. Second, even though such theories are moving to the centre stage in the social sciences' attempt to understand technology, their diffusion to the natural sciences, for example, seems to be limited. Third, these theories are still in a developmental mode, and are thus, in our view, flawed in some respects. This might be one of the reasons for the lack of diffusion to other spheres of society, even though there are surely also other forces at work here.

Let us start by looking at our point of departure for discussing the role of technology in society: the SCOT approach. The SCOT approach is a theoretical framework for studying the development and working of technological artefacts which has gradually developed from STS (science, technology, society) studies and study programmes. It is probably formulated in its most coherent form in Bijker (1995a).⁴ It takes its point of departure in the idea that there is no such thing as 'reality' per se, but that 'reality' is instead a social construction. This idea had already been put forward by symbolic interactionism in the 1960s (see i.e. Mead 1964; Blumer 1986), and brought into mainstream sociology by Berger and Luckmann (1966). As humans, we can only perceive the world around us through our own interpretation. The question of what 'reality' is then becomes a question of with how many other people we share the same interpretation, or, put differently, a question of the social context and the social interactions in which we find ourselves. If we accept this argument, technology cannot be regarded as a 'given' (as in technological determinism), but must be seen as socially constructed like all other social phenomena. The object of study for the SCOT theory is therefore the processes through which a given technology is socially constructed.

More specifically, the SCOT theory is inspired by semiotics, a linguistic approach dealing with the origin of meaning through an analysis of language and signs. A semiotic analysis takes its departure from the sign (an expression which represents content). If technology is approached from this angle, it can be seen as an expression with a content, i.e. not a neutral value. This approach makes it possible to analyse the processes of technological development as a sign around which meaning (content) is constructed through constant interpretation and reinterpretation. For the sign to make sense, it must be understood by more than one person; i.e. two or more persons must share the same code. Other groups can use and interpret the same sign, but have other codes attached to it. In the SCOT theory, technology is seen as an interpretable sign which only makes sense in relation to the social context it is a part of. Thus, technology is developed and becomes obdurate through social actions where actors (individuals, social groups) exchange messages about how a given technology should be interpreted. When a high degree of consensus (see below) about the interpretation of this technology has been reached, it becomes a 'reality' with characteristics that makes it look independent of the social groups participating in the shaping of the technology.

Methodologically, the SCOT theory departs from a given artefact (the bicycle, bakelite, the photoelectric lighting kit, etc.). The artefact is then deconstructed by considering the creation of the artefact through the eyes of the relevant social groups. A social group is relevant to the researcher as soon as it actively and explicitly takes a position in relation to a given technology (Bijker 1995a: 48). The method then seeks to identify different groups with different interpretations of problems and solutions which are said to constitute different technological frames. Those actors sharing the same interpretations are in the same relevant social group, and a certain technological frame is said to structure the interactions among the actors of a given relevant social group.

What Bijker attempts to demonstrate by this method is that a given technology can be interpreted in many different ways; or that what Bijker calls 'flexible interpretation' always exists. Actually it is possible, after the deconstruction process, to talk about the existence of as many artefacts as there are interpretations.

Having deconstructed a certain technological artefact, the SCOT analysis then moves to an analysis of the social construction of the artefact; or towards an understanding of how the degrees of freedom in interpretations are gradually reduced. This reduction takes place through two processes which the SCOT theory calls 'stabilisation' and 'closure'. Stabilisation can be determined by a rhetorical analysis first employed in science studies by Latour and Woolgar (1979). Bijker writes:

> They showed that in the construction of scientific facts 'modalities' are attached or withdrawn from statements about facts, thus connoting the degree of stabilisation of that fact. Thus the statements: 'The experiments claim to show the existence of X', 'The experiments show the existence of X' and 'X exists' exhibit progressively fewer modalities and thereby show progressively greater degrees of stabilisation of X.
>
> (Bijker 1995*a*: 86)

Closure is a process which takes place between the relevant social groups indicating a decrease in the flexibility which is used to characterise the artefact. A closure is the end of controversy about the interpretation of the meaning of the artefact. Thus, closure is about reaching consensus on the dominant meaning of the artefact. When a closure process has taken place it is almost irreversible.[5]

The processes of stabilisation and closure involve the merging of many relevant social groups and technological frames into one big structure called the 'sociotechnological ensemble'. The driving force in the creation of a given sociotechnological ensemble are power relations. These power relations are described as 'the power coin' with semiotic power, on the one side, and micro-politics, on the other side. Meaning is developed as a result of an abundance of micro-political forces: formulation of problem-solving strategies, theories and experiments. This mode of power is seen as anchored in the actors, and as liberating. Semiotic power, on the other hand, is seen as constraining. Semiotic power manifests itself when flexible interpretation is decreasing and the controversy is in its closing phase. When a sociotechnological ensemble reaches a state of obduracy, power relations are fixed and the technology's meaning 'forms part of an enduring network of practices, theories and social institutions' (Bijker 1995*b*).[6]

For our purposes there are many insights to be gained from the SCOT theory. First, in our view, the constructivism represented by this approach seems able to provide a much deeper and more multi-faceted understanding of the development of (a given) technology than for example the linear and teleological accounts produced by technological determinism. Second, the notions of 'interpretative flexibility', 'stabilisation' and 'closure' seems very useful for understanding the development of TMIPPs. Thus, most of the innovations we are discussing in the case studies still seem to be in an initial stage where interpretative flexibility is high, but where there are also attempts at stabilisation and closure by many different actors. This is especially clear in the case studies on the citizen card and closed circuit television. However, we will not be using these three concepts directly in our case studies, but will instead rely on the notion of *discourse* (see below), which encompasses all three concepts. There are two reasons why we find this notion better suited for our purposes than the concepts suggested by the SCOT approach. First, in our view the theory of discourse provides a better explanation of why 'closure' is never finite, or why no identity or meaning can ever be fully constituted, and is always open to rearticulation. Second, our aim is broader than the SCOT theory. Thus, we are not interested in the construction of technology per se, but in models of democracy for the information age. These include not only technology or a given technological artefact (type of ICT), but also ideas on what role this artefact should play in relation to citizenship and democratic procedures (see Fig. 3).

We are also intrigued by the SCOT theory's notion of the 'sociotechnical ensemble' and the idea of 'semiotic power' and 'micro-politics' as the two sides of the 'power coin'. However, we think there are several problems involved in what we see as an attempt to construct a dichotomy or analytical distinction between actor and structure. Thus, the idea of 'semiotic power' (as well as that of the 'sociotechnical ensemble') is clearly an attempt at constructing a concept of structure, while the notion of 'micro-politics' can be seen as an attempt at constructing a concept of actor. If this is the case, which we assume it is,[7] we do not understand why semiotic power is seen as constraining only, and micro-politics or micro-political power as liberating or enabling only. To us, structures (structural power) must be seen as both enabling and constraining, and the same goes for actors – or rather relations between actors. In other words what we imply here is that we see the way in which the SCOT theory tries to conceptu-

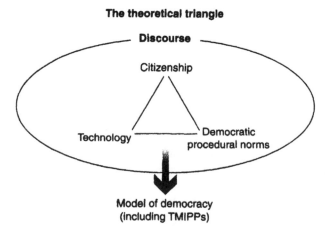

Figure 3 Models of democracy for the information age

alise the actor/structure duality as deficient. This deficiency is particularly pronounced as far as structure is concerned. However, we are convinced that the deficiency can be repaired by incorporating Giddens's idea of 'the duality of structure' (Giddens 1984: 25 ff.) as well as certain elements of new institutionalism in the SCOT framework (see below).

In our view there are two major criticisms of the SCOT theory. The first one, which we have already started discussing, is the faulty conceptualisation of the actor/structure duality. The other one concerns the problem of how the theory constitutes its object of analysis (i.e. technology).

Concerning the first criticism, Bijker has made clear that he is well aware of the enabling and constraining character of both structure and the strategies of actors. However, in their empirical analyses the adherents of the SCOT theory always seem to (over) emphasise the actor perspective, leading one to believe that a macro-system or an 'ensemble' is the sum of a long line of aggregated micro-events that are completely coincidental depending on who is signing up as 'relevant social actors/groups'. It is never mentioned that certain actors may have no choice but to take part in the construction process or are always left out, while others somehow always occupy central positions in the construction processes. As we noted above, we are convinced that this problem can be overcome by, at a general level, introducing the idea of the 'duality of structure', and introducing the concept of institution from the new institutionalism. The idea of the 'duality of structure' is that structures[8] must be seen as both objective forces and socially constructed phenomena. Objective in the sense that, qua the rules and resources they embody, they set the scene within which the social interaction between actors can take place. This social interaction, in turn, has the potential of changing (or reproducing) the structure(s) in question. Thus, structures must be seen both as the 'frozen' result of earlier social interactions but also as involved in current social interaction.[9]

The advantage of this approach to actor and structure is that it ends the fruitless discussions about the prioritising of actor or structure. Furthermore, it has the advantage of specifying more precisely (than, for example, the SCOT approach) what we should understand by structure (see note 8), and to introduce us to the importance of institutions. Thus, Giddens continues his discussion of structure by writing that 'The most important aspects of structure are rules and resources recursively involved in institutions. Institutions by definition are the more enduring features of social life. In speaking of the structural properties of social systems I mean their institutionalised features, giving "solidity" across time and space' (Giddens 1984: 24).

The concept of 'institution' is developed further and occupies a central position in the 'new institutionalism' of, for example, March and Olsen (1989, 1995). They define institutions as:

Collections of interrelated *rules* and routines that define appropriate action in terms of relations between roles and situations. The process involves determining what the situation is, what role is being fulfilled, and what the obligations of that role in the situations are.

(March and Olsen 1989: 160)[10]

Rules again are: 'routines, procedures, conventions, roles, strategies, organisational forms and technologies around which (political) activity is constructed'.

(ibid. 22)

Structure, perceived as a pattern of institutions, therefore cannot be seen as just a passive constraining or determining factor, but plays an active role in establishing islands of order in society, within which the interest and preferences of actors are formed, and within which they are therefore assumed to act according to a certain 'logic of appropriateness'. This does not mean that actors cannot 'act otherwise' but only seeks to explain how the horizon of actions are finite, formed as it is by the rules and resources of a given institution.

Thus, in our view the SCOT theory could gain a lot by seeing technological frames and sociotechnological ensembles as institutions, and stabilisation and closure as processes of institutionalisation. Such a perspective would provide the theory with a clearer understanding of how technological frames and sociotechnological ensembles are constraining/enabling the actions of actors through the rules and resources embodied in these institutions. The perspective would also enhance the SCOT approach's understanding of 'the obduracy of technology' which is better seen as rules and resources creating so-called 'path-dependencies' (Thelen and Steinmo 1992).

The second criticism of the SCOT theory has to do with the problem of how it constitutes technology as its object of analysis. Some refer to this problem as the 'black box' problem (Button 1993; Knights and Murray 1994) and claim that the SCOT theory does not pay enough attention to technology sui generis. This is also the line of criticism followed by Mayntz and Hughes, who claim that social constructivist perspectives on technology pay insufficient attention to especially large technical systems as institutions embodying a specific 'technological rationality' (Mayntz and Hughes 1988: 18–20).[11]

In our view this criticism touches on a soft spot in the SCOT theory but is nonetheless somewhat misplaced. Thus, it is simply not true that the theory pays insufficient attention to the working of a given technology. On the contrary, it takes great pains to analyse all the different possible uses and interpretations of a technological artefact, for example, the bicycle (Bijker 1995*a*: 19–100). In fact Bijker himself claims that he is establishing technology, or rather the 'sociotechnical ensemble' as an object sui generis. In so doing he tries to escape social reductionism, in which the technical is explained as a by-product of the social (ibid. 274).

It is, however, an open question if he is successful in this endeavour. Thus, the SCOT theory insists that a society should be seen as a 'seamless web', and that no a priori distinctions between for example the social, the technical, the scientific or the social world should be made (ibid. 13). To us, this is mistaking a normative (philosophical) position with the necessity of an analytical science to construct its object. The reason for this is simple: if science does not construct its object of analysis it remains unable to explain how the object makes a difference in the world.[12] The implication of this for our studies is that if we do not, a priori, define something we call technology (ICT), with certain differentia specifica we will remain unable to account for how this technology makes a difference. As far as we are concerned, we do not see any contradiction between this position, and the account of technology, or rather technological frames and sociotechnical ensembles, as socially constructed.

We can therefore now move to define technology which we do in accordance with Knights and Murray. They define technology in the field of ICT as:

A)   technological artefacts, such as computers and software;
B)   technological knowledge, in particular systems development skills;
C)   technological workers and managers who are engaged in particular systems development and information systems (IS) specialists;
D)   the culture of technology, or the signs, symbols and values brought to bear in discussing, using and developing technology.

(Knights and Murray 1994: 47)

Technology constitutes the first element in our theoretical triangle (see Fig. 3). The two other elements of the triangle are the different perception and practices of citizenship and of the different democratic procedural norms, which we believe exist in Western European societies. Articulated (interpreted and expressed) together these elements, in various versions, combine to form different models of democracy including different TMIPPs (or 'demo-technological ensembles' as we could also call them).

These processes can be seen as different institutionalisation processes. To us, an interesting question in this connection is whether the same technology (ICT applications) are used in different models (of democracy) or whether the institutionalisation processes (the stabilisation and closure) has already progressed as far as to 'link' some ICT applications more to one model than to others.

We will now move on to describe the other elements in the theoretical triangle: the perceptions and practices of citizenship and the different democratic procedural norms.

CITIZENSHIP AND DEMOCRATIC VALUES

Most current authors within the citizenship tradition recognise that there are three traditional perspectives on citizenship: the republican, the communitarian and the liberal (Mulhall and Swift 1992; Oldfield 1990). To this they will typically add one or more modern (postwar) perspectives labelled, as, for example, the radical democratic, the neo-republican or the social democratic perspectives/traditions. Here we will argue that there are five clearly distinct citizenship traditions: the three 'traditional' ones (which have all been continually updated), and two 'modern' ones: the radical democratic and the social democratic tradition (Andersen and Hoff 1999).

The republican citizenship tradition is connected with political philosophers such as Aristotle, Machiavelli, Rousseau, Hegel, Tocqueville, and, in more recent times, with Arendt and Habermas (Oldfield 1990). According to the republican ideal of citizenship, civic identities are broad. That is, citizens are strongly oriented towards the political community. Participation in public affairs is a way of life – a part of being a 'good citizen'. And citizen virtues give emphasis to moral duties: a good citizen is a loyal, active participant in politics, oriented towards the common good of the political community. The republican tradition shares with the tradition of participatory democracy the idea of the educative function of political participation, and, in particular, the belief that participation in associations and community affairs, as well as in the workplace, enhances the resources for citizenship at the national level (Held 1987). The republican tradition is rooted in a perception of politics as 'problem solving'. That is, finding 'good' and 'prudent' solutions for the political community as a whole. Thus, the dialogue over public issues in the public sphere is a central aspect of democratic practice. And, so far as democracy and democratic values are concerned, the republican tradition can be said to stress the values of political participation at all levels of society, as well as public deliberation and political rights and duties.

The modern communitarian school of thinking as it has been depicted by, for example, Mulhall and Swift (1992) is quite heterogeneous, and has formulated its point of view both in a direct criticism of modern liberalism, particularly as formulated by Rawls (see below), but also as a more encompassing criticism of Western morality and political culture. Particular attention has been paid to Rawls's work by the likes of Sandel (1982) and Walzer (1983), while the more general criticism of Western morality and political culture can be found in the work of Taylor (1990) and MacIntyre (1981, 1988). Despite the heterogeneity, these writers have enough in common to warrant the label communitarians.[13] First, like the republican tradition, the communitarians stress the importance of community for personal identity, interests and self-realisation. However, the important community here is not the 'artificial' political community of the republican tradition, but the 'real' historically specific and culturally diverse communities of language and everyday practices.

In contrast to the universalism of the liberal tradition, in terms of civil and political rights and justice, communitarians stress that such rights (as well as other 'social goods') are the inevitable product of a particular political, economic and cultural development. This particularism probably has its clearest expression in Walzer (1983). Second, and also in contrast to the liberal tradition, the communitarians think it possible to formulate common conceptions of 'the good'. Politics, and the state, are the vehicle for this common good, and in the case of conflict between the common good and individual life-projects, the common good must have priority. Thus, insofar as democracy and democratic values are concerned, the communitarian tradition can be said to stress the importance of community (local, virtual?) as the 'natural' reference point for developing an understanding of oneself, and society, and thus, also, as the 'natural' locus for the formulation of political demands and the implementation of policies.

Like the republican and communitarian tradition, the liberal tradition has many faces, from Locke (1963), through social liberals such as J. S. Mill (1982), to modern neo-liberals such as Nozick (1974). However, the paradigm statement of contemporary liberal theory is undoubtedly that formulated by John Rawls (1971, 1985) in a way which has (again) made discussions about liberalism unavoidable in social science. For Rawls, as for all liberals, personal autonomy or freedom is a dominant concern. The self is, as Mulhall and Swift put it (1992: 41, 158) 'antecedently individuated', and people's goals or preferences are formed independently of others. People should be free to define and pursue their own 'life-projects', although for Rawls it is also essential that all have equal opportunities to do that. This is guaranteed by the hypothetical social contract and the 'veil of ignorance', the assumption of which, for Rawls, makes citizens choose fair and just principles for the regulation of society.

This abstraction from citizens' social positions and particular conceptions of 'the good' is seen as necessary to allow room for cultural diversity. That is, not to prioritize any 'life-projects', or 'styles' over others. This also means that the state should be neutral; basically concerned with citizens (equal) rights and justice. In radical, neo-liberal versions politics are even regarded as evil, as any sort of binding collective decisions reduces the autonomy of the individual. Thus, neo-liberalism in particular stresses freedom of choice (exit) rather than influence on decision-making (voice). Liberal theories of citizenship therefore tend to see society as a venture necessary for mutual advantage; something in which people basically participate in order to derive personal benefits. For this reason theories of liberal citizenship put little, if any, stress on civic identities and civic virtues. Thus, democracy and democratic values in the liberal tradition, at least in its Rawlsian version, can be said to stress the importance of individual freedom in the form of civil and political rights in particular.

The social democratic citizenship tradition gives priority to equality, and to citizen rights rather than duties. Indeed, in T. H. Marshall's famous essay on 'Citizenship and Social Class' (1950), the fundamental question raised is whether the basic equality embodied in the formal rights of citizenship is consistent with the inequalities of social class? (1950: 50). As we know, Marshall's answer to this question was 'yes', even though he was aware of the way in which the concept of citizenship is used to legitimise social inequality. His conclusion is, however, conditioned upon the development of 'full citizenship', that is, full and equal participation of all citizens in public life.

In Marshall's teleological conception of citizenship, full citizenship marks the final stage of a development that begins with civil citizenship (individual and political freedom), which leads to demands for political citizenship (right of the people to take part in government as voters or representatives) which, in turn, is used as a vehicle for social citizenship (social rights). Social citizenship forms the basis of full citizenship. However, Marshall was well aware that the realisation of such full citizenship might be a rather utopian goal within a dynamic market or mixed economy. He wrote: 'The target (full citizenship) is perpetually moving forward and the State may never be able to get quite within range of it. It follows that individual rights must be subordinated to national plans' (Marshall 1950: 104). Thus, in social democratic thought (full) citizenship is seen as an ideal which might never be fully realised, but against which it is possible to measure social progress. In addition, and as Marshall's last sentence above indicates, social democratic political practice has always emphasised the attainment of equality more than formal citizenship status and participation. Thus, equality, as a prerequisite of 'real' freedom or 'real' democracy, has always been a core value of the social democratic tradition; a point which is also stressed by contemporary social democrats (see e.g. Hernes 1988; Rold Andersen 1984).

The radical democratic conception of citizenship is first and foremost associated with the works of Laclau and Mouffe (Laclau and Mouffe 1985; Mouffe 1991, 1992). Their point of departure is clearly the crises of class politics; the collapse of Soviet-style socialism, and with it the idea of the emancipatory potential of the working class and the revolutionary party. For Laclau and Mouffe this has led to a re-evaluation of liberal democracy, and thus to the formulation of a radicalised version of the modern liberal democratic tradition. Central to this formulation is the nature of the political community and the shaping of political identity (citizenship). While defending liberal pluralism (i.e. the concept of individual rights and the principles of justice), both the liberal and the communitarian conceptions of political community are criticised: the liberal conception for being instrumental, and the communitarian for being pre-modern and potentially totalitarian. Instead, an idea of political community is constructed where individuals are seen as linked to each other through the recognition of the authority of the condition specifying their common concern; a moral bond expressed through 'a practice of civility' (Mouffe 1991: 76).

However, for Laclau and Mouffe it is clear that a political community will always be shaped by conflict and antagonism, and it will therefore always be the product of, or represent, a given hegemony. In their discourse-theoretical understanding of the construction of political identity and hegemony this means that they come to see citizenship as 'an articulating principle that affects the different subject positions of the social agent, while allowing for a plurality of specific allegiances, and for the respect of individual liberty' (Mouffe 1991: 79). Thus, citizenship is not a concept with a completely fixed content, but a concept open to different and competing interpretations. The interpretation that Laclau and Mouffe suggest is one that radicalises the principles of liberal democracy – liberty and equality for all – and uses these as a point of departure for creating a radical political ideal meant to appeal to all repressed groups in society (Laclau and Mouffe 1985). Thus, democracy and democratic values in the radical democratic tradition can be said to stress the importance of individual liberty. However, what makes it different from the liberal tradition is that it puts a stronger emphasis on equality: first, that everyone should be guaranteed the same civil and political liberties. And, second, that one should be ready to accept that others might use their rights very differently from oneself. Thus, acceptance of diversity is also an important value in this tradition.

The reason why we have found it important to describe the different traditions of citizenship, and their inherent democratic values, is that they constitute the second out of the three elements in our theoretical triangle. Thus, what we are interested in seeing is how these traditions and values, which exist in different political and social communities, enter into existing and emerging democratic practices together with technology and different democratic procedural norms embodied in different political institutions, in order to both produce the characteristics of different TMIPPs and to constitute our models of democracy. In the next section we describe in some detail the third element in our theoretical triangle – the democratic procedural norms.

POLITICAL STEERING AND PROCEDURAL NORMS

While it is quite easy to describe the democratic procedural norms in the electoral chain of command this becomes much more difficult and tentative when we move towards governance modes of steering. What we do here, therefore, is examine the democratic procedural norms associated with the electoral chain of command, and then attempt a formulation of such norms for governance modes of steering. However, before we proceed we should make it clear that we regard all our four emerging models of democracy as representing governance modes of steering. In other words, they each seem to represent forms of network-oriented co-management and/or co-production arrangements, albeit in very different forms. Consequently, it is hard to believe that they should be governed by identical democratic procedural norms. However, as it is difficult to discuss these differences outside the more detailed discussion of the models themselves we shall leave the detail of this discussion until Chapter 2.

We commence by examining the electoral chain of command or the constitutional model. This basically seems to embody six democratic norms of a procedural character.

Equality in access to influence

It is a fundamental democratic norm that all members of the demos shall – at least in principle – have equal opportunities for exercising their influence. The norm is expressed in the 'one person one vote' principle laid down in the constitution or adjacent laws. Related to this principle is the idea that no-one should be exposed to political steering (laws, regulations) which they have not – at least in principle – had any influence upon. This is expressed through the principles of universal franchise and minority protection.

Public debate concerning political decisions

It is a basic idea that political decisions are taken on the basis of reasoned public debate in which everyone has – at least in principle – had an opportunity to participate, and in which the best argument wins. This is Kant's original idea on 'der reinen Vernunft' which among others Habermas has developed further in his theory concerning 'the public sphere' (Habermas 1989 [1962]).

The political authority's (government's) capability to act

In the constitutional model the political authority will most often consist of elected representatives, who are expected to exercise the mandate they have been given by making actual decisions (or non-decisions) as efficiently as possible. For these reasons constitutions or parliaments have rules on majority formation, rules concerning the passing of legislation, and so on.

The political authority's responsibility and accountability

In the constitutional model the political authority is bound by a set of rules and conventions it must respect; most notably the constitution. Thus, it is bound by these rules, and it normally takes special majorities, referenda or the like to change these rules. It is also a fundamental norm that the political authority is accountable. Its decisions should therefore be public and transparent. Importantly, there are also rules for how long a government can be in office, and how it is to be succeeded by another. Elections are regarded as events where governments and the individual representatives are ultimately held accountable for their performance.

The bureaucracy's responsibility and accountability

In the constitutional model the bureaucracy has a double responsibility. It must be responsible both in relation to the law and in relation to the political authority. The first type of responsibility is what we normally speak of as legal security ('Rechtssicherheit'). As we know, this principle can conflict with both norms for political loyalty and effectiveness. The second type of responsibility lies in the fact that the dispositions of bureaucracy can be controlled by the political authority (government, parliament), and citizens through such mechanisms as courts, the national auditor, the ombudsman or other regulatory systems.

Citizens' participation and political responsibility

In order for the five above-mentioned norms to be meaningful, and in order for the political steering to work democratically in practice, it is crucial that citizens play an active role. Thus, citizens are expected to play a role both in the process of political decision-making and in relation to the control of the legality and effectiveness of these decisions. To be able to live up to these roles citizens have – to a greater or lesser extent – to assume a personal responsibility for political steering. As we know, the character, extent and boundaries of this responsibility has traditionally played a major role in theorising (Western) democracy.[14]

Few authors have dealt with the question of democratic procedural norms in governance modes of steering. One interesting attempt at presenting such norms was undertaken by James March and Johan P. Olsen in their book on *Democratic Governance* (1995). They start the discussion about procedural norms by highlighting their importance for democracy:

> A discussion of modern democratic governance . . . is primarily a discussion of how . . . institutional frameworks [procedures] can be organised to achieve democratic ideals, and how institutions are constituted and changed within the processes they define.
>
> (ibid. 6)

They continue:

> . . . governance involves creating capable political actors, who understand how political institutions work, and are able to deal effectively with them . . . It involves building and supporting cultures of rights and rules that make possible the agreements represented in coalition formation. It involves building and supporting identities, preferences and resources that make a polity possible. It involves building and supporting a system of meaning and an understanding of history.
>
> (ibid. 28)

March and Olsen's claim is, therefore, that the craft of governance centres on four dimensions of steering:

developing identities;
developing capabilities;
developing accounts (of political events) and accountability; and
developing an adaptive political system.

Four types of capabilities are identified as being of particular relevance for governance: rights and authorities, (political) resources, (political) competencies and organisational capacity. Concerning accounts, March and Olsen regard the development of accounts and accountability as significant, as accounts define the meaning of history, the options available and the possibilities for action for all involved actors, whereas accountability is necessary in order for politicians, members, citizens and other actors, to keep track of how their organisations are performing in the network landscapes of governance. Finally, it is important to develop an adaptive political system. That is, a system which is able to cope with changing demands and changing environments. This involves creating accounts of history that make learning possible, and the provision of resources and capabilities for executing, interpreting and learning from experimentation.

On the basis of the argument so far, what democratic procedural norms can one develop which will be regarded as valid for governance modes of steering? March and Olsen do not answer this question themselves, but pose it as a question for further research. However, we think it possible, on the basis of their ideas on governance, to tentatively suggest what democratic procedural norms for governance models of political steering could look like. We think it possible to formulate four such norms:

- the development of the democratic identities of citizens and other political actors;
- the development of capabilities for appropriate political action among citizens and other political actors;
- the development of accounts and accountability for all political institutions;
- the development of an adaptive political system able to cope with changing demands and changing environments.

Although formulated broadly, these norms seem to suggest a framework within which it is possible to discuss more precisely exactly what norm(s) is dominant within our different models of democracy. Thus, the development of democratic identities seems particularly important in both the neo-republican and cyberdemocracy models. The development of capabilities seems important in both the consumer democracy model (rights) and in the cyberdemocracy model (political competences). And, finally, the development of an adaptive political system seems particularly pertinent in both the demo-elitist and neo-republican model (see Fig. 2).

ON DISCOURSES AND STRATEGIES

As we have claimed that our four models of democracy constitute both discourses and strategies, a word on our conception of both of these concepts is needed. Our conception of discourse is primarily inspired by the works of Laclau and Mouffe (Laclau 1977, 1990, 1991; Laclau and Mouffe 1985; Mouffe 1992) and Foucault (1977, 1978). Laclau and Mouffe define discourse as 'a given collection of phenomena through which the social production of meaning takes place' or as '[a] structured totality resulting from an articulatory practice' (Laclau and Mouffe 1985: 105). An articulatory practice is defined as 'any practice establishing a relation among elements such that their identity is modified as a result of [that] practice' (ibid). Discourses are therefore created through a number of articulations which establish a relation of difference among elements in such a way as to mutually modify their identity. Thus, a discourse can be seen as a relational system of differences in which the single element only has an identity in terms of its relation to the other elements. An example could be a 'family discourse' in which a 'father' is only a father because there are also mothers, sons and daughters. It is, in other words, through the articulatory practice that the meaning and identity of the elements and the discourse itself is established.

For our purposes this means that our models of democracy are constructed as discourses through the way in which the elements in our theoretical triangle (citizenship/democratic values, democratic steering/procedural norms and technology) are articulated in relation to each other and in this way given both meaning and identity. For Laclau and Mouffe, however, the concrete discourses existing at a certain time are only able to partially fix or freeze existing social identities or elements. The elements which at a certain time are not fixed in a discourse constitute 'the field of discursivity' (Laclau and Mouffe 1985: 111). These elements are also described as 'floating signifiers'[15] which, because of their surplus of meaning, it has not been possible to fix in a concrete discourse. These 'floating signifiers' with their surplus of meaning are seen as the raw material for the creation of new discourses or for the re-articulation of existing discourses. Thus, discourses are never closed entities and no identity can ever be fully constituted, nor can any meaning be ultimately fixed. What the discourses do is to partially fix meaning. In other words, what discourses do is create 'islands of order' in a sea of chaos by stopping the flow of differences and constructing a centre. Laclau and Mouffe refer to such centres as 'nodal points' or 'master signifiers'. The function of this point is to tie a number of elements together in a 'knot of meaning'. Thus, a nodal point becomes a kind of mirror in which the discourse can be seen in its totality (Laclau and Mouffe 1985: 112). While we have yet to analyse our different models of democracy, and it is, therefore, premature to begin guessing as to what their 'nodal points' might be, one hypothesis which could be advanced is that the 'nodal points' are the different (competing and conflicting) notions of citizenship.

A general critique of the work of Laclau and Mouffe is that they are too linguistically oriented, and therefore do not allow room for non-linguistic elements in their theory. This is a misplaced criticism, however, as they clearly state that a discourse contains both linguistic and non-linguistic aspects, and that the unification of these aspects is crucial in order to understand the 'totality' of a discourse (Laclau 1990: 100). Nevertheless, it is true that they focus on the linguistic aspects of discourses, and pay little attention to their material aspects. Foucault, on the other hand, pays considerably more attention to these material aspects of discourses even though he is also concerned with discourses as language (see e.g. *The History of Sexuality,* 1978). Foucault thus describes in *Discipline and Punishment* (1977), how disciplining techniques are developed in the school, the army, the workhouse, the capitalist factory and so on, and the way in which these institutional and organisational practices constitute knowledge, not as text, but as a very practical knowledge: a knowledge which disciplines the body, regulates the brain and brings order to feelings. Because these disciplining techniques produce knowledge of this type they are, according to Foucault, 'discursive practices' or parts of discourses, as much as any other type of knowledge. For the purpose of our analysis this means that when we study the way in which TMIPPs are produced by different discourses, we must explore both the way in which they express the articulation of elements in our theoretical triangle and how they express a production of knowledge.

For Laclau and Mouffe, as with Foucault, discourses are also expressions of power. As discourses are never closed entities there will always be different possibilities for action when different actors are trying to constitute or 'close' a certain discourse.

These types of decision are expressions of power, which always include the repression of other possible decisions (Laclau 1990: 34). Thus power can be seen as the setting or construction of (a set of) differences,[16] which constitute a 'field' in which certain actors can pursue their goals. Power is the creation of a demarcation line between a discourse and its surroundings, and the way in which this demarcation is made self-evident in the discourse. This is the reason why Foucault comes to see discourses as the simultaneous production of knowledge, truth and power.[17]

However interesting it might be, it is not necessary for our purposes to proceed further with this debate.[18] What we have done here has been to present our view on the concept of discourse, and illustrate the intimate relation between discourse and power. The consequences for our analysis of the different models of democracy as discourses is that in this analysis the question of power must also be fully recognised. Thus, in the competition and conflict between the different elements and models we must constantly ask ourselves the questions – by whom, for whom, with what effects and at what costs?

Our conception of strategy is inspired in particular by the way in which this concept has been formulated and used in organisation theory (e.g. Crozier and Friedberg 1980), and in the literature on the uses of ICT in public administration (e.g. Frissen and Snellen 1990). Our approach to the concept is what Frissen and Snellen refer to as a 'positioning approach'. That is, an approach which links strategy to the question of power. Thus, for us strategy is a concept that designates how an actor intervenes in a certain (policy) field in order to produce certain outcomes (Hoff and Stormgaard 1990: 109). Strategy can therefore be seen as an overarching concept for empirically observed patterns of behaviour. As strategies are almost always studied ex post, they can be said to be 'ex post rationalisations of certain attitudes and actions given a certain coherence and consistence (by the researcher) with the purpose of understanding how an organisation [society] works' (Crozier and Friedberg 1980: 25 ff.).

The question which then poses itself is what attitudes and actions to focus on or include when doing concrete research? We have dealt with this question elsewhere, and what we want to include in sorting out the strategies of e.g. different actors are statements of intent, as they are expressed in official reports and documents, attitudes (wishes) and norms and values, as they are uncovered by interviews (Hoff and Stormgaard 1990: 109). In principle the same goes for everyday practices or organisational routines (see March and Olsen 1989). For these forms of action it can, however, be debated as to whether they deserve to be referred to as 'strategies'. Normally one would demand that the acts of intervention are a result of deliberative processes in order to call them strategies. That is, that they can be discussed and argued for and against. This need not, and indeed most often is not, the case for everyday practices, which are based on routine acceptance of decisions (authority) and mutual tact and respect. However, we have decided to also include such forms of intervention here as possible strategies or, more likely, strategic elements insofar as they lie behind and enter into discursively formulated actions and statements.

This definition of strategy, and the proposed methodology, seems well suited to our aims for this book. However, working with strategies at the level of models of democracy only, will limit our analysis to a very high level of aggregation. To overcome this we will, therefore, also work with the notion of strategies at lower levels, and explore how different strategies enter into, support, and/or work against, the elements of the different models.

Notes

1 An 'artefact' is defined by Pelle Ehn (1988) as an object made by humans – often a tool. Artefacts can support both communicative and instrumental activities. An artefact both supports and expands human activity, but in many cases also replace human activity. Conditions for its use are built into the 'artefact' (see also Latour 1992). In Bijkers work (see below) 'artefact' is used consistently in reference to technological devices.

2 Even though mankind shows an extraordinary ability to change the patterns of action preinscribed in a certain artefact. Thus, we all know persons who have either rebuilt their car, tampered with their electrical devices or (tried to) reprogram standard software. For an interesting case on attempts at such 'de-inscription', see Akrich 1992.

3 The extent to which technological determinism really is embedded in Western culture is aptly analysed in Smith and Marx 1994.

4 See also Bijker, Hughes and Pinch 1987; Bijker and Law 1992.

5 Please note the resemblance between this account of the social construction of technology and our account of discourse below. This is of course no coincidence, as we see the social construction of (a given) technology as representing a discourse on this technology.

6 I am indebted to among others Johansson (1998) for this account of the SCOT theory.

7 This assumption is supported by Bijker's own awareness of the actor/structure duality. Thus, he writes: 'The conceptual framework should allow for an analysis of the actor-oriented and contingent aspects of technical change as well as of the structurally constrained aspects' (Bijker 1995*a*: 13).

8 Giddens defines 'structure' in the following way: 'Structure refers not only to rules implicated in the production and reproduction of social systems but also to resources. . . . As ordinarily used in the social sciences "structure" tends to be employed with the more enduring aspects of social systems in mind. . . . The most important aspects of structure are rules and resources recursively involved in institutions' (Giddens 1984: 23–24).

9 Concerning technology this point is brought home convincingly by Orlikowski 1992. She uses the idea of 'duality of structure' to stress how technology simultaneously assumes structural properties and must be seen as a product of human interaction.

10 Concerning resources, we adhere to Giddens's definition of these. Thus, he distinguishes between two different types of resources: allocative and authoritative resources. About these he writes: 'Allocative resources refer to capabilities – or, more accurately, to forms of transformative capacity – generating command over objects, goods or material phenomena. Authoritative resources refer to types of transformative capacity generating command over persons or actors' (Giddens 1984: 33). Giddens sees allocative resources as connected with economic institutions, and authoritative resources as connected with political institutions. Domination, he says, depends on the mobilisation of these two distinguishable types of resources (ibid.).

11 They write: 'the free-standing material-technical artifacts and what they do by themselves should be taken seriously. This means that their actual operations (not just their design) and the actual embodied norms (standards) governing these operations should be conceptualised as genuinely social processes of a particular kind' (ibid. 19).

12 The SCOT position on this point could be tenable if it limited itself to only interpretative science; to construct narratives that were unique for the single case. However, the ambition of the theory is bigger than that. Thus, in the course of analysis analytical categories are produced, which are claimed to be of general value (Bijker 1995a: 97, 100). At least they are used to analyse also other technologies than the one from which they are derived. Therefore the SCOT theory cannot pretend to be an interpretative science only, but also becomes an analytical (nomological) science. In so doing it requires an ontology; it must be able to establish the relation between itself, as science, and its object, otherwise its explanatory power is lost.

13 There are also communitarians who have dealt explicitly with the role ICT can play for both community and democracy; see Etzioni 1972, 1993.

14 For example in the discussion between the so-called participation democrats (see e.g. Pateman 1970) and the elite democrats (see e.g. Schumpeter 1976). For newer examples, see Barber 1984 and Etzioni-Halevy 1993.

15 The concepts of 'signifier' (content) and 'signified' (expression) is borrowed from Saussure (see e.g. Culler 1984).

16 Laclau and Mouffe talk about these differences as 'antagonisms'. For them a defining characteristic of politics is that it concerns the constitution of such antagonisms.

17 The same point is made by Bijker when he writes that 'I argued that the fixing of meanings that occurs during the formation of a technological frame is a form of power' (Bijker 1995a: 282).

18 However, what is interesting to note is the methodological ground rules for studying discourses which Foucault puts forward in *The History of Sexuality*. There are five such rules: (a) study the system of differences (e.g. laws, privileges, goods, etc.), (b) study the types of goals pursued by those who act on others acts (in relation to authority, profit, etc.), (c) study the means for the constitution of relations of power (knowledge, technology, surveillance, architecture, etc.), (d) study forms of institutionalisation, as institutions constitute privileged points of observation, (e) study degrees and forms of rationality and rationalisation (see also Dreyfus and Rabinow 1982).

References

Akrich, M. (1992) 'The de-scription of technical objects', in W. E. Bijker and J. Law (eds) *Shaping Technology/Building Society*, Cambridge, Mass.: The MIT Press, pp. 205–224.

Andersen, J. G. and Hoff, J. (1999) *Democracy and Citizenship in the Scandinavian Welfare State*, London: Macmillan (forthcoming).

Barber, B. (1984) *Strong Democracy*, Berkeley: University of California Press.

Berger, P. L. and Luckmann, T. (1966) *The Social Construction of Reality: A Treatise in the Sociology of Knowledge*, New York: Doubleday.

Bijker, W. E. (1995a) *Of Bicycles, Bakelites and Bulbs: Towards a Theory of Sociotechnical Change*, Cambridge, Mass.: The MIT Press.

——(1995b) 'Democratisation of technology: who are the experts?', The World Series on Culture and Technology. Downloaded from http://www.desk.nl/~acsi/WS/speakers/bijker2.htm.

——and Law, J. (eds) (1992) *Shaping Technology/Building Society*, Cambridge, Mass.: The MIT Press.

——Hughes, T. P. and Pinch, T. J. (eds) (1987) *The Social Construction of Technological Systems: New Directions in the Sociology and History of Technology*, Cambridge, Mass.: The MIT Press.

Blumer, H. (1986) *Symbolic Interactionism – Perspective and Method*, Berkeley: University of California Press.

Button, G. (1993) *Technology in Working Order: Studies of Work Interaction and Technology*, London: Routledge.

Crozier, M. and Friedberg, E. (1980) *Actors and Systems: The Politics of Collective Action*, Chicago: The University of Chicago Press.

——et al. (eds) (1975) *The Crises of Democracy*, New York: New York University Press.

Culler, J. (1984) *Saussure*, Glasgow: Fontana Press.

Dreyfus, H. L. and Rabinow, P. (eds) (1982) *Michel Foucault – Beyond Structuralism and Hermeneutics*, Chicago: The University of Chicago Press.

Ehn, P. (1988) *Work-oriented Design of Computer Artifacts*, Stockholm: Arbetslivscentrum.

Etzioni, A. (1972) 'Minerva: an electronic townhall', *Policy Sciences* 3: 457–474.

——(1993) 'Teledemocracy: the electronic town meeting', *Current* February: 26–29.

Etzioni-Halevy, E. (1993) *The Elite Connection*, Cambridge: Polity Press.

Foucault, M. (1977) *Discipline and Punishment*, Harmondsworth: Penguin.

——(1978) *The History of Sexuality: An Introduction*, Harmondsworth: Penguin.

Frissen, P. and Snellen, I. Th. M. (eds) (1990) *Informatization Strategies in Public Administration*, Amsterdam: Elsevier Science Publishers.

Giddens, A. (1984) *The Constitution of Society*, Cambridge: Polity Press.

Habermas, J. (1973) *Legitimationsprobleme im Spätkapitalismus*, Frankfurt am Main: Suhrkamp Verlag.

——(1981) *Theorie des kommunikativen Handelns*, Frankfurt am Main: Suhrkamp Verlag.

——(1989 [1962]) *The Structural Transformation of the Public Sphere: An Inquiry into a Category of Bourgeois Society*, Oxford: Polity Press.

Held, D. (1987) *Models of Democracy*, Cambridge: Polity Press.

Hernes, H. M. (1988) 'Scandinavian citizenship', *Acta Sociologica*, 31 (3): 199–215.

Hoff, J. and Stormgaard, K. (1990) 'A reinforcement strategy for informatization in public administration in Denmark', in P. H. A. Frissen and I. Th. M. Snellen (eds) *Informatization Strategies in Public Administration*, Amsterdam: Elsevier Science Publishers, pp. 107–132.

Johansson, S. (1998) 'Life between actor and structure: an analysis of constructivist approaches to technological development in a neoinstitutional perspective', paper presented to RC23 – Research Committee on Sociology of Science and Technology, ISA XIV World Congress of Sociology, 26 July–1 August 1998, Montreal, Canada.

Knights, D. and Murray, F. (1994) *Managers Divided: Organisation Politics and Information Technology Management*, Chichester: John Wiley and Sons.

Laclau, E. (1977) *Politics and Ideology in Marxist Theory*, London: Verso.

——(1990) *New Reflections on the Revolution of Our Time*, London: Verso.

——(1991) 'Community and its paradoxes: Richard Rorty's "Liberal Utopia"', in Miami Theory Collective (ed.) *Community at Loose Ends*, Minneapolis: University of Minnesota Press.

——and Mouffe, C. (1985) *Hegemony and Socialist Strategy – Towards a Radical Democratic Politics*, London: Verso.

Latour, B. (1992) 'Where are the missing masses? The sociology of a few mundane artefacts' in W. E. Bijker and J. Law (eds) *Shaping Technology/Building Society*, Cambridge, Mass.: The MIT Press, pp 225–258.

——and Woolgar, S. (1979) *Laboratory Life: The Social Construction of Scientific Facts*, Beverly Hills and London: Sage.

Locke, J. (1963) *Two Treatises on Government*, Cambridge and New York: Cambridge University Press.

MacIntyre, A. (1981) *After Virtue*, London: Duckworth.

——(1988) *Whose Justice? Which Rationality?*, London: Duckworth.

March, J. G. and Olsen, J. P. (1989) *Rediscovering Institutions: The Organizational Basis of Politics*, New York: The Free Press.
—— (1995) *Democratic Governance*, New York: The Free Press.
Marshall, T. H. (1950) *Class, Citizenship and Social Development: Essays*, Cambridge: Cambridge University Press.
Mayntz, R. and Hughes, T. P. (eds) (1988) *The Development of Large Technical Systems*, Frankfurt am Main: Campus Verlag.
Mead, G. H. (1964) *On Social Psychology*, Chicago: University of Chicago Press.
Mill, J. S. (1982) *On Liberty*, Harmondsworth: Penguin.
Mouffe, C. (1991) 'Democratic citizenship and the political community', in Miami Theory Collective (eds) *Community at Loose Ends*, Minneapolis: University of Minnesota Press.
—— (ed.) (1992) *Dimensions of Radical Democracy – Pluralism, Citizenship, Community*, London: Verso.
Mulhall, S. and Swift, A. (1992) *Liberals and Communitarians*, Oxford: Blackwell.
Nozick, R. (1974) *Anarchy, State and Utopia*, Oxford: Blackwell.
Oldfield, A. (1990) *Citizenship and Community*, London: Routledge.
Orlikowski, W. J. (1992) 'The duality of technology: rethinking the concept of technology in organizations', *Organisation Science* 3 (3): 398–427.
Pateman, C. (1970) *Participation and Democratic Theory*, Cambridge: Cambridge University Press.
Rawls, J. (1971) *A Theory of Justice*, Oxford: Oxford University Press.
—— (1985) 'Justice as fairness: political not metaphysical', *Philosophy and Public Affairs* 14 (3): 223–251.
Rold Andersen, B. (1984) *Kan vi bevare velfærdsstaten?* København: AKF Forlag.
Sandel, M. (1982) *Liberalism and the Limits of Justice*, Cambridge: Cambridge University Press.
Schumpeter, J. (1976) *Capitalism, Socialism and Democracy*, London: Allen and Unwin.
Smith, M. E. and Marx, L. (eds) (1994) *Does Technology Drive History? The Dilemma of Technological Determinism*, Cambridge, Mass.: The MIT Press.
Taylor, C. (1990) *Sources of the Self*, Cambridge: Cambridge University Press.
Thelen, K. and Steimo, S. (1992) 'Historical institutionalism in comparative perspective' in K. Thelen, S. Steinmo and F. Longstreth (eds) *Structuring Politics*, New York: Cambridge University Press, pp. 1–33.
Walzer, M. (1983) *Spheres of Justice*, New York: Basic Books.

2 Modelling electronic democracy

Towards democratic discourses for an information age

Christine Bellamy

The purpose of this second chapter is to elucidate the four models of information-age democracy which we introduced in Chapter 1: namely, the consumer, demo-elitist, neo-republican and cyberdemocratic models. As we emphasised in our opening chapter, these models are not to be understood as 'ideal-types' of electronic democracy, as logically coherent constructs neatly abstracted from specific social settings or from competing political values. Rather, the approach adopted in this book derives from a perspective which situates both the practice and rhetoric of democratic politics in their specific historical contexts. By extension, it seeks to ground differing notions of 'electronic democracy' in a set of rival discourses connecting democratic values to technological change. As they are hard-wired into technologically mediated innovations in political practices (TMIPP), these discourses are both embedding and constraining the ways we think about electronic democracy and moulding democratic futures for the information age.

My task in this chapter, then, is to construct a set of models to capture these discourses. In so doing, the chapter will reveal the complex interfaces between democratic ideals and their material base. Just as democratic thought is inevitably influenced by changing assumptions about the means of communicating information, so the rhetorics which shape technology are themselves influenced by dominant social values and intellectual paradigms, including those expressed through democratic ideals. These bundles of assumptions interface in TMIPP. Indeed, TMIPP can be conceived as 'actor-networks' (Callon 1987), as intermediaries bringing (perceptions about) the capabilities of ICTs, (ideas about) democratic values and (intended changes in) political practice together into new kinds of relationships capable of acting formatively on political institutions. The approach taken here focuses much more on assessing the meaning and theorizing the significance of such innovations than on the endless mapping of their alleged 'impact'. The contributors to this book share a common preoccupation with the strategic intentions lying behind these innovations, with the assumptions that are thus being revealed. TMIPP are being studied here, then, not only as reflectors of, but much more importantly as active agents in, the process through which the discourse of electronic democracy is being made and re-made.

The models developed in this chapter are hypothetical and provisional. They are brought forward tentatively, as a means of establishing an iterative process through which the process of constructing an analytic framework can both inform and be informed by the experience of specific cases. In other words, the opening version of this framework developed here is intended to provide a meeting point, a point of mutual engagement, between those involved in practical experimentation, the (multiple) authors of this book and, of course, its readers. By focusing discussion around the meaning of TMIPP, this approach will serve to bring to the fore, rather than to deny, the conflicting interpretations with which the very notion of electronic democracy is imbued. It has been said that ICTs are 'ambiguous' technologies, holding within them opposing tendencies, towards liberation and empowerment, on the one hand, and oppression and domination, on the other. Thus, some participants will interpret a specific case of innovation as holding out the promise of enhancing democratic values, so others will interpret it as offering significant threats. Others still will point out that the reading of these cases depends on what one understands by democracy as well as how one interprets the significance of technological change. My intention in this chapter is to acknowledge these competing readings of electronic democracy by presenting a range of models that enable exploration of the complex points of mutual reference between the disparate sources of democratic rhetorics, the contradictory properties ascribed to ICTs and therefore the contested meanings immanent in TMIPP.

My starting points for constructing these models lie mainly in two parallel sets of texts: the contemporary literature on citizenship and democracy, which is mainly grounded in political thought, and the contemporary literature on technology-mediated communications, much of which is grounded in the fast-growing discipline of media studies. Where these literatures interleave is in their preoccupation with institutions which have either colonised or emptied out the realm known as 'civil society'. Whether this preoccupation relates to the capture of political parties by bureaucratic oligarchies; the influence in government of 'iron triangles' and policy communities; the complex and untransparent processes of bureaucratic governance; or the power of the mass media, what connects all these concerns is that they focus on arrangements that are significantly mediated by webs of communications and interlinking information systems that shape the images and opinions, categories and identities that configure contemporary politics. This book has been prompted by the widespread conviction that there are new forms of ICTs that challenge the dominance of the technologies on which institutions are founded. The argument is that the emerging technologies of the so-called information age are technologies with different kinds of properties, properties that are at once capable of restoring the personal control, intuitive communication and authentic engagement that characterises face-to-face interaction and overcoming the limitations on human connectivity imposed by time and space. It is this apparent ability, at once to extend and to reverse the technological 'impact' of the 'first media age' (Poster 1995), that is nurturing so much interest in the democratic prospects of the second media age.

Our four models of information-age democracy are designed to capture four competing strategies for promoting electronic democracy that seem to be emerging from contemporary discourses. In so doing, they focus explicitly on the relationships between elements in those discourses that are capable of being tied into 'knots of meaning' through TMIPP. First, each model depends on a specific notion of democracy, founded on a particular conception of citizenship. Second, it is thereby associated with a particular set of procedural norms. Third, it is also associated with a more or less distinctive way of exploiting ICTs, built on a specific set of understandings about the nature of information and human communication and its significance for such norms. And fourth, each model is associated with a particular set of policy issues, reflecting specific readings of the opportunities and threats posed for democracy by 'new' ICTs. Each of these models may also be regarded as a reaction to specific problems in contemporary democratic practices, practices which have been shaped by the legacies of liberal constitutionalism. It is therefore with an examination of this legacy that I embark upon my task.

THE LEGACIES OF CONSTITUTIONAL DEMOCRACY

The countries from which we draw the cases in this book share a formal commitment to 'representative democracy'. Representative democracy may also be referred to as 'constitutional democracy', not simply because it is the model of democracy embedded in formal constitutional arrangements but because this term conveys, too, much that is important about the long-established hegemony of representative democracy and its contemporary legacies.

The centring of political power in Western Europe on representative institutions is commonly interpreted as the outcome of a liberal project designed to challenge and limit the growing powers of the absolutist state by defining a sphere in which civic rights – especially those relating to religious practice, to civil association and to private property and commercial enterprise – would be recognised and protected. Long-drawn-out struggles for constitutional reform resulted in a series of political accommodations with a range of 'possessive' interests (Macpherson 1962), in which economically powerful interests were gradually granted political recognition, mainly through the reconfiguration of parliamentary representation.

Constitutionalism is, in consequence, often associated with 'protective democracy', with the belief that political and civic rights are, first and foremost, to be valued as instruments for defending personal or sectional interest rather than for expressing an individual's essential humanity or for securing social justice (Macpherson 1966; Held 1987). Marxist historians, for example, regard the constitutional state as a bourgeois construct, as a crucial instrument in the emergence of capitalist domination (e.g. Habermas 1989; Macpherson 1977; Poggi 1978). Nevertheless, it is widely recognised, too, that liberal constitutionalism also provided the historical framework for the development of practices which have come to be widely valued in Western democracy. Indeed, so potent is its legacy that, as we will see, each of the first three of our models of information-age democracy may be regarded as an attempt to restore a particularly valued dimension of the constitutionalist tradition.

Liberal constitutionalism in a democratic age

A major contribution of constitutionalism to the development of democratic politics is that it made possible the emergence of what, especially following the English translation of Habermas (1989), is now referred to widely as the 'public sphere'. Habermas himself used the term to denote a sphere of human association which emerged in the specific conditions of the emerging nineteenth-century bourgeois state in and from 'civil society', that is in the space between the institutions of the state, on the one hand, and the private structures of kinship and domesticity, on the other. The main significance of the public sphere was that it underpinned the emergence of 'public opinion' as the expression of the rational, deliberate, critical voice of an independent, informed but non-partisan public. The emergence of the public sphere is, therefore, closely associated with the powerful and lasting belief that the 'public' is capable of exercising supervision over politicians and that the exercise of state power should – and, just as important, could – be limited by and judged by public opinion. In the constitutional model, it was the 'parliamentary chain of steering' that was the main conduit through which this process was supposed to occur.

Habermas's view is that the emergence of the public sphere was made possible not only by certain political conditions – specifically the growing economic independence and political recognition of the middle and professional classes – but also by a particular development in information technology, namely the emergence of print. The significance of print was that it enabled public discourse to transcend face-to-face communication: the public sphere was public rather than simply civic, cosmopolitan rather than local. It was not, however, a sphere of the masses. Its scope was limited, just as its coherence was promoted, by the shared discourse of the literate bourgeoisie. Its legacy consists in the belief that government can be criticised and supervised by 'the people', but the paradox is that this belief was realised most successfully in an era which preceded popular democracy. Indeed, for many students of modern democracy and political communications, including Habermas himself, the attempt to superimpose popular democracy on liberal constitutionalism was a project that failed. It failed to create a truly popular democracy but destroyed much that had been valued in the liberal constitutional state, especially its reliance on an independent-minded public. Universal suffrage led not to popular sovereignty but to the development of ever more sophisticated techniques by which party and bureaucratic elites secured increasing control over the expanding electorate. According to this reading, then, the melding of constitutionalism with popular democracy turned parliamentary institutions into instruments of government rather than agents of the people. Its most distinctive outcome was the 'elective dictatorship' of party-based government.

Much of the reasoning behind this pessimistic analysis turns on the belief that the extension of the franchise destroyed the public sphere as a competent, independent, critical source of public opinion. As a wider range of classes were given the vote, so the redefinition of the 'public' shattered the common value system of the public sphere, undermining the autonomy, coherence and potency of public opinion. Furthermore, what remained of an autonomous public sphere was further undermined by the pervasiveness of the administrative state. The development of the Keynesian welfare state (KWS) has often been regarded as a process by which the working classes were incorporated fully into citizenship because it secured the social rights – for example the rights to education and health care – which enabled working people to exploit their hard-won political and civic rights (Marshall 1970). In other accounts the KWS appears, rather, as an instrument for securing the continued legitimation of the capitalist state in an era when the masses came visibly to share economic and political power (e.g. Offe 1984). Whatever its true genesis, however, the growth of the KWS has substantially undermined the notion that there is a spontaneous sphere of civic action, separate from the state. Rather, the need to secure an increasingly precarious range of social and economic outcomes forced the (various tiers of the) state, corporate business, the associations of organized labour and a wide range of professional interests into ever closer relationships in an increasingly complex mesh of 'co-arrangements' forming the distinctive administrative structures of late modern governance (Kooiman 1993). Many of the sources of power in late modern society lie therefore outside the scope of the 'parliamentary chain of steering', in the impenetrable, interlinked networks of governance and corporate business. In effect these networks are private networks (Rhodes 1997) from which the voice of local communities, consumer interests and elected representatives have been excluded and which have served therefore to take important facets of collective consumption out of the political sphere.

These problems of constitutional democracy have been compounded, too, because faith has in any case been lost in the possibility of securing authentic popular expression through the parliamentary chain of steering. The argument is that the practical exigencies of mobilizing a mass electorate led directly to the establishment of mass political parties with oligarchical leaderships and increasingly centralised bureaucratic apparatus (Ostrogorski 1903; Michels 1915; Duverger 1959). The consequences are that free elections have amounted to little more than highly restricted choices between sets of leaders and programmes, and channels of political representation have fallen largely under the control of party machines (Schumpeter 1950). This massification of politics came to be strongly associated with the emergence of mass communication media (Adorno and Horkheimer 1972): the ills of modern democracy seem to be reflected in the trajectory of technological change. Studies of the democratic significance of mass media have dwelt on its potential for atomising individuals, undermining civil society, attenuating possibilities for collection action and 'refeudalising' relations between state and society. Public opinion has been reduced to so much market research data, while the power to manage democratic politics has steadily accrued among the corporate interests, the media moguls and the party apparatchiks who control the style, content and targeting of information carried on mass media (Garnham 1990). Popular democracy is better understood, then, as the apotheosis of 'managerial democracy' (Laudon 1977).

The key question to which all this leads is whether the new technologies of the information age – particularly new capabilities for computer-mediated communication (CMC) and electronic networking – are tending to intensify or challenge managerial democracy. The answer to this question is, as yet, far from clear. On the one hand, there is the well-established 'reinforcement of politics' thesis, which argues that technologies are ineluctably shaped by prevailing power structures: their main effects are, inevitably, to reinforce existing political practices (Danziger et al. 1982). This thesis was strengthened by the somewhat disappointing results achieved by teledemocratic innovations of the 1970s and 1980s, which, on the whole, failed to live up to the promises of their champions (Dutton 1992; Arterton 1987; Abramson et al. 1988). In the same way, studies of CMC in electoral politics have focused on the role of computer-aided market research techniques in shaping electoral behaviour and manipulating opinion formation (McLean 1989).

On the other hand, there are equally powerful champions of the view that this technological revolution is potentially different from those that have gone before, that the emergence of the cybertechnologies of the 'second media age' marks a profound break from the 'first media age' of mass communications (Poster 1995). One argument is that these are 'fetch' technologies rather than 'deliver' technologies, with all that this implies for personal control (Sawhney 1996). They permit individuals themselves to act as discriminating searchers of information and autonomous controllers of human connectivity, and by enabling information to be endlessly reproduced and circulated, undermine the commodification of information that has occurred in the industrial age. In profound ways, therefore, CMC challenges fundamental aspects of the political economy of communications. While the liberalisation of broadcasting and telecommunications markets and the promotion of the global information superhighway may appear to deliver political communications into the hands of global capital, the distinctive technologies of the 'networked society' (Castells 1996) are in practice proliferating and diversifying in ways that could take them beyond the control of governments or corporate business (Friedland 1996). Networked technologies are 'citizen technologies' (Winner 1993): 'those who previously had to make themselves presentable to the agencies of mass communication technologies . . . have begun to represent themselves' (Weston 1994: unpaged).

This optimistic reading of contemporary ICTs is nurtured, too, by those who argue that the hegemony of the mass media has never been complete, that the public sphere was never so coherent, so unified, or so exclusively dominated by bourgeois values as Habermas believes (Keane 1984; Curran 1991). By this reading, the recent history of political communication reveals not so much the attenuation of the public sphere but the persistence of a multiplicity of public spheres capable of sustaining the oppositional politics of working-class movements and, more latterly, the counter-cultural politics of the new social movements. Shaped as they are by these webs of political affiliation, new technologies could emerge as emancipatory technologies capable of supporting 'counterveiling networks of communications' reaching beyond and beneath the bureaucratic structures of the state (Keane 1991).

It is possible, of course, to take a more jaundiced view of the tendencies associated with electronic networks. For other writers, cybernetworks engender 'hyper-real' worlds detached from physical location and hence from grounded social support. Cyberspace is a space of signs, images and electronic games where individuals fall more easily prey to suggestion, propaganda and advertising (Baudrillard 1988) or become lost in their own, self-referencing fantasies (Robins 1995). For these writers, the political significance of the cyber age is that, rather than marking a sharp break from the era of mass communications, it could mark a significant extension of the 'already virtual' properties of industrial age communications (Holmes 1997). Cybernetworks could intensify the shift towards socially abstracted 'pseudo-communities' (Beniger 1986) offering no more than a transitory semblance of social belonging. At the same time, the more efficient targeting of CMC will combine with the increasing connectivity between the bureaucratic systems to strengthen the effectiveness of social control (Lyon 1997).

MODELLING DEMOCRACY FOR AN INFORMATION AGE

In the next section of this chapter, I move on to consider four models of information-age democracy which expose and explore the tensions between these contradictory visions of life among new technologies. These models have been arranged along a continuum (Fig. 2) depicting the varying degrees to which they tend either towards a narrow definition of democracy, one in which the parliamentary chain of steering still plays a critical part, or point to new kinds of democratic practice. Thus, the 'consumer democracy' model appears on the far left, as the model which most takes for granted existing parliamentary institutions, and cyber democracy appears on the far right, as that which challenges those institutions most radically. These models are also distinguished by the extent to which, and the ways in which, they continue to engage with the legacies of liberal constitutionalism. All these models except one, the cyber democratic model, can be regarded as reinventing a specific dimension of constitutional democracy. Thus, consumer democracy is closely allied to 'protective democracy'. Demoelitism captures strategies which are designed to renew the search for a more acceptable accommodation between the functional representation of specific interests, on the one hand, and the legitimation bestowed by popular elections, on the other. And neo-republicanism aims to reproduce the procedural norms of the 'public sphere', as a means of restoring the power of public opinion in contemporary democracy. In this schema, only the cyberdemocratic model captures the possibility of developing entirely new forms of democracy in the information age.

It follows that as we look from left to right in Figure 2, the modelling of information age democracy becomes less tightly conceived. Accordingly, I commence the detailed elucidation of these models with the consumer democracy and demo–elitist models, the models which many readers will regard as most realistic.

The consumer democratic model

Consumer democracy shares with demo-elitism an uncritical acceptance of many well-established features of constitutional democracy, including the role of parliamentary institutions, elections and parties. At the same time, however, there is a clear understanding that for most electors the public affairs of the modern state occupy a far lower place than the private concerns of family, home and work. These models reflect the work of Schumpeter, public choice theorists (Olson 1965; Downs 1967) and other 'realistic' accounts of modern democracy in supposing that the only important political action of most people is to cast a vote. These two models also place considerable emphasis on the growth of the bureaucratic state, recognising the increasing penetration of the administrative and regulatory functions of governance into the everyday lives of ordinary people. In the consumer democracy model, therefore, the main priority is to give individuals more information, more choice, and thus more power in dealing with public bureaucracy.

Consumer democracy builds particularly strongly on those parts of public choice theory that show that active participation in pressure groups, political campaigning or, even, voting is not for most people a rational strategy. It takes for granted but it therefore largely discounts the input side of the parliamentary chain of steering. Instead, it focuses on the reconstruction of the output side, on the interface between services and their consumers. In other words, consumer democracy aims not so much to challenge as to bypass the tired institutions of representative politics. It seeks, in effect, to recentre democracy from the political nexus, a nexus formed around parliamentary and electoral processes, onto the consumer nexus, a nexus formed largely around the consumption of public services. Consumer democracy can therefore be regarded as the culmination of a strategy for legitimating and controlling the growth of the administrative state, by establishing greater popular control over the consumption nexus. In this way, it is heir to such fashions as the ombudsmen movement of the mid-1960s, the public participation movement of the early 1970s, and the public service orientation of the mid-1980s. However, as it was manifest in the early 1990s, public consumerism also came to be specifically associated with the growing influence of the New Right, with checking the power of bureaucrats by introducing market-like mechanisms into public services and widening the scope of contractual relationships (Barry 1990; Pollitt 1993). In other words, consumerism sought to limit the power and scope of the administrative state not by restoring a civil society of *homo publicus* but by seeking to expand the realm of *homo economicus*.

Consumer democracy model shares with economic liberalism and rational choice theory the assumption that individuals are to be regarded as active, competent, instrumental and rational in the making of choices and the expressing of preferences, at least so far as their consumption of public services is concerned. It derives most closely from a utilitarian or 'protective' conception of liberal democracy and can therefore claim direct descent from the intellectual foundations of the constitutional state. It assumes that individuals' interests will be protected only if they possess the means to protect them, an assumption which establishes a powerful claim to equal political rights. In the context of the modern administrative state, this principle implies a strong claim to information about public service entitlements as well as to the means of enforcing those entitlements, whether this be political voice, market choice or legal contract.

The objection which is often raised to consumer democracy is that it channels preferences through a relatively narrow set of administrative arrangements concerned mainly with public service delivery. Its tendency is further to depoliticise the process of collective consumption. Indeed, the centring of democratic processes on the consumption nexus marginalises the possibility that citizens may have views on 'high' politics or that they may wish to engage in rational discussion with others who have equally powerful views. It fails to show how the high politics of national economic management, foreign affairs, or, say, law and order can be subjected to effective popular supervision. Nevertheless, consumer democracy also points to interesting facets of information-age democracy, highlighting in a particularly clear way the ambiguities surrounding innovations with ICTs.

Consumerism epitomises the old saw that 'information is power'. It seeks to redress the balance of power between producer and consumer by promoting such principles as choice, access, redress and voice. The effectiveness of these principles depends in turn, however, on a meta-principle: access to more and better information. Consumerism establishes as a fundamental procedural norm the principle that there must be effective flows of information to consumers, enabling service users to become more competent, more discriminating, more powerful clients of government. This model draws attention, therefore, to important questions of public policy: for example, what information can governments make freely available? How does this impact on policies relating to the commercial exploitation of information? How can ICTs enable consumers to become more active, more selective, more purposeful users of public service information?

As we model it here, consumer democracy also implies that governments address the converse question: how can consumers make their preferences known to governments? Herein lies an important rub. The most obvious answer to this question lies in the explicit harvesting of consumer opinion, through such devices as customer satisfaction surveys or focus groups. However, like other organisations in the information economy, public services have access to other, less obvious, sources of intelligence about consumer preferences, including the myriad of data which are inevitably surrendered as individuals interact with public services. Furthermore, as market-like arrangements spread throughout governance, so it becomes increasingly feasible to claim that market transactions could stand as legitimate proxy for other, less comprehensive, channels of popular voice.

Consumer democracy raises in particularly stark form, then, some key questions posed by new ICTs for democratic values. It exposes more explicitly than our other models the force of Lyon's proposition that the inevitable corollary of an individuals' participation in the information society is the surrender of a mass of data about their behaviour and preferences (Lyon 1994). Will governments be content to restrict the gathering of information from the public to overt means or does this process extend to the use of other, more covert, kinds of market intelligence? Is such intelligence being used as a proxy for political forms of democratic expression? What kinds of controls, if any, are being placed on the uses of personal data? Are these measures sufficient to maintain or rebuild popular confidence in the late modern state (Raab 1998)?

The demo-elitist or neo-corporatist model

Like the consumer democracy model, the demo-elitist model assumes that public opinion is less active than the constitutional model suggests, and that its prime function is to constrain and legitimate government rather than to steer policy. Originating as it does in social democratic thought, demo-elitism concedes that in modern welfare states, citizens' rights and demands are centred as much on social benefits and economic prosperity as on political participation or civic freedoms. It suggests that popular legitimation depends less on widespread agreement about procedural norms and more on policy outcomes than the liberal project acknowledges. It proposes, therefore, that successful welfare states are those that manage both to satisfy a sufficient range of wants, and to do so in ways that mediate most acceptably between competing claims.

This analysis therefore places more attention than does constitutional democracy on the role and composition of bureaucratic elites and on the relations between these elites and formal associations of civil society, such as the national organisations of corporate business, trades unions and professional bodies. It is alert, in other words, to the democratic issues posed by late modern governance. Demo-elitism gives a prominent place to the role of experts and external interests in meeting the demands imposed by the search for popular legitimation. The policy communities and issue networks that form around governments are not, therefore, to be easily dismissed as an excrescence on the body politic, but accepted as a normal, routine part of governing. It follows that they should also be fully integrated into accounts of contemporary democratic practice. Accordingly, this model places emphasis, too, on corporatist procedures as mechanisms for balancing as well as articulating political demands. The extended networks of contemporary governance systems (Kickert et al. 1997) are critical to the process of building consensus and cooperation between the interdependent interests that have become entangled in the modern state. In this model, then, the processes of representative democracy, on the one hand, and the institutions of governance, on the other, share responsibility for the quality of late modern democracy. The former serve to legitimate the state and act as a means of renewing political elites, while the extensive networks of functional constituencies provide the means of renewing the cooperation and accommodations which enable this legitimation to be sustained.

Despite this democratic rationale for demo-elitism, it cannot be denied, too, that this model also depicts a state of affairs which is prone to degeneration from a democratic point of view. Demo-elitism points equally well to an oligarchical form of government, in which a narrow range of self-perpetuating elites become steadily more detached from control by the constituencies they claim to represent. In this more pessimistic scenario, power over public policy comes to be concentrated in closed networks, just as techniques for managing the representative process are monopolised by party and media bosses. Whereas consumer democracy may be regarded as an attempt to bypass the problems of contemporary democratic practice, demo-elitism acknowledges the danger that the problems of mass politics will be intensified by ICTs.

Demo-elitism also captures, however, many reforms on the active agendas of contemporary governments. In the first place, the demo-elitist model is designed to acknowledge a range of proposals for enhancing the democratic quality of electoral politics, thus strengthening the representative side of the demo-elitist balance. These proposals range from the present British Government's proposals for allowing voting in unconventional locations – such as supermarkets and bus stations (Department of the Environment, Transport and the Regions 1998) – to proposals for putting party manifestos, candidates' voting records and position statements on the World Wide Web. More sophisticated innovations could offer voters enhanced opportunities for expressing opinions or better ways of forming opinion, including electronic support for interactive conversations with elected representatives, or experiments with innovations aimed at offering politicians 'strategic guidance', such as citizen juries, policy juries, deliberative opinion polls or city forums (Fishkin 1991; Adonis and Mulgan 1994; Percy-Smith 1995; Hirst 1996).

What is distinctive about the demo-elitist model is that it also emphasises the importance of reform on the elitist side of the demo-elitist balance. In part, our thinking here echoes the work of Etzioni-Halevy (1993) in proposing that contemporary democratic theory should focus on such questions as the responsiveness, accountability and openness of elites, and the extent to which elite structures are compatible with egalitarian values. In this respect, demo-elitism points up such issues as: the relative autonomy of elites (both from each other and the state); the circulation and interchange of elites, sub-elites and public; the inclusivity of corporatist structures; and the transparency of corporatist processes. In so doing, it raises several issues relevant to our concerns in this book. First, the emphasis on openness and transparency brings into play such policy issues as freedom of information and the regulation of the press. Second, it questions the extent to which the economic interests and social agencies which become enmeshed in neo-corporatist networks are themselves subject to democratic control and renewal. In the work of Etzioni-Halevy (1993) or Putnam (1993, 1995), for example, the efficacy of modern states in promoting a consensual, inclusive, effective style of governing is shown to depend on such factors as the inclusivity of neo-corporatist structures, the relative autonomy of economic and social elites, and the extent to which those elites are embedded in dense networks in civil society. As a model of information-age democracy, demo-elitism thus draws attention to the contribution which new information and communications technologies might make in building and invigorating such networks. Indeed, the complex, diffuse networks of modern governance could be controlled not simply by strengthening accountability through the electoral chain of command or by securing greater democracy within specific neo-corporatist structures. We would wish to explore, too, the possibility of countering the pervasive power of governance networks through the mobilisation of equally pervasive and flexible alliances between the clients of and stakeholders in these networks.

It should be clear that while demo-elitism gives some prominence to formal political processes centring on the parliamentary chain of steering, it also shifts the focus of democratic attention onto a wider set of relationships than those encompassed by a narrow, liberal definition of political institutions. It therefore resonates with the growing emphasis in neo-corporatist writing on the reinvigoration of civil society as a counter to the dominance of governance networks. Its multiple points of contact with (what is variously alluded to as) associational (Hirst 1994), stakeholder (Hutton 1995; Hirst 1996) or, even market-socialist democracy (Miller 1989; Le Grand and Estin 1989) shifts this model some way from the far left-hand side of the continuum in Figure 2. Nevertheless, it may be distinguished from neo-republicanism by its recognition that the autonomy of civil society from the state is relative at best, because of the irreversible interdependencies that now exist between governmental, economic and social agencies. Civil society no longer functions as a sphere of spontaneous, unregulated, unaccountable association, clearly separate from the state, but through extensive networks in which the government is often the strongest partner. As a model of information-age democracy, demo-elitism therefore focuses mainly on opening up and strengthening vertical rather than horizontal flows of information and communication: between voters and their representatives; between representative institutions and government; between government and external elites; and between elites and their stakeholders. It is preoccupied mainly with macro- and meso-level processes.

The neo-republican model

As this discussion has begun to make clear, neo-republicanism shares with demo-elitism an interest in enriching and pluralising the associations of civil society. Its primary focus is, however, somewhat different, for the neo-republican model takes as its point of departure not a focus on the legitimation of government, the openness of elites, and the balancing of public policy, but a concern with the quality of participation and engagement, especially at the micro and local levels of politics. Neo-republicanism is founded on the notion of 'active' citizenship, a notion which draws its contemporary influence from at least three important strands in political thought. Accordingly, this model is, perhaps, the most eclectic of the models developed in this chapter.

Most centrally, neo-republicanism draws on an organic rather than an individualist conception of citizenship, one which is currently brought forward under the communitarian banner (Mulhall and Swift 1992). It promotes the idea that the rationalities which individuals pursue and the values on which they draw are derived from traditions shared with other members of society. In contrast to the strict liberal position in which justice consists of (no more than) a set of procedural norms, a set of agreements about the rules under which individuals compete to further their interests, the attraction of communitarianism is that it offers the possibility of shared social values. In other words, communitarianism puts forward the idea that society can be organised around a common view of what aspirations are good, and can amount to much more than agreement about what procedures are fair.

The second strand of thought on which this model rests is that which conceives citizenship as embodying an ideal of 'civic virtue'. This conception may be variously referred to as a 'classical', 'republican' or 'Athenian' conception of citizenship (Miller 1995). It draws on the Aristotelian conception of the good life, a life lived within the polis, in which each citizen can realise fully his own capabilities and aptitudes, the highest of which is development of a moral capacity, a capacity for balancing his own desires against those of other citizens. The highest expression of civic virtue, therefore, is engagement with other citizens in decision-making for the polis. It was the re-emergence of this ideal in modern political thought, most obviously in ideas about 'developmental democracy' (Held 1987), that provided much of the moral underpinning for contemporary notions of participatory or 'active' democracy, by putting forward the notion that political rights, and the means of exercising them, should be regarded as the essential condition for developing the moral, social and intellectual qualities necessary for the full expression of individuals' humanity. Democracy is not simply to be valued as an expedient for protecting their material interests, but as a fundamental, and therefore as a universal, human right.

Third, the neo-republican model draws on a disparate set of ideas within the discourses of humanitarian Marxism and the radical left. These ideas are connected by the belief that the re-establishment of an autonomous civil society would be profoundly subversive of the modern state, challenging its extensive domination over economic, political and cultural forms. The public sphere is, by this reading, an emancipatory sphere. While Habermas has been roundly criticised for his apparent approval of the historical public sphere, founded as it was on a bourgeois, patriarchal society (e.g. Calhoun 1992), many writers on the left are nevertheless seduced by the normative implications of his work, that is, by the idea that there could be a sphere of rational human communication, independent of both state and capital, capable of acting as a source of criticism and, even, of protest. In this way, the growing interest in the notion of the 'public sphere' is also serving to promote a neo-republican conception of the human subject.

Contemporary neo-republicanism draws then on an eclectic range of ideas to construct a vision of an active citizen, busily engaging with others in a highly participative, highly inclusive form of politics. In the hands of many contemporary writers, this vision has come to stand as a critique of the thin, self-regarding, instrumental politics associated with the liberal project (e.g. Barber 1984). Neo-republicanism conceives politics as 'a shared activity which takes people beyond the individualism of the market' (Stoker 1994: 9) to work through their conflicts in a search for the social good. As a model of information-age democracy, it reflects the hope that the electronic media of the late industrial age could replicate many features of the Athenian agora or the New England town meetings of the colonial age. In the hands of contemporary communications theory, it conjures up a vision of a virtual public sphere, a sphere mediated by electronic networks, that could become 'a focal point of our desire for the good society, the institutional site where popular political will should take form and citizens should be able to constitute themselves as active agents in the political process' (Dahlgren 1991: 1–2). Such a vision clearly sits uncomfortably with dominant interpretations of mass communications. For this reason, the neo-republican model of electronic democracy is highly dependent on the belief that the 'new' technologies of the information age are radically different from those of the first media age.

Neo-republican discourse on electronic democracy is connected, then, by an ideal of active democracy governed by the procedural norms of the public sphere. At the same time it is divided by the differing aspirations of those who adopt it. As we have already seen, there is a growing corpus of work which argues that the new technologies of the information age could revitalise the 'oppositional' and 'counter-cultural' public spheres nurtured in the new social movements by providing electronic forums for a stronger politics of protest and emancipation. At the other end of the political spectrum, a discourse of neo-republicanism has emerged strongly in the new communitarianism of the civic networking movement, with its talk of electronic town halls and virtual public squares. The paradox is that many of the best-publicised examples of TMIPP in the literature to date (Bellamy and Taylor 1998; Tsagarousianou et al. 1998) focus on the development of civic networks and wired cities aimed at renewing local communities and reinventing local democracy. These networks are centred on specific geographical places and map directly onto the institutions of the local state, prompting questions about the connection of electronic politics with mainstream politics. For example, do neo-republican strategies assume that virtual public spheres can remain innocent of party politics? (How) does a virtual public sphere aggregate and shape opinion? (How) is virtual opinion articulated in the real-life polity? In other words, (in what ways) can neo-republican engagement contribute to the democratic steering of the state?

Another interesting question concerns the implications of neo-republican discourse for public policies concerning technological investment and regulation.

For example, its emphasis on near universal participation has led to the view that access to the information superhighway must be recognised as a fundamental social right, accorded to all citizens in the information age (Doctor 1994; Williams and Parvik 1994; Calabrese and Borchert 1996). This is a claim, however, that recognises that information-age democracy rests on building extensive technological infrastructures that are far beyond the resources of civil associations. Thus, the American civic network movement has lobbied hard for publicly supported telecomputing while, as we have seen, much of the growing literature on the public sphere is promoting the case for new kinds of public service networks. In consequence, this model is associated here with public policies aimed at establishing a new political economy of communications, but the dependence of the public sphere on public sponsorship must be regarded as a paradox whose ramifications need to be researched.

The most fundamental issue posed by this model, however, is not simply whether the wires can be put in place to create electronic networks, but why it might be supposed that these networks would amount to a 'public sphere'. In its classical usage, a public sphere is a sphere not only of participation but also of engagement. It assumes a shared commitment to procedural norms and political values, capable of mediating more personal, immediate or transient affiliations such as those of locality, interest or identity (Taylor 1995). This is an assumption, however, which is substantially undermined by counter interpretations of new electronic networks which see them as intensifying the one-dimensional, disembodied, instant communicatory experiences of the first media age. What involvement can there be between cyborgs? Why should electronic networks mobilise a sufficient sense of cohesion to provide a true point of political engagement in the fast-changing, complex world of late modern politics?

The cyberdemocratic model

This question is given added point because it resonates with one of the most pervasive themes in contemporary political thought: that this is an era that is particularly marked by social diversification and cultural turbulence. By this reading, the greatest threat to late modern democracy is not excessive political centralisation or managerial control, but a tendency to social fragmentation and alienation. We are witnessing, it seems, not an intensification of capabilities for channelling and managing politics, but the balkanisation of politics. The highly elaborated, increasingly differentiated, self-referencing networks of cyber society stand as powerful metaphors, indeed, for the growing irrelevance of the socially referenced 'objective' categories through which politics has been structured in modern times. In particular, the unifying concepts of nation, community, interest or class (MacIntyre 1988; Taylor 1989; Gray 1993) have given way to a focus on 'identity', a concept which draws attention to the fluid, contested, contingent categories through which social groupings are formed (e.g. Mouffe 1993). It is the possibilities and problems exposed by the intricate, unmappable webs of affiliation spreading through cyberspace, that we seek to bring into the discussion of information-age politics by offering up our model of 'cyberdemocracy'.

In putting forward this model, we are endeavouring to capture some of the most optimistic, and some of the most threatening, scenarios of postmodern politics. For some postmodern thinkers, the 'explosion of communication' is an important, even a key, factor in supporting the increasing range of 'micro-communities' capable of sustaining a new, emancipatory politics of identity (Leca 1996). For the very reason that they disembody communication, the new virtual communities of the new information age enable individuals to construct their own identities, allowing them to escape the 'categories of otherness' which have marginalised and ghettoised minority groups. The emergence of autonomous, self-referencing electronic networks could therefore play an important part in the 'pluralisation' of postmodern society, in the reconstruction of politics on a basis of mutual 'agonistic respect' in place of (what was at best) a patronising tolerance of otherness (Connolly 1991, 1995). By this reading, cyber communities could profoundly challenge the old politics, a politics which secured its fragile cohesion by stigmatising and excluding individuals whose 'difference' validated its own prevailing norms.

For many writers, this vision of a new, emancipatory kind of pluralism is at once highly seductive and deeply problematical. On the one hand, they welcome the prospect of freeing up politics from the homogenizing processes of cultural imperialism, from what Phillips has referred to as 'the conservatism of the undifferentiated norm' (1993). She looks instead, for example, to a truly inclusive 'democracy of difference', capable of giving full expression to the rich diversity of human talents, identities and interests. On the other hand, there are also deep concerns that cultural pluralisation will simply reinforce tendencies to political fragmentation and social atomism. Rather than opening up an expansive, inclusive domain of public-spirited, outward-looking citizens, the networking of cyberspace would thus give rise to a proliferation of confined and narrow public spaces, inhabited by beings whose sense even of their own identity is slippery and transient (Sassi 1996). The danger is that cyberdemocracy will consist of no more than the constant multiplication of isolated groups, with no channels, and more importantly, no commensurable cultural norms or political values that could enable their claims on each other or, indeed, on the wider society to be articulated, recognised or reconciled. Worse still by this reading, the diffuse and transient means of human connection that characterise the information age will serve not only to emphasise the disintegration of shared cultures and the fracturing of long-established political traditions but will itself contribute to decentring the self as an agent of purposeful, socially referenced, action. The undermining of the narratives that give meaning to human life, and the dissolution of a sense of belonging to a wider whole, will negate the possibilities for human beings to engage in collective action, recognise political obligation or sustain social commitment (Whitebrook 1995).

There are two main kinds of responses to these sorts of worries. The first is to regard this whole line of thought as an expression of the difficulty which (even) postmodern theorists experience in escaping from the Weberian paradigms of politics and state which have dominated modern thought. For such writers, this recoiling from the death of modern politics is symptomatic of a failure of imagination, a failure to conceive of a genuinely virtual democracy liberated from the constraints of territoriality, temporality and the categories of the nation-state. The very point of cyber society is that it is intellectually emancipatory as much as it is political liberating. For Poster even to use the term 'democracy' is to imprison our conception of cyberspace in an outmoded modernity. For him the essential point about the 'second media age' is that it promises to displace human connectivity from its institutional location, returning the very formation of culture into the people's power (Poster 1997). The idea that cyberdemocracy could be modelled *a priori* is oxymoronic.

A more usual kind of reaction, however, has been to worry away at the problems of conceptualising postmodern communities (Jones 1995). The most common theme in all this work is how to give scope to the widest range of interests and identities while preserving a shared foundation for citizenship. It centres on the immensely difficult problems of reconciling pluralisation with justice, diversity with belonging, democracy with difference. As scepticism grows with the communitarian project, so one important line of thought is simply to revert to the quasi-liberal search for a basic set of procedural norms, a 'framework of common practices' through which disparate groups could at least interact (Phillips 1993). However, even this limited aspiration is brought into question when the very grounding of the self is so heavily under challenge. We are forced, then, to examine the processes by which societies define belonging and construct identity, as a precursor for exploring how identities do and should address one another in a new democracy of difference (McClure 1992).

My own view is that this task would be considerably aided by jettisoning the slippery and unhelpful metaphor of 'virtual community' in favour of a theoretical concern with the subjective interconnectivity that is possible through 'networks' (Holmes 1997). Rather than worrying away at the paradoxes of social cohesion in the postmodern world we might do better to focus social theorizing on the multiple points of intersection in the webs of connection formed between identities. This strategy would at least permit us to acknowledge the negotiated quality of human connectivity and the intersubjective nature of social relationships. It would force us, too, to acknowledge that the negotiation of identity is the negotiation of meanings. In the second media age, no less than the first, these meanings are conveyed through texts and signs which are technologically mediated. The electronic networks of the cyber age stand, then, as crucial intermediaries in the profoundly political processes through which identities are constructed. Cyber networks not only focus attention on the range and nature of interfaces between the disparate, overlapping connectivities proliferating in cyberspace but, even more fundamentally, they bring into view the political significance of the communications through which identities are recognised and sustained.

This perspective has, of course, some important methodological implications both for the modelling and for the investigation of cyberdemocracy. In the first place, it renders obsolete the assumption that democracy can be articulated around settled procedural norms. It carries, too, important implications for understanding the significance of information and communications. Whereas our other models focus mainly on information and communication as material resources, pointing the student of TMIPP towards issues about control over and access to their technological base, the cyberdemocratic model directs attention to content, to the signs and meanings embedded in the structures and formats of electronic communications. More than any other model, it problematises information and its communication as political and thus as powerful phenomena. It leads us, too, to question how open and endlessly negotiable these phenomena can be. Are there forms of censorship – or indeed self-censorship – operating in cyberspace? Are there forms of information brokerage that privilege certain kinds of meaning and therefore certain kinds of identity? Are there, in other words, subtle accretions of power that could threaten the apparently open, turbulent, flexible networks of cyberspace with the kind of institutionalised closure that could shut out difference and limit pluralisation?

Towards empirical investigation

This chapter has shown how the process of modelling electronic democracy exposes different sets of discourses on electronic democracy. Our models have also raised several different sets of questions. In the next part of the book we use a series of case studies of TMIPP to explore the usefulness of these models and questions, before returning to further theoretical discussion in Chapter 11.

References

Abramson, J. B., Arterton, F. C. and Orren, G. R. (1988) *The Electronic Commonwealth: The Impact of New Media Technologies on Democratic Politics*, New York: Basic Books.

Adonis, A. and Mulgan, G. (1994) 'Back to Greece: the scope for direct democracy', Demos 3: 2–9.

Adorno, T. and Horkheimer, M. (1972) *The Dialectic of the Enlightenment*, New York: Herder and Herder.

Arterton, F. C. (1987) *Can Technology Protect Democracy?*, Washington, DC: Roosevelt Center for American Policy Studies and Sage.

Barber, B. (1984) *Strong Democracy: Participatory Democracy for a New Age*, Berkeley: University of California Press.

Barry, N. (1990) 'Markets, citizenship and the welfare state: some critical reflections', in R. Plant and N. Barry *Citizenship and Rights in Thatcher's Britain: Two Views*, London: Institute of Economic Affairs.

Baudrillard, J. (1988) *Selected Writings*, (ed.) M. Poster, Cambridge: Polity Press.

Beniger, J. R. (1986) *The Control Revolution*, Cambridge, Mass.: Harvard University Press.

Bellamy, C. and Taylor, J. A. (1998) *Governing in the Information Age*, Milton Keynes: Open University Press.

Calhoun, C. (ed.) (1992) *Habermas and the Public Sphere*, Cambridge, Mass.: The MIT Press.

Calabrese, A. and Borchert, M. (1996) 'Prospects for electronic democracy in the United

States: rethinking communication and social policy', *Media, Culture and Society* 18 (2): 249–268.

Callon, M. (1987) 'Society in the making: the study of technology as a tool for sociological analysis', in W. Bijker (ed.) *The Social Construction of Technological Systems*, Boston: The MIT Press.

Castells, M. (1996) *The Rise of the Network Society: Economy, Society and Culture*, I, Oxford: Blackwell.

Connolly, W. (1991) *Identity/Difference: Democratic Negotiations of Political Paradox*, Ithaca, NY and London: Cornell University Press.

——(1995) *The Ethos of Pluralization*, Minneapolis: University of Minnesota Press.

Curran, J. (1991) 'Rethinking the media as a public sphere', in P. Dahlgren and C. Sparks (eds) *Communication and Citizenship: Journalism and the Public Sphere*, London: Routledge.

Dahlgren, P. (1991) 'Introduction', in P. Dahlgren and C. Sparks (eds) *Communication and Citizenship: Journalism and the Public Sphere*, London: Routledge.

Danziger, J., Dutton, W., Kling, R. and Kraemer, K. (1982) *Computers and Politics*, New York: Columbia University Press.

Department of the Environment, Transport and the Regions (1998) *Modernising Local Government: Local Democracy and Community Leadership*, Consultative Paper, London: DETR.

Doctor, R. (1994) 'Seeking equity in the national information infrastructure', *Internet Research* 4 (3): 9–22.

Downs, A. (1967) *An Econonomic Theory of Democracy*, New York: Harper & Row.

Dutton, W. (1992) 'Political science research on teledemocracy', *Social Science Computer Review* 10 (4): 55–61.

Duverger, M. (1959) *Political Parties: Their Organization and Activity in the Modern State*, 2nd edn, London: Methuen.

Etzioni-Halevy, E. (1993) *The Elite Connection: Problems and Potential of Western Democracy*, Cambridge: Polity Press.

Fishkin, J. (1991) *Democracy and Deliberation: New Directions for Democratic Reform*, New Haven: Yale University Press.

Friedland, L. A. (1996) 'Electronic democracy and new citizenship', *Media, Culture and Society* 18: 185–212.

Garnham, N. (1990) *Capitalism and Communication: Global Communication and the Economics of Information*, London: Sage.

Gray, J. (1993). *Post-liberalism: Studies in Political Thought*, London: Routledge.

Habermas, J. (1989) *The Structural Transformation of the Public Sphere*, trans. T. Berger, Oxford: Polity Press and Blackwells.

Held, D. (1987) *Models of Democracy*, Cambridge: Polity Press.

Hirst, P. (1996) *Reinventing Democracy*, London: The Political Quarterly Publishing Co. Ltd.

——(1994) *Associative Democracy: New Forms of Economic and Social Governance*, Amherst: University of Massachusetts Press.

Holmes, D. (1997) 'Virtual identity: communities of broadcast, communities of interactivity', in D. Homes (ed.) *Virtual Politics: Identity and Community in Cyberspace*, London: Sage.

Hutton, W. (1995) *The State We're In*, London: Jonathan Cape.

Jones, S. G. (ed.) (1995) *Cybersociety: Computer-mediated Communication and Community*, London: Sage.

Keane, J. (1984) *Public Life and Late Capitalism: Towards a Socialist Theory of Democracy*, Cambridge: Polity Press.

——(1988) *Democracy and Civil Society*, London: Verso.

——(1991) *Media and Democracy*, Cambridge: Polity Press.

Kickert, W. J. M., Klijn, E.-H. and Koppenjan, J. F. M (eds) (1997) *Managing Complex Networks*, London: Sage.

Kooiman, J. (1993) *Modern Governance: New Government-Society Interactions*, London: Sage.

Laudon, K. (1977) *Communications Technology and Popular Participation*, New York: Praeger.

Leca, J. (1996) 'Questions of citizenship', in C. Mouffe (ed.) *Dimensions of Radical Democracy*, London: Verso.

Le Grand, J. and Estin, S. (1989) *Market Socialism*, Oxford: Clarendon Press.

Lyon, D. (1994). *The Electronic Eye: The Rise of the Surveillance Society*, Cambridge: Polity Press.

——(1997) 'Cyberspace sociality: controversies over computer-mediated relationships', in B. Loader (ed.) *The Governance of Cyberspace*, London: Routledge.

McClure, K. (1992) 'On the subject of rights: pluralism, plurality and political identity', in C. Mouffe (ed.) *Dimensions of Radical Democracy*, London: Verso.

MacIntyre, I. (1988) *Whose Justice? Which Rationality?*, London: Duckworth.

McLean, I. (1989) *Democracy and New Technology*, Cambridge: Polity Press.

Macpherson, C. B. (1962) *The Political Theory of Possessive Individualism*, Oxford: Oxford University Press.

——(1966) *The Real World of Democracy*, Oxford: Clarendon Press.

——(1977) *The Life and Times of Liberal Democracy*, Oxford: Oxford University Press.

Marshall, T. H. (1970) *Social Policy in the Twentieth Century*, 3rd edn, London: Hutchinson.

Michels, R. (1915) *Parties: A Study of the Oligarchical Tendencies of Modern Democracy*, trans. from the Italian by E. and C. Paul, London: Jarrold and Sons.

——(1962) *Political Parties*, trans. E. Paul and C. Paul, New York: Free Press.

Miller, D. (1989) *Market, State and Community: Theoretical Foundations of Market Socialism*, Oxford: Oxford University Press.

——(1995) 'Citizenship and pluralism', *Political Studies* 43 (3): 432–450.

Mouffe, C. (ed.) (1992) *Dimensions of Radical Democracy: Pluralism, Citizenship and Community*, London: Verso.

Mulhall, S. and Swift, A. (1992) *Liberals and Communitarians*, Oxford: Blackwell.

Offe, C. (1984) *Contradictions of the Welfare State*, London: Hutchinson.

Olson, M. (1965) *The Logic of Collective Action: Public Goods and the Theory of Groups*, Cambridge, Mass.: Harvard University Press.

Ostrogorski, M. (1902) *Democracy and the Organization of Political Parties*, trans. from the French by F. Clarke, London: Macmillan.

Percy-Smith, J. (1995) *Digital Democracy: Information and Communication Technologies in Local Politics*, London: Commission for Local Democracy.

Phillips, A. (1993) *Democracy and Difference*, Cambridge: Polity Press.

Poggi, G. (1978) *The Development of the Modern State: A Sociological Introduction*, London: Hutchinson.

Pollitt, C. (1993) *Managerialism and the Public Services*, 2nd edn, Oxford: Blackwells.

Poster, M. (1995) *The Second Media Age*, Cambridge: Polity Press.

——(1997) 'Cyberdemocracy: the Internet and the public sphere', in D. Holmes (ed.) *Virtual Politics: Identity and Community in Cyberspace*, London: Sage.

Putnam, R. (1993) *Making Democracy Work: Civic Traditions in Modern Italy*, Princeton: Princeton University Press.

——(1995) 'Bowling alone: America's declining social capital', *Journal of Democracy* 6 (1): 65–78.

Raab, C. (1998) 'Electronic confidence: trust, information and public information', in I. Suellen and W. van de Donk (eds) *Public Administration in an Information Age: A Handbook*, Amsterdam: IOS Press.

Rhodes, R. A. W. (1997) *Understanding Governance*, Milton Keynes: Open University Press.

Robins, K. (1995) 'Cyberspace and the world we live in', in M. Featherstone and R. Burrows (eds) *Cyberspace/Cyberbodies/Cyberpunk: Cultures of Technological Embodiment*, London: Sage.

Sassi, S. (1996) 'The network and the fragmentation of the public sphere', *Javnost* 3 (1): 25–42.

Sawhney, H. (1996) 'Information superhighway: metaphors as midwives', *Media, Culture and Society* 18 (2): 291–314.

Schumpeter, J. (1950) *Capitalism, Socialism and Democracy*, 3rd edn, New York: Harper Row.

Stoker, G. (1994) *The Politics of Local Government*, London: Commission for Local Democracy.

Taylor, C. (1989). *Sources of the Self: The Making of Modern Identity*, Cambridge: Cambridge University Press.

——(1995) 'Liberal politics and the public sphere', in his *Philosophical Arguments*, Cambridge, Mass.: Harvard University Press.

Tsagarousianou, R., Tambini, D. and Bryan, C. (1998) *Cyberdemocracy: Technology, Cities and Civic Networks*, London: Routledge.

Weston, J. (1994) 'Old freedoms and new technologies: the evolution of community networks', paper given to the Free Speech and Privacy in the Information Age symposium, University of Waterloo, Canada, November 1994 (available from the Teledemocracy Programme of NPTN at http://www.nptn.org.80/cyber.serv/tdp.

Whitebrook, M. (1995) *Real Toads in Imaginary Gardens: Narrative Accounts of Liberalism*, Lanham, Md.: Rowman and Littlefield.

Williams, F. and Parvik, J. V. (1994) *The People's Right to Know: Media, Democracy and the Information Highway*, Hillsdale, NJ: Lawrence Erlbaum Associates.

Winner, L. (1993) 'Beyond inter-passive media', *Technology Review* August–September: 69.

Part II

Case studies

3 Danish political parties and new technology

Interactive parties or new shop windows?

Karl Löfgren

INTRODUCTION

This pilot study provides the first opportunity to report on some preliminary findings from research studying the general use and strategy of information and communication technologies (ICTs) within Danish political parties. The objective is to identify whether the political parties have set up certain strategies[1] for using the new technologies in their communication with the electorate/citizens, as well as for intra-party communication with their members. The intention is to show how the political parties perceive the adaptation of ICTs *vis-à-vis* the electorate and members, and if this changes the connection between the party leadership, on the one side, and the members and the electorate, on the other. The data used for answering these questions will be interviews with the political spokespersons and 'webmasters' of the four major political parties represented in the Danish parliament ('Folketing').[2]

Furthermore, our intention is also to give a brief inventory of certain public electronic software applications which the political parties are making use of in contacts with their members, voters and citizens. This inventory has been carried out through on-line research on the four political parties' different software applications in order to study the resources. In order to study these applications we have chosen to categorise the different aspects of the investigation into two different parts: *information* and *communication*, where the first refers to the websites of the parties, and the latter to the two investigated Bulletin Board Systems (BBS).

We depart from a hypothesis stating that the political parties in Denmark are seeking to invigorate party-politics within a reconstituted contemporary polity based on 'governance' (cf. Kooiman 1993; Rhodes 1997). ICT plays an important role in this connection by 'reinventing' the party with its ability to increase the dissemination of information and enhance the level of communication between voters/members and the party leadership. However, this 'reinvention' does not signal a single clear-cut democratic strategy; indeed we seldom find considerations on the way in which the use of new technology might affect democracy. Whereas pre-defined strategies are rare in our study, it is however, possible to identify intrinsic, only sometimes deliberate, considerations (through the parties' own statements) on why the parties have adopted ICTs. Mainly, the parties consider having their own website as a mode to secure symbolic values for the organisation. With regard to the actual use, the interactive features of new technologies are mainly limited to those members subscribing to the services (which in turn, are few), whereas the voters and the citizens are offered new forms of top-directed political propaganda.

Although this study will mainly show examples of new forms of 'old' vertical connections between voters and politicians stressing image, effectiveness and 'service obligations', we are also witnessing signs of more horizontal participatory connections. Our conclusion is that the current strategies and utilisation of ICTs in relation to the voters and citizens will reinforce the tendency towards professional party organisation, where the political party is centred around a leadership, and where the new technology is used for top-down dissemination of information. Conversely, we are able to perceive that the members in a small scale among themselves are utilising the new technology to create their own political discourses through the interactive forms of new technology, albeit detached from the political leadership within the parties and without any effective influence on the decision-making process.

Political parties in decline?

The decline of the political parties' role as 'mass organisations' has been of research interest since the 1960s. Traditionally, our Western constitutional system has since the gradual acknowledgement of parties as the key actor in representative democracies throughout the twentieth century, included the political membership party as the most important institution for mediating the 'people's' will and aspiration into the political world. The classical membership parties, through a whole network of local branches, and based on societal linkages, were able to emancipate the citizens into membership organisations (Duverger 1954). However, this traditional picture of the constitutional democratic model has eroded with a decreasing number of citizens taking part in the political parties' activities in terms of number of members in the parties, as well as the emergence of professional, managerial and centralised party organisations (Panebianco 1988; Katz and Mair 1995).

Like many other Western constitutional democracies Denmark has not been undisturbed by these tendencies. With only a small proportion of Danish citizens actually taking part in political party work, there is clearly a deterioration of the political parties' traditional function as 'intermediators'. Whereas the proportion of voters who were members of a political party in Denmark by the beginning of the 1960s reached 21.1 per cent, the similar figures by the end of the 1980s had declined to only 6 per cent (Katz and Mair 1992: 334).

Simultaneously, the party organisation has passed through major transformations. The traditional Danish 'membership party', has like other European equivalents, been replaced by a more professional and managerial organisation incorporated in the state-system – 'the cartel party', thus becoming more detached from the civil society (Katz and Mair 1995; Bille 1994, 1997). Contact with voters and citizens has been transferred from the membership party to the mass media. Furthermore, the political parties' leaderships are becoming less dependent on both financial and voluntary labour support from the members due to public funding and increased employment of professional party workers. Hence, we can conclude that the parties per se are not in decline, but that the classical function of the party as intermediator between people and government is in decline.

It is possible to perceive this general trend of party organisational development with the advent of new ICTs (in particular the World Wide Web). While the majority of literature to date on ICTs and the political world has been concerned with searching for these more participatory forms of democracy in the realms of civil society, but, with some notable exceptions (see, e.g. Smith 1998; Ward and Gibson 1998; Casey 1996) there is less written on political parties.

Depla and Tops (1995) have suggested that the new technologies may offer two possible successors of the political party as a mass organisation. First, the *modern cadre party*, where the new technologies foster new forms of political participation through functional discussion forums.[3] Second, the *professional electoral association* where the political parties are organised around a single political leader, and where the new technology is used to strengthen the temporary campaign association set up for promoting the leader. Whereas the former party model can be perceived as a 'reinvention' of the membership party, the latter bears a lot of resemblance to the 'cartel party'. These two models of parties in the information age can also be perceived in the light of the democratic models as set out in this volume (see Chapter 2). Whereas the first is a new democratic party form, stressing the emancipatory attributes of the TMIPP, very much like the 'cyberdemocracy model', the second party model is barely a continuation of already existing demo-elitist democratic practices. The question here is thus what trajectory the Danish parties are following. Depla and Tops suggest in their conclusion that 'for the future of political parties . . . it will be of importance whether or not the interactive features of the new media is used. With these features, political parties are able to bring up discussions and to involve members and sympathisers in their organisation in a new way' (1995: 176).

This paper will focus on these interactive features of the new ICTs.[4] In response to the advent of the new technologies, the Danish political parties have gradually entered the information age with the establishment of party websites on the World Wide Web, and by setting up BBSs. From an international perspective, Danish political parties have been relatively 'latecomers' in adapting new technologies compared to political parties in many other European countries. This despite the fact that the country holds a high position internationally when it comes to the diffusion of Internet access among the population.

The following inventory gives a brief presentation of the different electronic applications that the political parties in the study currently use.

Table 1 ICT applications in the Danish political parties

Political parties	ICT applications
The Social Democratic Party (Det Socialdemokratiske Arbejderparti)	Website, BBS 'Net•dialog', Press-service (SNT; mailing-list)
The Liberal Party (Det Liberale Parti Venstre)	Website, Press-service 'Venstres Pressetjenste' (mailing-list)
The Socialist People's Party (Socialistisk Folkeparti)	Website, BBS 'Hotlips'
The Conservative's People's Party (Det Konservative Folkeparti)	Website

Note
All of the 10 political parties currently represented in the Folketing have websites, but only SP and SPP have internal conference systems

STRATEGIES

Our study shows that the political parties have entered the world of new technology almost without any predefined, explicit strategies. In most of the cases the initiative to adopt new ICTs came from individuals within the political parties' leaderships and/or party bureaucracy, without any prior internal discussion in the party organisation, mainly as a result of other parties' adoption of websites and the general public rhetoric on the information society. This, and claims from the spokespersons of the parties that there was some resistance within the parties towards the implementation of new ICT, imply that new technology is still a not very well integrated part of the parties' activities.

However, this does not mean that the parties are acting totally blindly. Rather, they conceive it more as an integrated part of their over-arching information strategy, which, in turn, relates more to the above-mentioned professional party organisation, than to any transformations in the party linkages. A typical trait is that the size of the political parties affects the resources spent on developing new ICT projects. The two big political parties – the SP and the LP – have far more resources and this is reflected in the magnitude and maintenance of the websites. The findings of the interviews follows.

The Social Democratic Party (SP) was the only party who had some kind of predefined strategy on this area. The SP have made a clear distinction between services for members and services for voters and citizens. With respect to its members, the SP joined a BBS run by the Danish Federation of Trade Unions (LO) named 'net•Dialog' in 1996 (originally set up in 1994), which also operates as an intranet between the different 'associations' within the labour movement. All members of the SP, the trade unions with affiliated associations, and subscribers to the daily Social Democratic newspaper 'Aktuelt' can join the 'net•Dialog' conference service. The estimated number of users in 'net•Dialog' is approximately 8,000 people, which makes it one of the biggest (non-Internet) on-line services in Denmark. The different conferences are all moderated by somebody who is acknowledged to be 'suitable' for the specific area, typically a spokesperson, or a chairman of a party committee.

The website was established in 1996 as an initiative from the party headquarters and the reason was mainly that it was considered to be a 'natural step' in the 'modernisation' of the party.[5] The website is mainly directed to non-members and the webmaster estimates the number of hits to between 30,000 to 50,000 every week, and it is maintained by external consultants. The strategy for the future is to improve the homepage with respect to user-friendliness, to decentralise the maintenance and to use new visualising formats (such as video and audio applications). What is even more interesting is that the party has identified certain 'target groups' which the new homepage is to be directed to:

- Pupils in primary and secondary school
- Potential members
- Members
- Professionals (librarians)
- Other political parties and groups
- Local activists
- Journalists and professional mass media people
- Labour Union and their local shop-floor representatives

(Larsen 1997: 3)

What we can conclude from this strategy is that the website will mainly operate as a 'service provider' supplying interested groups with information about the party, rather than generating public debates. Since we did the interviews (in May 1997) the strategy seems to have changed somewhat as selected conferences from the net•Dialog system at present are mirrored in the website, and opened up for postings from non-members.

The Liberal Party (LP) was the first party to establish a website in Denmark (September 1995). The adaptation of a website is considered to be an attempt to appear as a 'young and vital party' as their ICT-spokesperson presented it. The initiative to enter the Internet actually came from the party chairman, and most of the discussion and planning around the adoption of new ICTs has been informal and unstated. There are two central officials in charge of the maintenance of the website; one for the parliamentary group, and one from the party organisation headquarters (both are originally press and liaison officers).

As for the party's own brief statement on strategy, the main issue has been to decentralise the maintenance of the website. There is thus a high degree of freedom with respect to what the individual MPs can publish on their individual homepage as long as they stick to the party's templates. The future strategy is mainly concentrated on rapidly increasing the volume of the homepage with new material and to maintain the accuracy of the pages. The party has made attempts to use their website for consultative discussion conferences where a topic is presented (by the party chairman) and where the 'visitors' are welcome to make a comment within a limited period of time. This is a feature which is likely to continue. As one of the webmasters argued: 'there were some serious contributions to the debate, so we are likely to maintain these discussion groups'.

The Socialist People's Party (SPP) has in their use of ICTs been motivated by the experiences of different grass-roots associations and their Free-nets (they mention 'Alternative for Progressive Communication' (APC) as an example). This is clearly stated in one of their pamphlets: 'a modern socialist strategy shall exploit the possibilities of the new technology' and 'the left wing shall actively use the information technology in favour of a de-centralisation of power' (Socialistisk Folkeparti 1994: 11). The initiative for adopting new technologies in the party originally came from a member of the parliamentary group. However, the SPP has so far not accomplished any specified strategy regarding how to exploit the new technology for external contacts. The BBS – 'Hotlips' – is thought to be the internal communication link in-between the members, whereas the website is supposed to work as the platform for external communication.

'Hotlips' was set up in May 1995 (and was the first of its kind in Denmark), and there are somewhere between 400 and 500 users. The website was established in May 1996. The webmaster's impression of the users of the website is that it is primarily young members who are connected to the services. It is interesting to notice that much of the responsibility for both the BBS and the homepage is placed at one person's desk, i.e. the webmaster. There exists a certain party committee to track new technology development but the webmaster is to a large extent the person responsible for the daily maintenance.

The Conservative People's Party (CPP) established their website in May 1996 after pressure from local branches. Until now, the party has not adopted any special strategy for using ICTs in the party. The party's website was set up rather fast and since it resulted in over 200 new members (in addition to the normal applications for membership) the party's headquarters soon became aware of the importance of being 'on the net'. According to the webmaster, the future plans are to improve the design of the website with new applications such as video and audio clips. New interactive applications are, however, not on the agenda for the moment. This issue has been discussed, but so far there are no resources for setting up a more interactive application (such as a BBS or a news group). The webmaster stated that one of the obstacles for increasing the use of ICT within the party, was that many of the members of the parliament still contested the use of new technology – 'many still use their typewriters deliberately'. Like the SPP there was a problem of lack of resources for developing a more long-term strategy for the development and use of new ICT.

USE

As mentioned above, all Danish political parties have within a very short period of time acquired homepages on the World Wide Web, and two of them even provide BBSs. We studied the homepages on the World Wide Web for a three-month period (between April and June 1997) where we regularly (once a week) downloaded the resources from the different websites and checked the accuracy of the content. With respect to the BBSs we collected a random sample of four of the conferences from each BBS and studied the communication over time. A distinct period of time would not have provided us with sufficient data. This study will not clarify the whole range of communication that takes place in the two BBSs since we are only examining a minor part of them.

The conferences we chose to study on net•Dialog were all debate conferences, whereas two were on 'general politics' and two on more specific topics – 'Education' and 'Health'. On SPP's 'Hotlips' we studied one on politics in general and two on specific issues – 'European Union' and 'Education', and fourth, a conference on the annual congress of the party. This chapter will not include the member's closed conferences, since we were not granted access. Non-members can obtain limited access to most of the conferences. There is, however, practically no 'desire' from either of the parties to grant access to non-members.

THE WORLD WIDE WEB

This first category refers to *information* resources which are *unidirectional* without any immediate possibility to respond. With the information part we refer to the interfaces where there are no urgent requests for possibility to reply immediately, which was the normal content of the parties' websites. This should not be interpreted in ways that the audience is composed of merely passive consumers of information. All websites of course have the possibility for the 'audience' to respond to either some in the party or the webmaster, and all the parties stress that they appreciate being in contact with citizens and that they also receive responses from those who visit their homepages.

Following some general guidelines for how to assess information resources in general on the Internet,[6] we have picked some criteria which we believe could be useful for visualising the political parties' use of WWW. The criteria which we choose are as follow: (a) content, (b) currency and (c) workability. Below we will present the criteria and the findings.

Content

Most of the content of the political parties' homepages had been abstracted from the parties' standard official material, e.g. the party charters and the party history. The material on the websites was clearly directed to non-members seeking to obtain more information about the party. There were very few examples of material exclusively produced for the website. A lot of the published texts on the websites lacked authors, which made it difficult to find out the actual author of the text – was it an individual or was it the whole party organisation? We also found that the parties had organised their websites almost in the same hierarchical way and we chose to sub-categorise the content as follows:

News – weekly/monthly updated material addressed to a general audience with the latest comments from the central leadership on contemporary political topics. All of the parties (except the SP) had a regular newsletter (usually weekly) from the party leader (or a highly ranked person in the party leadership) with comments on the current topics. News from the press-services of the LP were also mirrored at their website (approximately 20 each week). Furthermore, there were special newsletters from the 'European Parliamentary' group in the LP and the SP (which also had an international section). The LP's and the SP's websites also contained a number of current speeches from the parliament.

General presentation of the party – general information such as history of the party, more or less rich information on the members of the parliament, on-line versions of party charters, declaration of principles, etc. Only a minor part of the resources has been produced especially for a web-edition.

The LP, in addition to the above-mentioned official material, had a large number of working papers, speeches and articles. As mentioned earlier their strategy was to decentralise the maintenance of their website, so the personal homepages differed a lot. Some contained just some minimum information on the person, whereas others where quite extensive, containing whole speeches and links to other places of interest. The SP had a similar version containing only e-mail addresses and their positions in the party.

Contacts – How to join the party, how to obtain more information, who is in charge of the website (webmaster), telephone numbers, e-mail addresses, etc. All the parties provided the possibility to contact them via e-mail and to order material from the party headquarters. Also common for all the parties was the urge for joining the party as a member on-line.

Links – to local branches, to national/international sister parties/associations and youth organisations websites. The normal hypertext links were connected to the international sister parties in Scandinavia and Europe. The SPP's homepage contained a massive list of links (20) to all sort of 'affiliated' websites with more or less political content. In addition, the SPP's website also contained a list of links to the different ministries and the LP's website included a clickable map to all local branches in Denmark.

Debate forum – the LP had a discussion forum on their website for a short period (three weeks – on the topic 'ICT in primary school'), which was initiated by the party chairman. There were around 20 annotations to his urge, whereas most of the annotations supported the chairman's original announcement. None of the other parties had anything similar.

Contemporaneity

A major problem from which the analysed websites suffered was out-of-date material. This appears to be a chronic problem for websites in general and Danish political parties' websites are not exempt. A lot of the material we downloaded from the websites had been put there without being updated and/or the material had after a time become obsolete. The worst example we found was the 'News from the European Parliament' on the SP homepage which had not been updated since December 1996, and was still not updated in July 1997. All the political parties' websites however, suffered from this problem. This was not always easy to detect because there were hardly any signs when the material had originally been placed on the website.

Workability

This includes features such as:

- *user friendliness*: Most of the studied homepages were easy to navigate in. The main exception was the SPP homepage that was very anarchistic in its design and there the idea was to read all the different pages from A to Z. All of the parties had some information in English, usually the party history.
- *searching*: Here the political parties' websites made a good impression. The websites were all organised in different categories and you could easily click yourself to the relevant information. The LP's website also provided a search engine, but it was of the more simple type thus making it harder to find what you were searching for.
- *connectivity*: In the studied period there were hardly any problems in accessing the websites with standard browser software.

Bulletin Board Services

The second category – *communication* – refers to the network-based conferencing services (such as the BBS) where you can identify a more distinct *bidirectional* discussion. This includes software interfaces where questions, annotations, etc., are asynchronous replied via a 'moderator' or directly to the whole, or parts of, the group of participants.

The two BBSs we studied – 'Hotlips' and 'net•Dialog' – were quite different from each other – both in terms of content and size. This seems quite logical keeping in mind that there are some rather important differences in terms of organisational manners between the two parties – the Social Democratic party and the Socialist People's Party. Whereas the first is a classical Western European Social Democratic party, i.e. the archetype of a classical membership party; the latter is a small leftist party, more settled in a grass-root organisational style and having a participatory party organisation.'

'Net•Dialog' is run as a joint venture between the Social Democratic Party and the Federation of Trade Unions in Denmark, and is operating as both an electronic post and a conference system. The service is divided into two 'appearances': 'net•DiAlog' – the edition that the Social Democratic party uses, and 'net•DiaLOg' which is the edition for the trade unions. As a user, one has access to both parts, the different organisations are responsible though for the content of the conferences in their part of the system. The daily technical operation is run by one company 'Net-medier A/S' which is a division of the Social Democratic media group – 'A-press'.

The debate conferences which we especially focused on, were only a small portion of the overall content of the net•Dialog. All major official documents from both the Social Democratic party, as well as the trade unions, are published in categorised conferences which are built up hierarchically. Furthermore, there are daily articles and chronicles from the major SP papers and media, databases of the speeches in the parliament, current activities, etc. There is also something named the 'marketplace' which not only refers to normal buying and selling, but also provides the means for more 'social' communication between the members. One of the more interesting features of the system is the conference on the European Parliament where everybody is free to ask questions directly to the group of Social Democratic members of the European Parliament and where the members of the Parliament try to reply directly to the conference. This part did, however, not attract much attention from the users in the studied period.

All the debate conferences were moderated by a person who (in most cases) was elected by those who participated in the conferences and were in many cases also initiated by the same persons. There also exists some general rules and guidelines for how to behave in the conferences (Landsorganisationen 1996: 53 ff.). The user is encouraged to keep up a good tone of communication with others and avoid contributions that can possibly harm, or be misinterpreted by others. We did not however, find any interference from the moderator in the conferences during the studied period. Nevertheless, there had been a previous case where the moderator had to intervene into the discussion (according to the webmaster).

The two conferences on 'politics in general' were subject to more intensive posting than the specific issue-related conferences. However, this was mainly because the general conferences had a high proportion of press releases, drafts, etc. from different branches and the affiliated associations of the party. This type of 'editorial' material was actually a dominant feature in all of the studied conferences. It was usually sent by members of the parliament, high-ranking politicians in some of the associations and/or the local/regional governments. Surprisingly, this sort of posting was seldom annotated by the other users, although the messages were usually read. The few debates which sprung out of the individual members' contributions were very often written in a 'to-the-editor-style'. However, many of these individual contributions were not annotated at all, which was usually the case with the short (and maybe not very well-reasoned) notices. Where some response occurred, the tone was almost always friendly and the involved participants encouraged each other to continue to write or to find solutions to the topic. There was only one debate in our study that fostered a more vivid debate. A woman wrote a contribution on men's lack of responsibility in relation to the welfare of children. This developed into a dispute between the sexes on custody where the participants became rather aggressive and where personal feelings came out in the open.

While this study could by no means grasp the total content of all the conferences, it was rather easy to detect some patterns. First, high-ranking politicians (for example, members of the parliament) never took part in the debates, but simply conveyed their press releases to the conferences; a form of 'recycling' of old material, rather than addressing new issues in front of the members. Second, that the normal contributors to the discussions were to be found in a rather narrow circuit of people; 'the old guard' of the party. Third, that the people who took part in the debates in many cases knew each other from other activities within the party, and that the political positions were very often settled in advance. Hence, from our small samples of the debate we could perceive that the net•Dialog service did not open up for new communicative connections between the members and the party elite. Rather, it reinforced the connections between the members themselves.

It is possible to interpret this finding as another sign of the decline of the membership party. But one can also perceive this type of new connections as something positive where the members maintain and reinforce a political discourse of a political party as a membership organisation. Another thing we observed was, that the new technology also had a positive effect in the sense that political experiences from different parts of the country could very rapidly be shared with the rest of the members. This implies that the members in their internal communication can 'bypass' the central leadership despite geographical constraints, and that geographically 'isolated' members to a larger extent can experience 'belonging' to a political party.

The SPP's 'Hotlips' has a lot in common with net•Dialog in terms of the technical design. But it does not contain the same amount of information resources and number of conferences as the latter. The number of users are also, as mentioned earlier, less than on net•Dialog. There are closed conferences for members, but as we will demonstrate, the membership debate is not as confined as at the Social Democratic equivalent. Whereas the conferences on net•Dialog are moderated, this type of steering does not exist on Hotlips. People are free to write whatever they like, and it is only through the members own interference that an intimidating or racist contribution can be stopped. This has however never been the case. The somehow 'open' grass-root style of the Socialist People's party has thus also affected their conference system.

In addition to the general debates, Hotlips has a joint conference with the Danish daily paper *Politiken* (which also runs a BBS called 'Pol Online') so that the subscribers of Pol Online can participate in debates with people from Hotlips and vice versa. The conference ('SPP on Pol Online') was set up in May 1997 and the number of contributions exceeds all the other conferences of the political parties. Typically, this specific conference has been dominated by political issues in the periphery of the dominant political discourse. In this case the most overwhelming issue in the first month was 'free drugs/hashish'.

Like in net•Dialog, the conference on politics in general obtained more postings than the conferences on specific issues. Surprisingly, we did not find very much debate at all in the conference on politics in general. Most of the contributions to the conference were of the 'to-the-editor' style without any annotations, rather similar to the findings from net•Dialog. Actually, some of these contributions were letters to the press which had been published elsewhere, or had been refused by the editors of the daily papers. The contributions where one could trace a bilateral communication had in most cases its origin in the closed 'members conferences'. Something that did make a difference in relation to Net•Dialog was the higher proportion of contributions from the central leadership, who actually took themselves time to answer questions and respond to critique. In the specific issue conferences there were signs that the debates had been more vivid last year, but somehow they were almost dead by now. For example, the posting to the conference on education was maintained by one single person.

Conversely, the conference on the annual national congress, contained an aggressive debate on the party auditor's role in relation to the youth league. After the congress the debate continued where almost all details on the correspondence between the auditor and the leadership of the youth league before and after the annual national congress was revealed and debated, and where the accusations scattered back and forth. While this conference was the only one where we were able to witness any signs of a vivid debate, this sort of open and frank discussion shows the potential of the media. It also stresses that prior organisational forms, where the SPP since the foundation in the 1950s has stressed the participatory linkages within the party organisation, plays a more important role than the technology per se.

CONCLUSION

This pilot study has analysed a sample of the Danish political parties' use of two specific applications of new technology. Since the area is constantly changing, it is hard to predict anything about what lies around the corner and, therefore, this study can be seen as an early inventory of a new field of research. Already since we carried out our study in the spring of 1997 some changes with regards to the specific applications have occurred.

While the parties' use of ICT is still in an initial and trial-and-error mode, and where the adaptation of new technologies has not penetrated the party organisation on a large scale, the findings here suggest certain patterns in the use and strategies of new ICTs within the parties. The current implicit strategies of the investigated parties are leading one's thought in the direction of the party attempting not to end in a backwater in relation to future political communication infrastructures.

The main objective in the development of websites by the parties has been the production of nice-looking 'shop-windows' for the parties to present mainly standard party information to the electorate and citizens. Basically, Danish parties' use of websites until now have neither embodied new interactive features, which might promote new horizontal flows of communication between the party elite and the members/electorate, nor challenged established forms of party organisation.

When it comes to the two examined bulletin board services the situation is slightly different. The objective here has been to create a new forum of debate, preferably for the members. We have been able to witness signs of a free and open discourse among the members that could entail the potential of inverting the membership party. However, the low proportion of members actually participating in these debates, as well as the absence of participation from the party leaderships, and the predominance of 'the old guard' of the parties suggest that new technology is unlikely to alter the power structures within the party organisations.

Overall, the findings here suggest that the parties' use of new ICT is reinforcing the current trends of professional party organisations with top-down dissemination of information, whereas citizens and members are provided with new channels for individualised and consultative participation, but without any real influence. Even though there are some minor indications of new bidirectional connections, the overall picture does not lead one to believe that the parties' adaptation of new technology will change the overall picture of a demoelitist discourse embedded in the Danish political parties' strategies and use of new technology.

Notes

1 For a definition of 'strategy': see Chapter 1.
2 Sonja Mikkelsen, MP (the Social Democratic Party), Jens Løgstrup Madsen, MP (the Liberal Party), Henriette Kjær, MP (the Conservative People's Party), Sven Bastrup, webmaster (the Socialist People's Party), Benny Damsgaard, webmaster (the Conservative People's Party), Kim Larsen, webmaster (the Social Democratic Party), Martin Vith, webmaster (the Liberal Party), Finn-Erik Enderlein, webmaster (the Liberal Party).
3 Similar trains of thought in the shape of 'party-based direct democracy' can be found in Budge 1996.
4 We will however use the term 'bidirectional' instead of 'interactivity'. Interactivity has unfortunately in much of the literature on ICT become an underdefined 'buzz-word' encompassing all sorts of human communication conveyed by telematics. A richer definition can be found in Rafaeli (1988): 'Formally stated, interactivity is an expression of the extent that in a given series of communication exchanges, any third (or later) transmission (or message) is related to the degree to which previous exchanges referred to even earlier transmissions' (Rafaeli 1988: 111).
5 However, the fact that the Liberal Party had just launched their website is also mentioned.
6 Smith 1996; Rettig 1996.
7 The party was founded in 1959 after a struggle within the Danish Communist Party, partly as a reaction against the centralist and traditional communist party organisation ('democratic centralism'). One of the parties first internal initiatives was therefore to increase the members' influence in the organisation through e.g. members' direct influence on the composition of the central party committees (cf. Bille 1997: chapter 6).

References

Bille, L. (1994) 'Denmark: the decline of the membership party?', in R. S. Katz and P. Mair (eds) *How Parties Organize: Change and Adaptation in Party Organizations in Western Democracies*, London: Sage.

——(1997) *Partier i Forandring: En analyse af danske partiorganisationers udvikling 1960–1995*, Odense Universitetsforlag: Viborg.

Budge, I. (1996) *The New Challenge of Direct Democracy*, Oxford: Polity Press.

Casey, C. (1996) *The Hill on the Net: Congress Enters the Information Age*, Chestnut Hill, Mass.: Academic Press Inc.

Depla, P. F. G. and Tops, P. (1995) 'Political parties in the digital era: the technological challenge', in W. B. H. J. van den Donk, I. Th. M. Snellen and P. W. Tops *Orwell in Athens – A Perspective on Informatization and Democracy*, Amsterdam: IOS Press.

Duverger, M. (1954) *Political Parties: Their Organization and Activity in the Modern State*, 2nd edn, London: Methuen.

Katz, R. S. and Mair, P. (eds) (1992) *Party Organizations in Western Democracies 1960–1990: A Data Handbook*, London: Sage.

——(1995) 'Changing models of party organization and party democracy – the emergence of the cartel party', *Party Politics* 1 (1): 5–28.

Kooiman, J. (ed.) (1993) *Modern Governance: New Government – Society Interactions*, London: Sage.

Landsorganisationen [The Danish Federation of Trade Unions] (1996) [on-line version] *Introduktion & brugervejledning til Net•Dialog* [cited 1 July 1996: available from net•Dialog BBS].

Larsen, K. (1997) *Ny Website*, unpublished internal working paper for a Social Democratic internal conference in Roskilde, April 1997.

Panebianco, A. (1988) *Political Parties: Organization and Power*, Cambridge: Cambridge University Press.

Rafaeli, S. (1988) 'Interactivity: from new media to communication', in R. P. Hawkins, J. M. Wiemann and S. Pingree (eds) *Advancing Communication Science: Merging Mass and Interpersonal Processes, Sage Annual Reviews of Communication Research* 16: 110–134.

Rettig, J. (1996) *Beyond Cool – Analogue Models for Reviewing Digital Resources* [on-line – cited 1 July 1997], available from World Wide Web: < http://world wide web.onlineinc.com/online/online/onlinemag/SeptOL/rettig9.html>.

Rhodes, R. A. W. (1997) *Understanding Governance: Policy Networks, Governance, Reflexivity and Accountability*, Milton Keynes: Open University Press.

Smith, A. (1996) *Criteria for Evaluation of Internet Information Resources* [on-line – cited 1 July 1997], available from World Wide Web: <http://world wide web.vuw.ac.nz/~agsmith/evaln/index/htm>.

Smith, C. (1998) 'Political parties in the information age: from mass party to leadership organisation?', in I. Snellen and W. van de Donk (eds) *Handbook in the Information Age*, Amsterdam: IOS Press.

Socialistisk Folkeparti (1994) *Det må gerne være sjovt*, pamphlet from the Socialist People's Party.

Van de Donk, W. B. H. J. and Tops, P. W. (1995) 'Orwell or Athens? – Informatization and the Future of Democracy', in W. B. H. J. van den Donk, I. Th. M. Snellen and P. W. Tops, *Orwell in Athens – A Perspective on Informatization and Democracy*, Amsterdam: IOS Press.

Ward, S. and Gibson, G. (1998) 'The first internet election? UK political parties and campaigning in cyberspace', in I. Crewe, B. Gosschalk and J. Bartle (eds) *Political Communication and the 1997 General Election*, Ilford: Frank Cass (forthcoming).

4 British political parties

Continuity and change in the information age

Colin Smith

INTRODUCTION

Contemporary analyses of the role and actions of political parties criticise both their claim to continue to occupy a central position as primary mediators in the polity, and their performance as agents of democracy. Parties, along with other traditional representative mechanisms, are widely understood to have become displaced from their role as the dominant input channels in the political system, both by new forms of participation, and new methods for governments to discern popular opinion. The emergence of interpretations of democracy differing from the once-dominant constitutional model has been a common consequence of this.

Political parties can be conceived of organisationally as sets of information flows, linking the parliamentary leadership to central party officials, through to governing bodies of the party and on to the basic units of organisation, the constituency and branch parties.[1] Parties have informational relationships with the general public of varying importance at each of these junctures; through direct contact, traditional media, and now also new technologically mediated innovations in political practice (TMIPP), supported by new information and communication technologies (ICTs). While TMIPP has not reached an advanced stage within all, or arguably within any, of the informational processes which are enmeshed around British parties, it is also arguable that any use of technologies concerned with the processing, storage and exchange of information must necessarily affect existing information flows (Smith and Webster 1995).

While the existence of emergent TMIPP around parties can already be said to be important, what is less clear is the significance of these relationships in understanding the contemporary role and place of parties in the polity. Almost inevitably, parties attempt to depict an avowed orientation towards new technologies as expressions of organisational and political vitality. A closer examination of the manner in which elements within parties have taken up and applied capabilities offered by ICTs reveals a much more interesting set of emergent trends and outcomes than that which parties often seek to portray.

If parties no longer occupy the ground between citizenry and government in the way that they once did, do TMIPP around parties provide evidence of attempts to restore themselves to a dominant position? In the process, might this involve the promotion of aspects of democracy characteristic of either a modified constitutionalism or new emergent democratic forms such as demo-elitist, neo-republican, consumer or cyberdemocracy? Case study research of four of the main parties in the UK (Conservative, Labour, Liberal Democrat and Scottish National Party) carried out during and since the period of the British general election campaign of 1997 points to a complicated pattern of emergent relationships; however it does not suggest a simple attempt to reinvigo-rate constitutionalism, a model of party, and of democracy, which is now uncharacteristic of contemporary political processes in the UK.

The overarching objective of this chapter is to explore political parties' use of ICTs by identifying the general strategies and discourses which have informed the variety of innovations which the chapter identifies. Within this are three key interrelated aims; first, to highlight the uptake of capabilities offered by ICTs within and around parties, describing and analysing some of the main technolo-gies and their applications. The second aim is to explore emergent relationships within and around parties facilitated by new technologies, relationships which may be suggestive of changing forms of party organisation and competition. Finally, the question of whether such emergent relationships provide evidence to support a possible redefinition of the relationships between citizens and parties will be explored, relating back to the discussion of models of democracy contained in Chapters 1 and 2. The chapter begins by discussing the evidence illustrating the 'crisis of democracy' as it manifests itself at the input channel of the democratic process, namely the concept of party decline.

PARTIES AND THE 'CRISIS' OF DEMOCRACY

The constitutional model of democracy is associated with the classic political party; the mass party. In the archetypal mass party model, the fundamental units of political life are pre-existing and well-defined social groups (Neumann 1956), and the operation of politics is primarily manifest through the competition and cooperation of these groups. Political parties are the agencies through which these groups, and their memberships and supporters, participate in politics by making demands upon the state and attempting to place their representatives in key offices. Parties, then, provide an essential linkage between citizens and the state (Lawson 1980). There is a strong current in the literature on party organisation presenting the mass party as the standard against which every other form of party should be measured and analysed. However the mass party relates to a particular conception of democracy, and to a particular idea of the structure of society, neither of which are of great contemporary relevance (Katz and Mair 1995).

The decline of almost every aspect of the mass party has been noted since the 1950s. The evidence in support of dealignment, the weakening and fracturing of the linkages between social class and party identification, is particularly strong. For example, the proportion of 'very strong' identifiers with any political party fell from 47 per cent in 1964 to just 16 per cent in 1987 (Denver 1994: 54), and the results of such attitude surveys have been substantiated by the concrete evidence of election data.[2] One response to this was seen in the emergence of catch-all parties (Kirchheimer 1966) a new form of party organisation aided by economic growth and the establishment of welfare states which helped cut across socio-economic groups. The development of a mass media was also a significant factor, since parties were able for the first time to engage not just with their own memberships but with the electorate at large, composed of voters 'learning to behave more like consumers than active participants' (Katz and Mair 1995: 7).

Compelling evidence for the party decay thesis can also be found in the decline in party membership. British political parties, like many of their European counterparts, are finding it difficult to recruit and retain members; individual membership of all three principal parties is estimated to have fallen by at least a half since 1974 (Katz and Mair 1995: 113–117).[3] A growth in the membership of the Labour Party to around 370,000 since Tony Blair became leader would have to continue unabated for some time before the party could claim to have a truly mass membership, while Labour's determination to further weaken its links with trades unions will continue to reduce the importance of affiliated membership of the party through union membership (Pinto-Duschinsky 1997).

The evidence in favour of party decline is convincing; but that evidence relates specifically to the mass party archetype, not the concept of political party per se. Contemporary parties are still an enormously important feature of the political landscape; they continue to be the central organs for generating candidates, for fighting the elections that put them into office, and for determining the character of a country's governing body (Finer 1984: 1). However, since the demise of the mass party was partially conditioned by the rise of a mass media facilitated by a changed technological context, it seems probable that further technological advance, represented in this case by new media, must continue to relate to emergent party organisational forms.

PARTIES AND NEW TECHNOLOGY: EXPLORING THE CAPABILITIES

As suggested in the introduction to this chapter, one of the most fundamental questions in an examination of TMIPP around political parties is in locating the source (in technological terms) of the most meaningful innovation, and identifying where the result of any innovation is best exhibited. What technologies, with which applications, and what outcomes are actually changing our understanding of political parties? Many studies of the role of new technologies in parties concentrate on the ways they use the Web. In doing so, however, a decision is made to study some aspects of 'information age' parties to the neglect of others, particularly the role and importance of more basic ICT-supported relationships and complementary technologies such as dedicated communications networks or database applications.

A thorough investigation also requires an understanding and awareness of the organisational and institutional bases of the practice of politics and democracy. The emergence of the Internet, and the rise in popular consciousness of this 'network of networks' is undoubtedly an important development with huge economic, social and political ramifications. However, a blinkered focus upon its use to the exclusion of an appreciation of more basic networking around parties (often unconnected to the Internet) has led to a lacuna in terms of both theory building and empirical research on the relationships between new media and established political institutional arrangements and procedures.

Further, a focus on examining the Web and the neglect of the wider range of technologies used by parties could be understood as being characteristic of a form of technological determinism. This is manifest through a tendency to take the ICT application as the focus, rather than the organisation in which its use is embedded, in this case the political party, and the institutional arena which the party occupies. Instead of examining parties' use of new technology in the widest possible sense, and drawing conclusions and developing theory from that point onwards, the scope of investigation becomes limited to the uses which parties make of the Web. In contrast, the approach taken in this case study is to investigate party use of the Web only as a starting point in the process of beginning to understand the relationship between parties and new technologies.

Some literatures on political parties and ICTs break through the deterministic strait-jacket to illustrate scenarios where outcomes are conditioned by choice, organisational factors and social shaping. In the Netherlands, Depla and Tops (1995) have speculated upon the contribution of ICTs in the emergence of either modern cadre parties or professional electoral associations in the American model. The first scenario suggests that new media could contribute to a renewal of participation, decision-making and communication in parties, reinventing them not as classical mass parties but rather as modern cadre parties (Duverger 1954) focused upon issues and political leaders. The second suggested scenario is the emergence of electoral associations (Panebianco 1988) organised around a single leader. While either outcome is dependent on a variety of institutional factors, it also involves a degree of technological choice around whether and in what manner parties choose to exploit the interactive features of ICTs. This supports a view that technology is essentially neutral; it does not embody any defining characteristics necessarily favouring one set of organisational or democratic outcomes over another.

PARTIES, THE 'WEB' AND CYBERDEMOCRACY

The potential of the Internet to support new forms of participation and decision-making through virtual social arenas has contributed to the formation of theories on emergent forms of cyberdemocracy. Cyberdemocracy is often used to describe the potential of new media such as the Web to 'free' individuals from physical and psychological barriers to participation around traditional forms of democracy, and to perfect flawed decision-making processes. Much of the argument in favour of cyberdemocracy is premised upon a belief that existing social infrastructures for the support and encouragement of public debate and political action have been severely undermined (Tsagarousianou, Tambini and Bryan 1998: 5), often encapsulated in terms of an erosion of the public sphere (Habermas 1989). However, a focus on the ability of the Internet in particular to provide a new arena for democratic engagement is often accompanied by a particular view of the technologies; crediting them with an inherent transformational potential which can lead directly and quickly to dramatic or radical change in the operations and form of patterns of governance. Such assumptions have to be subjected to further analysis, given the inherent determinism in the viewpoint and the lack of supporting evidence, particularly in the practice of party politics, for such overt and dramatic change through TMIPP. An analysis of the use of the Web by political parties illustrates this well.

The possibility of the Internet supporting a new public sphere for democracy has implications for the role and operations of political parties, since many conceptions of the role of parties understand them as seeking to provide opportunities for discourse and participation within their structures. To explore the relationship between political parties and the Web, a study was made of the use of the Web by a sample of four parties (Labour, Conservative, Liberal Democrat and Scottish Nationalist Party) during and after the 1997 general election, with the analysis divided into two categories.[4] The first, focusing upon the inter-party nexus, aimed to identify any aspects which might inform an understanding of how parties are using the Web in order to advance their aims and aid their election campaigns. The second, examining the intra-party nexus, aimed to identify instances of the Web being used to enhance party organisation and create opportunities for membership involvement and participation.

Information Systems Managers (or their equivalent[5]) from the parties in the sample participated in interviews on the role of the Web for recruiting support and votes for the party. These interviews strongly suggested that the parties expected only those with a pre-existing interest to enter their sites; such as floating voters wishing to discover more information about a party in order to make an informed choice of who to support. However, three out of the four parties stressed that it was important for them to be *seen* to be engaging with the Internet and exploiting its capabilities in a confident manner; since it contributed to a public perception of them as up-to-date and relevant. Much mention was made of the youth vote in relation to this point, yet only two of the parties provided special sections devoted to the youth vote (Labour and the Conservatives). Overall, efforts to recruit floating voters via the Web were limited to providing information and opportunities to contact elements of the party concerned. There was no evidence that parties were using their websites in order to attempt to gather data on the political opinions and policy preference of individuals who visited the sites.

The provision of information to the public was one of the main purposes identified by parties for establishing their sites. The Scottish National Party

(SNP) made greatest use of this possibility by hosting an extensive on-line library of textual material relating to the party, from the current manifesto through to party policy documents and discussion papers. The other parties were more cautious in the material made available to the public. Labour and Conservative sites were conspicuously 'on-message' during the election campaign, concentrating on the themes they wished to address in their campaigns and offering a more restricted (if perhaps more elaborate) range of information than the other two parties in the sample.

A number of sites provided additional information about marginal constituencies, including electoral statistics, constituency search facilities, contact names, and profiles of candidates. Constituency parties in marginal seats which they hoped to win occasionally had their own campaign websites, often established with the help of party headquarters. This was confirmed through subsequent case-study research, where it became apparent that such assistance varied from party to party from casual help to more formal arrangements. In each case, headquarters were usually very interested in both the form and content of the information a constituency party put on its site. There were resulting tensions because of alleged interference from central party officials such as 'key seat organisers', party officers sent in to manage the campaign in crucial marginal seats.[6] A number of those sites which were established for the general election campaign in April 1997, have since been mothballed or completely withdrawn, indicating that the establishment of the site was merely a component of a short-term campaign strategy.

Membership recruitment as opposed to voter recruitment was a low priority for party websites. Only one of the parties, the SNP, had a facility allowing potential members to join on-line. The other parties asked potential members to e-mail a request for a joining pack, to be delivered by conventional mail. The SNP was the only party which when subsequently asked, admitted to monitoring such membership requests, and figures from the party suggest that relatively few new members joined this way. A strong impression was gained that the sites were aimed at the general public rather than the party member, and this was largely confirmed in subsequent interviews.

Interviews suggested that parties value their websites for the ability to provide feedback, however, 'upward' communication was not, on the whole, valued as highly as the possibilities offered for downward communication, such as information provision and the education of voters. The ability to solicit the support of the public was given more importance than the ability to gain the views of party activists, or indeed, facilitate greater levels of participation in the party on the part of members. Subsequent investigations confirmed that the parties do not, at present, see the Web as a mechanism through which they can build a 'stronger' party organisation.

While the websites offered extensive opportunities to contact party officials, office staff, and politicians, whether such contacts would be read, acknowledged or even addressed was questioned by subsequent research suggesting that only ad hoc arrangements have been established to respond to electronic communication. Members may be allowed more direct access to party information and politicians/staff, but the form of response is regulated and controlled by the party elites. On the whole, the findings tend to suggest that the Web is not being used by parties to facilitate any significant increase in intra-party discussion, debate or 'democracy'. While the parties recognise the interactive opportunities that the Web offers, they consider its capacity for downward dissemination of information to be of greater importance.

There was absolutely no evidence of party use of the Internet supporting the idea of the Internet as a new public sphere; none of the parties provided public on-line facilities to allow the discussion of either specific policy proposals or wider political issues, between or within the memberships and the public. Instead, websites were 'shop windows' for the parties, providing an opportunity to put their policies across in a manner which they can control completely, and to present themselves as modern, computer-literate organisations. It is notewor-thy that party priorities for their sites seem to lie in attracting the attention of floating voters, providing information in the hope of soliciting their support, rather than engaging with the party member or activist. The Web is generally used as a top-down communication device to present information straight to the voters, avoiding the distorting effect of the traditional media.

The Web does not represent the source of dramatic change around parties or party politics. Its innovations are limited to the provision of information to the general public and attempts to garner the support and opinions of voters rather than party members. Providing such resources and mechanisms does not equate to a meaningful shift in the internal balance of power within parties, especially when much more effort goes in to providing resources and communication channels for the general public. There is great difficulty, then, in relating this to substantive ideas on party organisational change.

That the Web has had minimal impact upon the operation of parties in the UK is difficult to square with the heady images of transformation with which it is widely associated. This could be understood in terms of 'barriers to change', yet together such barriers encapsulate the expectations, norms and traditions which are embedded in the institutional realities of parties and the party system. As such, their power to mediate and shape outcomes is far greater than that which is usually assigned to them. Choosing to emphasise the supposed ability of new technology to quickly and radically alter the processes and organisational forms within the polity underestimates the ability of existing political institutions to adapt to, and also to shape, the new media. While the possibilities the Inter-net offers for reconfiguring political life are considerable, the transformative power is moderated with reference to the institutional and organisational bases of politics and democracy both in the UK and elsewhere.

Although parties largely do not see the Web as a suitable forum for enhancing membership involvement, case-study analysis revealed that they have set up other systems which allow membership dialogue and participation in party activities. These range from proprietary e-mail networks which during the period of the investigation were not part of the Internet, such as the Labour Party's Poptel

(Popular Telematics) system, and the LibDems CIX (Compulink Information Exchange) system, through to the Conservative Party's little-used Demon Internet e-mail system and the SNP's e-mail bulletin boards on the closed area of their Web pages. The role of such systems is examined in the next section.

CATALOGUING VIEWS AND TRANSMITTING INFORMATION

If the Web has not provided a platform for a radical reconfiguration of the operations of parties, relations between parties and the electorate have been transformed by stealth through other manifestations of TMIPP. The development of cheap and easy to use desktop publishing systems, which when linked to databases systems containing details of the local electoral register have proved to be a formidable campaigning tool. The large-scale activity of canvassing, identifying the support a party enjoys in the electorate, has also been modified. Telephone canvassing rivals the more traditional method of activists knocking on doors in order to identify the party's supporters, and even where doorstepping is still resorted to, the information gathered at the doorsteps is written onto pro-formas generated by desktop publishing packages, often to be entered into electoral database systems at the local campaign headquarters at a later date.

Telephone canvassing operations have become especially sophisticated. For example, the Labour Party set out to influence floating voters after their disappointing result in the 1992 general election, when a post-election inquest showed canvassing in crucial seats had been poor and patchy. Between October 1993 and 1996, party activists canvassed over 80 per cent of voters in ninety Conservative-held marginal constituencies by telephone in order to identify and influence 'floating voters'. Thereafter, electoral database software linked to desktop publishing packages allowed candidates to 'personally' keep in touch with potential supporters, and invite them to meetings when major Labour politicians visited. Although the party officially denies that its capabilities ever reached such an advanced state, party activists have confirmed that voter profiles in certain marginal seats could be produced for canvassing teams at the touch of a button. In the event, Labour won all but one of these marginals, which went to the Liberal Democrats.

During the 1997 general election campaign, constituents in marginal seats were treated to a flurry of personalised communications through their letterboxes, purporting to come directly from the leader of a political party, or some other party luminary. Party database systems held extensive personal details of constituents allowing quite detailed constituency profiles to be generated, information which was used to help decide which issues to address, and how. One striking example was the Conservative-held but marginal constituency of Edinburgh Pentlands, where the Labour Party was able to send out differing messages through leaflets to different Wards in the constituency, targeting the concerns of upper-middle class voters, on one hand, while also addressing the issues affecting residents of the deprived Wester Hailles housing estate. Labour went on to win the seat comfortably.

Campaigning also has an internal dimension, however, and ICTs are becoming an aspect of the transmission, processing and storage of information within political parties. The main parties in the UK all now enjoy facilities to transmit information via dedicated communications networks, utilising e-mail and bulletin board systems to exchange information in forums ranging from open conferences between any activist with facilities and subscription, and who cares to log onto the system, through to restricted channels used by the party leadership to issue campaigning information. While there is evidence of party central offices attempting to encourage constituency parties to take advantage of these communications networks, take-up so far is limited. Often cited reasons for this include the scarcity of financial and skills resources to purchase and use the equipment.

The role of such private communication networks, which are often wrongly described as Intranets (in terms of their sophistication, few of the systems currently in use come anywhere near these private areas of the Web protected by 'firewalls') is more difficult to interpret. The party IT managers were extensively questioned about these systems, which, because of their divergent nature, were given the generic name Computerised Information Systems or CIS. These systems enable transmission of information throughout the party structure, typically allowing constituency parties and individual members to receive and send information promptly, make use of party bulletin boards to access useful information, and take part in formal and informal party discussion forums. The sophistication of such systems varies from party to party, although all the systems presently used share the same basic facilities.

While CIS have the potential to become quite important mechanisms for large-scale membership involvement in parties, research suggest that their greatest impact has been in disseminating campaign information to individuals and key constituencies during election campaigns (Smith 1998: 182). Indeed, case-study research of each of the parties suggests that party CIS are used by very few individual members or constituency parties. The exception to this is those constituency parties which were placed onto the systems by party headquarters, because they were vital 'key seats', or marginals which the winning party had to take to win the election campaign. What meaningful activity there was around CIS in the constituency parties during the last general election was largely a result of headquarters' intervention and direction, lasting only for the duration of the campaign.

EVALUATING MODELS OF DEMOCRACY

The fundamental question addressed in this book is the continuing relevance of the traditional constitutional model of democracy, as evidenced through new TMIPP, compared to variant and emergent forms of democracy such as demo-elitist, neo-republican, consumer or cyberdemocracy. British political parties provide a particularly interesting case study to explore, because of the complexity of the emergent relationships around new technologies which they display. Whether such relationships provide evidence to support the continuing relevance as a descriptive and analytical tool of constitutionalism or any of its amended forms is best explored with specific regard to two models: demo-elitism and consumerism. The highly managed nature of political parties' use of ICTs is redolent of a demo-elitist model of democracy, but this is augmented by a concern with reflecting the preferences of the electorate which sees parties recast as responsive organisations. This can be understood in terms of consumer democracy, which argues that the key democratic role for the citizen is to express and register preferences which are then taken account of by other bodies, in this case by political parties.

Democratic elitism

The management of political communication around parties is now one of the strongest characteristics of their dominant organisational and democratic processes, and an increasingly important role in this is played by techniques adopted and imported from commercial organisations. The extent to which parties now behave like the market research organisations which they also employ is striking. Parties have applied new capabilities in order to better explore the electoral landscape, in order to identify sources of potential support. They have then used the results of such operations in order to reposition themselves and to 'sell' their new position to the consumers of the policies, the public.

The actual running of campaigns is now often dominated by electoral register software packages, which process canvass returns and produce constituency profiles and mailing lists. Yet the party leadership is often cautious about the extent to which local parties should be left to use these systems on their own. The Labour Party's fears about the technical competence of the majority of its constituency parties led to the use of their 'Elpack' system being suspended for the actual polling day on 1 May 1997, and traditional paper-based systems were resorted to instead. Meanwhile, in those seats identified as winnable key marginals, systems to map the opinions of the electorate and concentrate the resources of the party were put to most intensive use. While the Labour Party was by far the best organised in terms of headquarters' steering of constituency operations, similar patterns were evident in the other parties' operations.

The centrality of these strategies within political parties signals a deviation from the dominant constitutional electoral chain-of-command where, although the parties provided linkage between citizen and public, they did not attempt to steer and shape political outcomes to as great an extent. In this instance, the continued applicability of the constitutional model to parties is therefore in doubt, replaced by a managed and populist approach to democracy where TMIPP around parties provides evidence of attempts to use marketing techniques to identify important issues, modify policies, attract particular groups of voters, win elections and gain or maintain power. This is demo-elitist in character, since the political process is managed through an expert discourse which applies ICTs to facilitate a top-down control of democratic expression.

Parties and consumerism

However, demo-elitism cannot alone explain and interpret the contemporary democratic place of parties; there is also evidence supporting the importance of the consumerist model to explain and understand events, though a consumerism which is located at the 'political nexus' (the boundary between politician and citizenry) rather than at the 'consumption nexus' (the boundary between government and citizen).

While parties encourage innovation around new technology to be reported in terms of organisational renewal, research suggests that ICTs are not being used within parties in any considered manner to reinvent or rejuvenate a mass party organisation. Instead, significant emergent relationships around parties facilitated by ICTs are those which are based upon campaigning; specifically, improving and developing forms of campaigning which make very little recourse to the role and initiative of a mass membership.

The concept of consumerist democracy is usually centred upon the state, and stresses the increased ability of the state to solicit the preferences of the consumers of its services, the general public, and hence satisfy them. However, parties use of ICTs reveals themselves to be acting in an increasingly consumerist manner, using new capabilities to survey the electoral landscape, gauging public opinion, and sending out targeted messages to distinct groups of voters (Smith 1998). In the process there are distinct echoes of Downs's (1957) rational choice conception of party competition, where parties appear willing to apply new informational capabilities in order to get a better sense of public opinion, transmit information strategically around their organisations, and then present themselves to the electorate within a constituency to maximum effect. ICTs are not just used simply in order to 'get around' the problem of insufficient membership activity, rather a form of campaigning is being promoted which actively excludes a role for the initiative and participation of the ordinary membership. Most meaningful developments around ICTs have been concentrated at the centre, in the parliamentary leadership and national headquarters, and are focused upon discerning public opinion and presenting party policies to the greatest possible effect.

This case has provided evidence that TMIPP around British political parties can be understood both as forms of demo-elitist democracy, which anticipate that ICTs will be utilised to bring about enhanced top-down control of democratic expression, and consumerist democracy where parties concentrate efforts in anticipating and discerning opinion, and deploying informational resources to their best return. The use of ICTs around parties tends to reinforce the role and power of the professional party organisation *vis-à-vis* the other elements of the party, with the two main forms of activity being the discernment of public opinion and the identification of possible party supporters, and also the organisation and dissemination of that 'winning message' throughout the party. While ICTs are also being used in ways which might suggest greater potential for membership discussion and exchange of ideas (such as through the Web), the extent to which this impacts upon established processes of decision-making in the party is negligible.

CONCLUSION

The extension of the suffrage earlier this century necessitated the emergence of mass parties, organisational structures capable of mobilising the electorate. However, the establishment of popular sovereignty was accompanied by developments within parties mitigating against them performing their democratic role to the greatest possible extent. Particularly, processes of oligarchy occurred within parties through psychological and technical factors inherent in bureaucratic forms of organisation (Michels 1949) with the result that party leaders became progressively insulated from the demands of the membership. While much activity around ICTs around parties reflects the initiative of the leadership over the passivity of the wider party, there is more to the information-age party than a simple restatement of that internal oligarchy.

In much of the literature a casual and unexamined assumption is made that technological innovation leads to social change. Given the available evidence, we should instead emphasise the social shaping of the technologies and their applications, since: 'it is important to recognise that the information age is being shaped as much by the economic, social and political arrangements from which it has emerged, as it is by the technological innovations on which so much emphasis is placed' (Bellamy and Taylor 1998: 19). Therefore, any 're-engineering' of the internal organisational arrangements of a party in a manner suggesting a radical redistribution of opportunities for participation and power, would be an occurrence of huge significance. And similarly, with regards to the inter-party locus, it would be highly unlikely that the form and pattern of competition between parties could be quickly and thoroughly reconfigured through ICTs.

However, patterns of organisation and competition between and around parties are changing, and much of that change is evidenced through new TMIPP. The outcomes are far from those that would be envisaged by a deterministic view of new technologies. Political parties and the practice of politics is not being recast as cyberdemocracy through the Internet. Instead, the more subtle changes which are manifest in the consumerist behaviour of parties are both conditioned and reflect the institutional and organisational norms of party politics.

Notes

1 Political parties in the UK are organised to reflect the constituency basis of the electoral system. One Member of Parliament is elected for each constituency, and each political party has a constituency party with a membership drawn from that

constituency. Larger constituency parties are further subdivided into branches.

2 The percentage of the eligible electorate which actually votes has fallen in recent years. Turnout for general elections in the UK is always much greater than that for local elections, which averages well under 50%. Turnout at national elections fell from 85% in 1959 to 75.3% in 1987, and although there was some recovery to 77.3% in 1992, this is still a remarkable decline in the context of the increasing media coverage. The 1997 General Election saw the turnout hitting a low of 71.3%, implying that 28.7% of those eligible to vote had chosen not to do so. Therefore, the much heralded 1997 landslide for the Labour Party with 44.4% of the vote against the Conservatives with 31.4%, Liberal Democrats with 17.2% and others on 7%, hides much less impressive figures of support. Labour actually attracted the support of only 31.66% of those eligible to vote, the Conservatives 22.38%, Liberal Democrats 12.26% and 4.99% for other parties.

3 Conservative Party membership fell from a claimed peak of 2.8 million in 1953, to 1.5 million in 1976, to a recent estimate of between 350,000 and 400,000, half of what it was in 1992 (Pinto-Duschinsky 1997). Over the same period, Labour's declined from a total of over 6 million, including over 1 million individual members (the rest enjoying membership through affiliated trades unions and other societies), via an all-time peak of 7.2 million members in 1979, including 660,000 individual members, to under 5 million in 1992, of whom just over 300,000, or roughly 6%, were individual members (Butler and Butler, 1994; Katz and Mair: 113).

4 Three types of data were gathered and analysed. The first was a series of semi-structured interviews with party Information Systems Managers (or their equivalent) which provided overarching information on each party's use of new technologies, including the Web. Second, a survey of the websites of the four parties in the study was carried out during the British general election campaign of April 1997. Finally, data from the case studies of each party also illuminated party approaches to and use of the Web. The data therefore allows a comparison of situations pre-, post- and during the actual election campaign.

5 These were: Roger Hough, Information Systems Manager, The Labour Party
Michael Russell, Chief Executive, Scottish National Party and Chair of SNP Internet Services Group
Charles Cohen, Head of Office and Assistant to the President, Liberal Democrats
Geoff Boon, Webmaster, The Conservative Party

6 Under the British first-past-the-post electoral system, the individual (usually a party member) who attracts the biggest vote in each constituency wins the seat and is returned to parliament. A 'key seat' or a 'key marginal' is a constituency which a party deems to be capable of winning, and targets for special attention.

REFERENCES

Almond, G. and Verba, S. (1963) *The Civic Culture: Political Attitudes and Democracy*, Boston: Little Brown.

Arthur, C. (1997) 'Parties keep tight rein on cyberspace debate', *The Independent*, 18 April: 12.

Bellamy, C. and Taylor, J. (1998) *Governing in the Information Age*, Buckingham: Open University press.

Butler, D. and Butler, G. (1994) *British Political Facts 1900–1994*, London: Macmillan.

Carr, J. (1997) 'Excalibur, democracy's defender', *New Statesman*, 17 January: 18.

Daalder, H. (1983) 'The comparative study of parties and party systems: an overview', in Hans Daalder and Peter Mair (eds) *Party Organisations: A Data Handbook*, London: Sage.

——(1993) 'A crisis of party?', *Scandinavian Political Studies* 15 (4): 269–288.

Denver, D. (1994) *Elections and Voting Behaviour in Britain*, 2nd edn, London: Harvester Wheatsheaf.

Depla, P. F. G. and Tops, P. W. (1995) 'Political parties in the digital era: the technological challenge', in W. B. H. J. van de Donk, I. Th. M. Snellen and P. W. Tops (eds) *Orwell in Athens: A Perspective on Informatization and Democracy*, Amsterdam: IOS Press.

Downs, A. (1957) *An Economic Theory of Democracy*, New York: Harper and Row.

Dunleavy, P. (1991) *Democracy, Bureaucracy and Public Choice: Economic Explanations in Political Science*, London: Harvester Wheatsheaf.

Duverger, M. (1954) *Political Parties*, London: Harper and Row; first published in French in 1951.

Finer, S. E. (1984) 'The decline of party?', in V. Bogdanor (ed.) *Parties and Democracy in Britain and America*, Praeger: New York.

Game, C. and Leach, S. (1993) *Councillor Recruitment and Turnover: An Approaching Precipice?*, Luton: LGMB.

——(1995) *The Role of Political Parties in Local Democracy*, Commission for Local Democracy Research Report no. 11 (May).

Garner, R. and Kelly, R. (1993) *British Political Parties Today*, Manchester: Manchester University Press.

Habermas, J. (1989) *The Structural Transformation of the Public Sphere*, Cambridge: Polity.

Katz, R. S. (1990) 'Party as linkage: a vestigial function?', *European Journal of Political Research* 18: 143–161.

——and Mair, P. (1993) 'The evolution of party organizations in Europe: The three faces of party organisation', *American Review of Politics* 14: 593–617.

——(1995) 'Changing models of party organization and party democracy: The emergence of the cartel party', *Party Politics* 1 (1): 5–28.

Kirchheimer, D. (1966) 'The transformation of the Western European party systems', in J. La Palombara and M. Steiner (eds) *Political Parties and Political Development*, Princeton: Princeton University Press.

Laver, M. and Schofield, N. (1990) *Multiparty Governments: The Politics of Coalition in Europe*, Oxford: Oxford University Press.

Lawson, K. (ed.) (1980) *Political Parties and Linkage: A Comparative Perspective*, New Haven: Yale University Press.

——and Merkl, P. (eds) (1988) *When Parties Fail: Emerging Alternative Organisations*, Princeton: Princeton University Press.

Lipow, A. and Seyd, P. 'Political parties and the challenge to democracy: from steam-engines to techno-populism', *New Political Science* Winter 1995–1996, nos 33–34, 'After Thatcher' Special Issue on Contemporary British Politics.

Macintyre, D. (1995) 'Party politics turns Britain into an "apathetic" nation', *The Independent*, 23 November.

McKenzie, R. (1963) *British Political Parties: The Distribution of Power within the Conservative and Labour Parties*, 2nd edn, London: Heinemann.

Mair, P. (1993) 'Myths of electoral change and the survival of traditional parties – the 1992 Stein Rokkan Lecture', *European Journal of Political Research* 24 (2): 121–133.

Mair, P. (1994) 'Party organizations: from civil society to the state', in R. S. Katz and P. Mair (eds) *How Parties Organize: Change and Adaptation in Party Organizations in Western Democracies*, London: Sage.

Michels, R. (1949) *Political Parties: A Sociological Study of the Oligarchical Tendencies of Modern Democracy*, Glencoe, Ill.: Free Press.

Neumann, S. (1956) 'Towards a comparative study of political parties', in S. Neumann (ed.) *Modern Political Parties*, Chicago: Chicago University Press.

Ostrogorski, M. (1902) *Democracy and the Organisation of Political Parties*, London: Macmillan.

Panebianco, A. (1988) *Political Parties: Organization and Power*, Cambridge: Cambridge University Press.

Parry, G., Moser, G. and Day, N. (1992) *Political Participation and Democracy in Britain*, Cambridge: Cambridge University Press.

Pepinster, C. (1997) 'Hello floating voter, Harriet calling', *The Independent*, 25 March: 1.

Pinto-Duschinsky, M. (1997) 'Tory troops are in worse state than feared', *The Times*, 6 June: 15.

Rentoul, J. (1996) 'Lib Dems appeal for candidates', *The Independent*, 12 January.

Richardson, J. (1994) *The Market for Political Activism: Interest Groups as a Challenge to Political Parties*, Jean Monnet Chair Papers no.18: The Robert Schuman Centre at the European University Institute.

Smith, C (1998) 'Political parties in the information age: from "mass party" to leadership organization?', in I. Th. M. Snellen and W. B. H. J. van de Donk (eds) *Public Administration in an Information Age: A Handbook*, Amsterdam: IOS Press.

——and Webster, W. (1995) 'Information, communication and new technology in the political parties', in J. Lovenduski and J. Stanyer (eds) *Contemporary Political Studies 1995*, York: Political Studies Association.

Tsagarousianou, R., Tambini, D. and Bryan, C. (eds) (1998) *Cyberdemocracy: Technology, Cities and Civic Networks*, London: Routledge.

Walter, N. (1997) 'Don't vote, don't care', *The Independent*, 24 April.

Webb, P. D. (1994) 'Party organizational change in Britain: the iron law of centralization?', in R. S. Katz and P. Mair, (1994) (eds) *How Parties Organize: Change and Adaptation in Party Organizations in Western Democracies*, London: Sage.

Whiteley, P. Seyd, P., and Richardson, J. (1994) *True Blues: The Politics of Conservative Party Membership*, Oxford: Clarendon Press.

5 Political websites during the 1998 Parliamentary Elections in the Netherlands

Pieter W. Tops, Gerrit Voerman and Marcel Boogers

INTRODUCTION

The Dutch General Elections of May 1998 were particularly notable for the beginning of the use of the World Wide Web in Dutch election campaigns. Just like American and British political parties, the Dutch parties conducted their campaign not only in the streets and on TV but also in cyberspace. Nearly all of them established an election site where a range of information concerning the party's candidates, manifesto and campaign could be obtained. Although most of these sites had already been set up, the Internet really gained momentum in Dutch politics during the election campaign. This was highlighted by the introduction of all kinds of non-partisan election sites. The impact of these websites on the election results was not very significant, but still they constitute a new element in the political process.

Websites – partisan and non-partisan – can be considered as innovations in political practices for elections. They are mediated by technological possibilities that arise from the developments of the Internet. Thus the use of websites in election campaigns is an excellent example of a technologically mediated innovation in political practice (TMIPP). The question which we shall address in this chapter is how these innovations can be interpreted in terms of the democratic models discussed in Chapter 2. That is, in what political strategies do the websites play a role? And how are they embedded in discourses on democracy?

This chapter provides a description of the activities involving Dutch political parties and non-partisan sites on the Internet during the 1998 elections, including developments prior to that time. An endeavour has been made to reconstruct the outlines of these sites by interviewing the different parties' webmasters, by reading coverage in party magazines and by systematically observing their sites. The chapter starts by explaining the context regarding the Dutch political party system. An extensive description follows of the development of partisan websites. Next we address the question of the emergent strategies behind the development of the sites: why did the parties develop websites? Then we describe the non-partisan sites on the Internet. Finally we make some concluding remarks with regard to the meaning of the websites in the context of the models of democracy.

THE DUTCH CONTEXT: POLITICAL PARTIES AND ELECTORAL COMPETITION

The Dutch party system, firmly based on an extensive system of proportional representation, has been stable for a long time. This stability was linked to the pillarisation of Dutch society. Protestants, Catholics, socialists and to a lesser extent liberals operated within separate networks of like-minded organisations and institutions (Lijphart 1968). However, in the 1960s the pillarised system began to break down. The integrated social machinery became disturbed by increasing wealth, individualisation and secularisation. Voting behaviour became less determined by religion, social class and inter-party competition increased (Andeweg 1982). This caused a lot of electoral turbulence and volatility in the 1960s and 1970s.

After a period of relative tranquillity during the 1980s, Dutch politics began to be restless again. In the 1994 elections two government parties (the CDA and the PvdA) both lost twenty and twelve seats, respectively (on a total of 150 seats in parliament). Both liberal opposition parties, the VVD and D66 won nine and twelve seats, respectively (Anker and Oppenhuis 1995). The increasingly strong electoral volatility and inter-party competition was also apparent in the 1998 elections. The losers were D66 and again the CDA. The winners were the PvdA and the VVD. Small parties like the environmentalist GroenLinks (Green Left) and the traditional socialist party SP also gained a significant amount of votes.

This electoral volatility is – in contrast to the 1960s and 1970s – not only induced by changing political moods, but also by growing indifference about and a weakening ability to discriminate between the position of the different parties. Just like in other countries, Dutch political parties have to face a diminishing appeal. The decreasing number of party members (from 10 per cent of the electorate in 1960 to less than 3 per cent in 1995; see Koole, 1994) is the most obvious aspect of the changing significance of political parties. Parties are heavily criticised for their detachment from civil society, their inability to organise and integrate political debates and their strong orientation on governmental decision-making (Depla 1995). These criticisms are partly inspired by old, sometimes romantic views on the position of political parties, but they also reflect fundamental changes. They provoked a lot of debate in the Netherlands, as elsewhere in Europe was the case (Katz and Mair, 1995). Parties are searching for new roles and practices to legitimatise their position as an intermediary institution between citizens and government. In this search ICTs are getting more and more attention.

PARTY WEBSITES

Although the 1998 election campaign was carried on for the first time on the Internet, most political parties had been active in cyberspace for quite a while. This chapter presents a general account of the sites according to their appearance up to mid-1998 as well as their development prior to that time in as far as there is information still available. Generally, it can be stated that the use of websites has spread from the left wing to the right wing of the system. Apparently the leftist parties were more open to this new medium. GroenLinks took the lead by opening a site in 1994, the PvdA followed later that year. Subsequently D66, CDA, SP and the VVD followed suit. There are two parties which are an exception to the stipulated trend from left to right. First was the extremist right-wing party CD (Centre Democrats), which made an early appearance in cyberspace but whose site has for a long period of time has been mostly closed for maintenance. In addition, the SP is not on the list of the left-wing groups of early pioneers.[1]

GroenLinks (environmentalist party, 7 per cent of the votes in the 1998 elections)

As already mentioned GroenLinks was the first to start a website as one of the parties represented in parliament. When the GroenLinks site went on-line in 1994, it looked very modern and up to date. However, the party did not have the means to maintain the site. Furthermore, the party's members of parliament appeared to be reluctant to provide information.[2] As a result, GroenLinks became a victim of its own success and soon after its debut on the Internet other parties appeared with sites that were more modern. In anticipation of the parliamentary elections in 1998, GroenLinks modified its website and gave it a modern outlook. As far as content, the site was geared towards the May 1998 elections showing the party manifesto, the campaign newsletter and agenda. In addition, some of the key points in the party manifesto were explained and photographs of the party's candidates were presented.

An interactive element on the GroenLinks site is an invitation to vote for (or against) a draft statement of the party, by which the party's standpoints can be tested. The organisation of this poll however, left much to be desired. At the beginning of April 1998 the proposal concerning the right to part-time work was still on the web, although according to the accompanying text a response should have been received the month before. From the start the GroenLinks site has had a discussion list for party issues such as the automobile problems, disarmament and anti-racism. The party is not interested in the admission of participants: sending an e-mail is sufficient for one to be added to the mailing list. At the beginning of March 1998 there were 170 people registered (this figure had not changed a month later). The discussion is unmoderated. Everyone can submit a discussion subject and there are no rules. In a certain way this reflects the relatively more radical grass-roots character of the party in which the top-down influence of communication is met with suspicion.

PvdA (social democratic party, 29 per cent of the votes in the 1998 elections)

The PvdA opened a site on the Internet in 1994. For the most part, this site was maintained and run by volunteers. The site provided detailed information about the party's political standpoints and party activities. Visitors to the site could automatically receive a selection of the available information by subscribing to an e-mail list. In addition, an editorial board was set up so that it could keep information as up to date as possible. After establishing the site, the PvdA attempted to promote the use of the Internet within its own organisation. The party offered its members an Internet subscription for fifty guilders a year. Apparently the party foresaw an important role for the Internet to improve communications within their party.

For the 1998 elections the PvdA launched a new and extensive election site with rapid screen filling animation and sound. The website took on a more professional appearance courtesy of an external IT agency. This led to a number of conflicts concerning the significance of the site for the party. The volunteers who created the original site criticised the modification of their site and resigned. They believed that the new site offered little opportunity for an open political debate.[3] This conflict was not just a conflict between volunteers and professionals, but it also reflected different views on the democratic meaning of websites. The party professionals saw the websites as a new campaign instrument that could show the up-to-date character of the party and could be instrumental in attracting young voters to the party. For the original website volunteers, this was not only a threat to their position as webmasters of the party but also a violation of their norms and ideas concerning the use of websites in the party. These norms and ideas revolved around using the Internet as an instrument to renew and enhance party discussions and party democracy (Depla and Tops 1995). The first view is more related to a demo-elitist view on democracy, while the second one comes closer to a neo-republican view. The promoters of the first view managed to win the conflict.

The latest news about the party is on the PvdA's homepage. Additionally, the site offers information concerning the party's history, its organisation, its members of parliament and last minute information about the PvdA campaign meetings. It also shows the main subjects of the party manifesto and presents its candidates. Furthermore, the site provides the opportunity to purchase all kinds of merchandise – from a baseball cap to a bicycle bell, a raincoat and a mouse pad which all have the party logo on them.

The PvdA site provides the opportunity to debate PvdA manifesto topics. The debate is not entirely unrestricted: in contrast to some other election sites visitors to this site cannot choose their own subject. They are pre-selected by party officials. That may be one of the reasons that a rather low number of persons participate in discussions: there were no more than approximately 30 contributions during the whole election campaign. The website as such was visited much more frequently. The PvdA used a web count function to gather information on the number of people who visited the website. On election day and on the two days before about 3,000 people a day visited the website. In the weeks before the elections this number averaged about 1,000 people a day.

D66 (radical democrats, 9 per cent of the votes in the 1998 elections)

After GroenLinks and the PvdA the next to start a website was D66. This was opened in mid-1995. D66 attempted to increase the speed and accessibility to party information and thereby improve communications and involvement within the party. The sites design and layout were simple and text-based. Six months prior to the parliamentary elections, the site was radically changed although the text remained the same. The three-column presentation of the text makes it look like a newspaper which is somewhat strange considering that the Internet is a modern media but has been used like an old-fashioned one.

Part of the D66 website is the Digital Political Café. The political café offers the chance to send an e-mail to party members and supporters to discuss current political subjects. In order to begin a Café one must be a member of D66 but one can participate without being a member. D66's Digital Café is therefore not an open news group whereby different subjects can be read by a visitor, but a shielded discussion which can only be accessed by those who are on the e-mail list. Despite this closed character, it is explicitly stated that D66's administration is not responsible for the Digital Café.

CDA (Christian Democrats, 18 per cent of the votes in the 1998 elections)

The Christian Democratic party opened its website in February 1996. It consisted of speeches, addresses to the parliament, notes, reports, press reports, articles from the party's magazine and the like. Just like many other parties, the site was completely redesigned and renewed on the eve of the parliamentary elections. Much of the previous old information was left but restyled and more attractively presented. In addition, a topic called campaign was added which was geared towards the party's agenda.

The CDA's site emphasises the provision of information. A lot less attention is given to the possibility of discussion and exchanging thoughts and opinions. The only possibility for debate at the CDA site is to react to a political proposal, as took place in April 1998 regarding the expansion of the police's legal powers to search for weapons. The suggested statement is connected to the political themes of the moment and is prepared by one of the party's members of parliament. These members receive any reactions. In general there are not many: ten to twelve in the course of three weeks during the time that a statement is on the site. Discussion is open and in principle unmoderated – everyone can participate.[4] In contrast to other political parties where an allowance is made for mutual debate between members and supporters, one can only respond to politicians statements on the CDA site.

SP (traditional socialist party, 4 per cent of the vote in the 1998 elections)

The SP appeared on the Internet on 16 November 1996. The SP's objective was to use the new media to approach potential voters who would otherwise be more difficult to contact such as the school-going youths, students and young intellectuals. The site's primary objective was an electoral one. The site was considered less useful to its own supporters because the use of Internet was relatively low as far as SP members were concerned. Staff might find the site useful because of the archive option (for example for articles which had previously appeared in the party's magazine). The SP site also contained the party manifesto as well as the present views of the party and information concerning its local committees and representatives in municipal councils, provincial councils and parliament. The column called *Tegenstem* (vote against) provided a short summary of the SP's history. In addition, just like the PvdA, party merchandise such as stickers, pins, and so on, could be purchased and reports could be ordered. Finally, the visitor could participate in an IQ test on politics or send political jokes/cartoons by e-mail. The site was adapted in anticipation of the then coming elections – visitors could obtain information about the SP's campaign and its candidates.

There are many interactive possibilities on the SP site which clearly fit in well with the activist approach of the party and its unfailing interest in the opinion of ordinary people . Visitors can check in by registering their name in the guest book called *Web Site Story* and can comment on the SP site. On special pages visitors can participate in a debate on the manifesto and activities of the SP. Several hundreds of people used this feature. It was also possible to initiate or contribute to a debate. Digital debates on SP sites are unmoderated. Scandalous language is not removed and neither are subjects which criticise the party such as: *SP is undemocratic?* or *the SP is a party full of empty promises.* There is also the opportunity to select the E-Alarm option whereby SP visitors can confidentially, if they wish, report corruption, scandals and injustice. By completing a special e-mail form, visitors to the site can register for a visit to the party's MPs office in the Hague.

VVD (conservative liberals, 25 per cent of the votes in the 1998 elections)

The national VVD site was opened in the Spring of 1997. It provided information on the party manifesto and the regulations concerning the election of candidates for all elections (from local council to the European Parliament). In comparison to other party sites the VVD site utilised a lot of the graphic possibilities of the Internet. Textual information was relatively scarce. For example, there are no articles from the party's magazine or even text from other party publications.

The VVD is the only party which has set up an (independent) special election site – besides the normal party site – which is totally geared to the elections of the municipal council and parliament. The election site provides up-to-date information on campaign news, newsletters and campaign speeches. In addition, Dutch nationals who live abroad (estimated to be more than a half a million by the Ministry of External Affairs) are made fully aware of the fact that they can vote at the elections. All these expatriates have to do is to register themselves before a certain date (this can be done on-line through the website of the Ministry of External Affairs or through the Embassy). Apparently the Conservative Liberals anticipate a lot of support from these external resident compatriots. During the General Elections in 1994, 21,000 of these expats voted, 40 per cent of which voted for the Conservative Liberals. It appears that the Conservative Liberals are fishing for voters abroad in much the same way as the British Labour and the Conservatives parties did on their websites during their election campaigns in the Spring of 1997. Indeed, the fact that the Internet is used all over the world makes it an ideal medium for such purposes.

The VVD site gives visitors the opportunity to send private e-mail to the party's secretary. Furthermore, visitors can participate via the so-called interactive forum in discussions on a chosen subject (successive responses can be followed by choosing the threads option), or any possible subject. The debate is not monitored which means that subjects can be brought up which may not be in line with the party's views. The VVD independent election site also offers interactive participation which surprisingly enough, has little or nothing to do with the party. The election site indicates how one can reach the general election site of the Digital City (Amsterdam) or chat sites. In effect the interactivity of the VVD election site was not narrowly focused: the objective was to provide more service and entertainment rather than to tighten the links with the electorate and the VVD representatives.

STRATEGIES

During the 1994 elections, there was only one virtual voting booth on the Internet for visitors to the Digital City. Four years later it appears that the political momentum of the Internet has dramatically increased. Although these developments parallel the growing social significance of the Internet, the elections have played an important role in these developments. For those parties which were not or rarely active on the World Wide Web, the election campaign became a window of opportunity to establish or moderate a site so that Internet opportunities could be (further) developed. The campaign made it possible to put technologically mediated innovations on the agenda. It resulted in all kinds of coalitions between divisions of a party's staff, members and politicians. It also brought conflicts, like the one about changing the PvdA site. It shows that by using ICTs, fundamental questions arise regarding the manner in which these new technologies correspond with new political practices. For the time being, no revolutionary choices have been made in this respect. Many sites reflect the image the party has of itself. Because of its design and the way in which the party site appears on the Internet, the PvdA presents itself as a modern peoples party which is determined to 'conquer' the electorate by using every technological means possible. The VVD is shown as a light-hearted party aiming to entertain. And the SP as an activist party trying to convince the electorate to take up arms against injustice and abuse. The GroenLinks site, with its different discussion platforms, reflects the grass-roots character of the party. While the CDA with its ordinary and scarcely interactive site affirms its position towards traditional values and standards.

From interviews conducted with the party sites webmasters, it appears that Internet activities are not a central part of a political or electoral strategy. The most important reason for developing a site is indirectly electoral: to show that the party is up-to-date. Reasons such as to keep up with technology are also often heard. It is also not considered necessary to have an effective plan for the development of a website because of its relatively low costs. The fact that other parties already have a homepage is very often enough reason to also set up one (see Roper 1997; Voerman 1998). 'If it does not any good, it does not any harm either', seems to have been the view of many Dutch parties during their on-line election campaign. Relative ignorance about the Internet also plays a role. For the majority of parties cyberspace is a fairly new area. Some actors within the parties saw the election campaign – when political parties' social and political activities reach a climax – as an ideal opportunity for electorate and candidates to get acquainted with the Internet. The rapid development of websites during the election campaign served not only as an electoral target but parties hoped in this to be able to learn how Internet facilities could be of use for them.

Considering that most of the sites are set up or modified around election time, a party's site is predominantly used as a campaign instrument especially for the electorate (Voerman and de Graaf 1998; McLean 1989; van de Donk and Tops 1995). In this respect the introduction of websites is mainly inspired by the search for new communication channels between politicians and the electorate, a search that is so typical for demo-elitist conceptions of democracy. Websites are then primarily used to inform the electorate about party informa-tion. Election manifestos are publicised and explained in order to convince the electorate of the party's range of ideas. Visually appealing animation and links to chat sites are aimed at tantalising the electorate to return to the site. The Internet gives the opportunity to present the party's programme in a captivat-ing manner. According to some webmasters as a result of this, the party's ideology could gain impact in the campaign. After TV has focused on the appearance of political leaders in the campaign (White 1982; Wattenberg 1991), the Internet will lead to a greater attention to the ideological content of the campaign such as the party manifesto. Webmasters consider the new possi-bilities to present the party's political statements as a counter tendency to what sometimes is referred to (in the Netherlands) as an Americanisation of politics.

Party sites are not only for the electorate but also used to maintain contacts with party members. The first parties to open a website (GroenLinks, PvdA and D66) therefore have the most experience regarding the use of Internet technol-ogy and also use the site for internal communications. GroenLinks allows members and supporters to debate in a discussion group regarding some party subjects and quantifies opinions on party proposals through Internet elections. The PvdA has a discussion platform which only party members are allowed to use. Whereas D66 members can discuss matters with each other on a semi-closed Digital Café. Furthermore, these three parties keep their members informed about party matters through other electronic means, such as by e-mail and fax. These initiatives are partly inspired by the search for new public spheres in which to organize political debates in and around political parties. In this we recognise neo-republican conceptions of democracy, although there are always tensions with the interests of the party elites, who do not want to loose control of party discussions, especially not at election time.

Party sites are also used for the press. Although party sites do not require the intervention of the press to come into contact with the electorate, it obviously still remains a simple and effective way in which up-to-date campaign information, such as the text of speeches, data from party meetings and other campaign activities can be circulated. Whereas the PvdA webmaster praises his site as a means to undertake unmediated politics, his VVD counterpart sees his site as a tool to keep the traditional media informed about the latest developments. And thus a paradox situation arises whereby unmediated politics can also be used by the traditional media.

NON-PARTISAN INITIATIVES

The political use of the Internet was expanded by all kinds of non-partisan sites which gave ample attention to the elections. The national newspapers *NRC-Handelsblad* and *De Volkskrant* also opened their own election sites as did the *NPS* television broadcasting organisation. The *Digital City* (DC) and the *Dutch Center for Civic Education* (Instituut voor Publiek en Politiek, IPP) opened sites with news and information on the election campaign. Sites and lobby organisations began debates about the elections, such as the seniorweb of the Dutch associations for elderly people. Finally, there were several bulletin boards on Usenet which discussed the elections and in particular, a discussion group called *nl.politiek*.

Traditional media

The *NRC-Handelsblad* and *De Volkskrant* newspapers started their own election site highlighting campaign news from the newspaper. In addition, quite a lot of attention was given to the results of different election polls. The *NPS* site concentrated entirely on these. In contrast to *The Guardian*'s election site during the 1997 British elections, Dutch traditional media did not have discussion platforms. They were just virtual libraries providing all kinds of information about the election campaign. Those who wanted to have a lively discussion about party manifestos or about the election campaign should subscribe to a discussion group on Usenet or visit the pressure groups sites or DDS or IPP's special election sites.

Non-partisan discussion platforms

The most open discussions on politics and the elections took place on different Dutch discussions groups on Usenet. The best place to express one's opinion about the reactions to political items was through the discussion group called *nl.politiek* where all kinds of political matters could be discussed. Discussion groups which also dealt with other subjects (such as environment, motorbikes or household pets) periodically paid attention to politicians statements on that particular subject. In total approximately 2,700 discussion contributions were delivered in the weeks before the elections by an estimated 300 people.

Social organisations also made room available on their sites during the elections. In particular the seniorweb of Dutch associations of elderly people paid a lot of attention to the elections. With the support of IPP discussions were held at this site for four weeks with senior citizens and politicians regarding subjects of interest to the elderly. Thirty politicians including party leaders participated in this discussion.

About the time of the elections, the Digital City (DC) and the Institute for Public and Politics (IPP) jointly and individually opened sites which were totally committed to the campaign. The DC site presented various opportunities to discuss political matters with other voters or politicians whereby the potential of the Internet was fully utilised. For example, during the month before the elections, live interviews with prominent politicians were broadcast through WebTV. Users were given the opportunity to ask them questions. The DC also started a number of think tanks in which a number of politicians discussed various issues with pre-selected citizens. These discussions were lead and moderated by an anchorman who acted as host and kept the discussion on the right track. While the DC site concentrated on the debate between the voters and politicians, the IPP concentrated, in particular, on providing objective information regarding the different parties standpoints. The IPP site provided among other things, a tailor-made comparison of parties in which the user could select which party manifestos and which issues were to be compared. It also provided information about the views of several pressure groups concerning these issues. In addition, it was possible to read by e-mail a daily summary of campaign news from the newspapers.

In terms of the models on democracy these non-partisan discussion groups can be seen as being inspired by neo-republican notions of democracy. They try to stimulate interactive discussions on political matters between citizens themselves and between citizens and political parties, without politicians being in charge of the organisation or the issue selection of the discussion (Rheingold 1995).

Voter compasses

The major attraction to the IPP site was the voter compass which the IPP had developed together with *Trouw* newspaper. By using the voter compass, visitors to the site could determine which party coincided best with their political views.

There were two other sites with vote compasses which appeared at about the same time as the IPP, the consultancy organisation *Bolesian* and that of the writers organisation called *Writers Block*. These three voter compasses all worked along the same lines. After comparing the personal opinions of the user with the political parties views, the visitor was given a suggestion regarding which party suited him best. The IPP's voter compass was the most elaborate because it included all current parties whereas the *Bolesian* and *Writers Block* were only able to give advice on the five largest parties. Furthermore, the IPP voter test also included recent politician statements in its system. The other two vote compasses concentrated entirely on party manifestos. The results of the voter compasses came as quite a surprise to some visitors. At the introduction of the IPP voter compass, three out of eight politicians were advised to vote for another party instead of the one they represented.[5] If three vote compasses were filled in exactly the same, each one gave a different result (Schalken 1998). It appears that not only the electorate, but also politicians and computers had difficulty in making a choice between the different parties.

The voter compasses attracted considerable attention. The voter compass of *Bolesian* was visited 28,000 times, the IPP's 12,500, and the *Writers Block* compass had 4,500 users (*NRC-Handelsblad*, 5 May 1998). Apparently they appeal to ideas and wishes that people have with regard to politics and elections. In terms of the democratic models they can be analysed in two different ways. One interpretation, the one preferred by the people that developed the voter compasses, is that they enable voters to receive information in an attractive and concise way, on the contents of the party manifestos. They are, according to these people, a counterweight to the official campaigns that are concentrated more and more on the behaviour of politicians; instead they tend to pay more attention to the person behind the politician than to the ideas they are supposed to stand for. In this respect, a voter compass can be seen as a new instrument to fill the vertical relationship between politicians and voters in a demo-elitist model. But another interpretation is also possible. The use of voter compasses can be interpreted as a development towards a consumer form of democracy, where voters are shopping on the electoral market. A voter compass gives voters information on which party will best serve his needs and interests. The casting of a vote is not seen as an activity that results from political discussions or from ideological ties, but as the aggregation of a certain number of pre-existing consumer preferences.

CONCLUSION: WEBSITES, ELECTIONS AND MODELS OF DEMOCRACY

Although party sites reflect the present culture and procedures of Dutch political parties, they do bear traces of technologically mediated innovations of political practices. These possible innovations can be interpreted in different ways. Most changes or potential changes point to the direction of demo-elitist democracy. Party sites are mainly geared towards vertical communications between party elites, party members and the electorate. As the above description of party sites shows, the World Wide Web is used mainly as a new medium to advise the electorate about candidates and party manifestos. Any opportunities towards interaction between candidates or the party headquarters can be seen as an attempt to improve vertical communications. In contrast several non-partisan sites support more elements of consumer democracy and neo-Republican democracy. Voter compasses can be seen as a means by which the enfranchised consumer is assisted in making a choice on the electoral market. Discussion platforms can be perceived as the realisation of the republican ideal of free and critical political debate. Whether the present developments will lead towards the boundless (and still unknown) opportunities of cyberdemocracy is unknown.

Notes

1 It is not exactly clear when the CD (Central Democrats) appeared on the Internet. For that matter CP 86 (an extreme right-wing party) also had a site quite early on. Extreme right-wing parties quickly saw an advantage in a site, no doubt because of the problems they had making their political standpoints known to the general public through the traditional media.
2 Telephone interview with W. Rubens, webmaster of GroenLinks, 9 October 1997.
3 Statement on PvdA website, 13 February 1998.
4 Telephone interview with J. Jeroense, 17 April 1998.
5 *The Volkskrant*, 25 April 1998.

References

Andeweg, R. B. (1982) *Dutch Voters Adrift: On Explanations of Electoral Change (1963–1977)*, Leiden: Leiden University Press.
Anker, H. and Oppenhuis, E. V. (1995) *Dutch Parliamentary Election Panelstudy 1989–1994: An Enterprise of the Dutch Political Science Community*, Amsterdam: Steinmetz Archive/SWIDOC.
Benjamin, G. (1992) 'Innovations in telecommunications and politics', in G. Benjamin (ed.) *The Communications Revolution in Politics*, New York: Academy of Political Science.
Depla, P. (1995) *Technologie en vernieuwing van de lokale democratie* ('Technology and Renewal in Local Democracy'), The Hague: VUGA.
—— and Tops, P. W. (1995) 'Political parties in the digital era: the technological challenge?', in W. B. H. J. van de Donk, I. Th. M. Snellen and P. W. Tops (eds) *Orwell in Athens: A Perspective on Information and Democracy*, Amsterdam/Oxford: IOS Press, pp. 155–177.
—— (1996) 'Nieuwe technieken, nieuwe uitdagingen', in L. Bolsius, e.A. (red.) *CDA-Jaarboek 1996–1997*, The Hague, pp. 83–88.
Donk, W. van de and Tops, P. W. (1995) 'Orwell or Athens? – informatization and the future of democracy, a review of the literature', in W. B. H. J. van de Donk, I. Th. M. Snellen and P. W. Tops (eds) *Orwell in Athens: A Perspective on Information and Democracy*, Amsterdam/Oxford: IOS Press, pp. 13–31.
Katz, R. S. and Mair, P. (1995) 'Changing models of party organization and party democracy – the emergence of the cartel party, *Party Politics* 1(1) 5–26.
Koole, R. (1994) *De opkomst van de moderne kaderpartij: veranderende partij-organisatie in Nederland*

('The Rise of the Modern Cadre Party: Changing Party Organisation in the Netherlands'), Utrecht: Het Spectrum.

Lijphart, A. (1968) *The Politics of Accommodation: Pluralism and Democracy in the Netherlands*, Berkeley: University of California Press.

McLean, I. (1989) *Democracy and New Technology*, Cambridge: Polity Press.

Rheingold, H. (1995) *The Virtual Community: Finding Connection in a Computerized World*, London: Minerva.

Roper J. (1997) 'New Zealand political parties online: the World Wide Web as a tool for democratisation or political marketing?', *New Political Science*, nos 41–42: 69–84.

Schalken, C. A. T. (1998) Stemadviezen op het Internet, een vergelijking, at: http://www.publiek-politiek.nl/nmbb/inhoudi.htm.

Voerman, G. (1998) 'Dutch political parties on the Internet', *ECPR news*, no. 4: 8–9.

——and de Graaf, J. D. (1998) 'De websites van de Nederlandse political partijen 1994–1998' ('The websites of Dutch political parties 1994–1998'), in G. Voerman (ed.) *Jaarboaek Documentatiecentrum Nederlandse Politieke Partijen*, Groningen: RUG.

Wattenberg, M. P. (1991) *The Rise of Candidate Centred Politics: Presidential Elections of the 1980s*, Cambridge, Mass.: Harvard University Press.

White, T. (1982) *America in Search of Itself: The Making of the President 1956–1980*, New York: Harper & Row.

6 When democratic strategies clash

The citizen card debate in Denmark

Jens Hoff and Jacob Rosenkrands

INTRODUCTION

The electronic citizen card has been on its way since 1991. Various plans by a number of actors have been set up in order to exploit the potentials of so-called 'smart card' technology, which encompasses such things as personal identification, encryption technology and digital signature. Generally the plans have reflected major shifts in the attention and climate of the Danish ICT debate. Also the debate has revealed different, and even conflicting, strategies regarding the citizen card.

This chapter describes the history and debate of the Danish citizen card and discusses how various chip card functions correspond with strategies adopted by key actors in the Danish debate. Two main strategies are identified: an efficiency-oriented strategy supported by certain government branches, and a citizen-oriented strategy supported by among others the Danish Board of Technology. The chapter then discusses the democratic implications of these strategies. It is argued that the first strategy seeks to increase the steering capacity of bureaucracy and to transform public service in accordance with the model for consumer democracy discussed in Chapters 1 and 2. The second strategy is concerned with traditional constitutional questions such as the integrity and rights of citizens. To some extent this strategy has also brought new visions into the debate, focusing on how to digitally empower citizens. Thus, this strategy contains elements of a cyberdemocracy model.

The development of a Danish political strategy for the information society has raised a number of questions about key democratic values and relationships. The most important ones concern the balance between government efficiency and citizen integrity, openness in public administration, and the future relations between public officials and citizens. The questions call for new terms to describe democracy in the information age.

BACKGROUND: THE CITIZEN CARD

In the period from 1992–1997 the national political ICT agenda has broadened considerably. Thus, the debate on the citizen card has developed in a path-dependent way characterised by an ongoing struggle between existing and emerging political goals and rationalities for the use of ICT in different political practices (March and Olsen 1989). Three major shifts in the debate on the citizen card can be identified (Rosenkrands 1998). Initially, in the early 1990s, a rather narrow focus on ICT as a means of rationalising and modernising the public sector served as a common denominator. It even appeared as an explicit goal in the first government strategy on ICT presented in 1992 (Ministry of Finance 1992).

When the debate on an electronic citizen card was initiated by a joint group of state and municipal authorities in 1991, the main focus was to create a public *multi-purpose ID card*. The card was not only to be used as a means of visual identification, but also as an electronic key to the Danish (Central) Persons Register (CPR) which contains exclusive information on every citizen. In principle data did not need to be visible or included in the card, rather the card was seen as an instrument of the authorities to access specific information needed in the encounter between citizen and official. The leading supporters of the multi-purpose ID card were the National Association of Local Authorities in Denmark (Kommunernes Landsforening) and the Ministry of Interior, which is the administrator of the CPR, and also the branch of government responsible in relation to the citizen card. They stressed that substantial budget savings could be gained as soon as the citizen card replaced other public cards such as social security cards, drivers licences, student cards and library cards as well as a number of applications and forms issued to citizens to gather personal data.

The technological potential of the citizen card was not spelled out in full until the debate took its second shift in 1994. A comprehensive Danish national ICT strategy was presented with the government plan, Info 2000 (Ministry of Research and Information Technology 1994). In this strategy the citizen card was spoken of as a *client card* which could play a pivotal part in a new public infrastructure made up by a practically 'paperless' administration: 'The Public Service Net'. The strategy aimed at electronically connecting various branches of public administration, thus allowing authorities to share public data and to communicate more easily. In addition citizens were invited to use self-service systems from personal computers or public terminals.

In this respect the citizen card should serve as a means of identification for users when accessing the self-service systems. In the longer run the chip card could also lead to digital signature solutions which are necessary if citizens are to conduct legally binding transactions. Info 2000 – in connection with the development of more user-friendly interfaces with the Internet – brought new concerns onto the ICT agenda. Citizen influence, openness and equality was now openly debated as a democratic foundation on which the national ICT strategy should be built (Ministry of Research and Information Technology 1994).

Despite the fact that democratic principles remained unreflected and were only vaguely implemented in the specific ICT initiatives – the bulk of which still focused on rationalising administration – it paved the road for the third major shift in the debate on the citizen card. In the years following the release of Info 2000 a more citizen-oriented approach to the citizen card was developed.

The card was increasingly promoted as a *personal security key* which because of its encryption function would make up a comprehensive security asset in electronic communication – both in relations between administration and citizens and among private people. It was also suggested that the card could be used as a tool for citizens to control bureaucracy, i.e. by accessing and checking data registered about themselves. This view was put forward most powerfully by the Danish Board of Technology (Board of Technology 1994).

At first the idea that electronic communication would spread to most corners of society was rejected as almost utopian by the Ministry of Interior which wanted to keep the focus on the prospects for realising a multi-purpose ID card. However, due to fierce public resistance to the citizen card bearing any resemblance to a mandatory or even partly mandatory ID card, described as Big Brother measures, the plans for an ID card were soon abandoned. Not least the annual debates on information technology in the Danish Parliament (Folketinget), which were introduced in 1995, made it clear that only a citizen card issued as an optional offer with focus on personal security would be considered legitimate by most members of parliament.

When in the spring of 1996 the government suggested that a legal draft on the citizen card should be given top priority, substantial amendments had been made (Ministry of Research and Information Technology 1996). Years of speculation on the proper use for a public chip card were put to an end. The proposal stated that the citizen card should be optional and used for identification in relation to self-service systems, and as a security asset which should strengthen public trust in electronic communication. By observers this was seen as a fine compromise between the concerns of the authorities and of citizens, respectively, acknowledging the democratic values put forward in Info 2000.

However suddenly, a few months later, it was announced that due to problems on settling on technical standards, the introduction of the citizen card was postponed for an undefined period of time. Instead, the government stated that digital signature would be pursued as a separate policy. On the one hand, this seemed to provide the device for personal identification which was obviously needed if public self-service systems should work. On the other hand, experts on ICT security regretted that citizens' security was left unattended, since comprehensive access to encryption technology will not be brought about by the citizen card. The current status of the citizen card will be discussed in a section below.

THE CITIZEN CARD AND THE MODELS OF DEMOCRACY

In sum three basic models for the citizen card have been debated, each of which gives primacy to separate technological functions:[1]

1   A *multi-purpose ID card* for visual or 'plug-in' identification. Most important functions: digital code for personal identification and information visible on the card.

2   A *client card* for public electronic self-service systems. Most important function: digital signature.

3   A *personal security key* for communication. Most important function: encryption technology.

It is also possible that a fourth model should be included, that is the citizen card as a *tool of control* to be used by citizens for accessing and retrieving public information and safeguarding personal data. This model would probably need to contain devices for both personal identification, digital signature and encryption. However, as this model is more a vision than a proposal, it has played a remote role in the debate, and therefore it cannot be counted as one of the basic models of the citizen card. However, the view on the citizen card as a tool of control will not totally be left out of the following discussion.

From the three possible functionalities of the citizen card two main hypotheses can be derived: a first hypothesis which states that the citizen card could play a role in redirecting the polity towards *demo-elitist* or *consumerist* forms of democracy. This hypothesis is linked to the multi-purpose ID card and the client card. It is supported by the fact that such use of the citizen card would enhance bureaucratic resources. Most importantly, the citizen card in connection with the Danish (Central) Persons Register (CPR), would strengthen or at least facilitate the authorities' access to personal data. Instead of citizens showing cards, certificates or filling out forms, information would be accessed directly in databanks by means of the unique identification made up by a citizen card in combination with a personal PIN code.

Critics have argued that this could blur the citizen's insight into information which is stored and transferred in specific situations (Stripp 1995*a*). In principle this concerns – and threatens – the principle that data on citizens belong to themselves. On top of that, the question of control and surveillance has been brought into the debate. As Moreno, the inventor of smart card technology, stated, a chip card can easily become a 'little helper' for 'Big Brother' (Stripp 1995*b*). Thus, many people seem worried about the prospect that in the long run the citizen card could become a mandatory ID card for everybody, or for specific groups of citizens.

The hypothesis that the citizen card could facilitate consumerist aspects of democracy is validated by the client card. Such a card would be necessary to fully develop the amount of public information and interactive self-service applications on the Internet. The citizen card could make life easier for busy people by allowing them to settle their dealings with the public administration electronically 24 hours a day. In addition it could cause a reduced workload in the administration, when citizens begin to do work which was formerly carried out by civil servants, such as, for example, handling and typing paper applications and forms. In the first National ICT plan, this type of self-service was described as 'making the client an employee' (Ministry of Finance 1992).

Primarily, this development towards self-service systems would gain momentum from the option of the chip card to make digital signatures. 'Document authenticity', which confirms the proper sender of the message, and 'document integrity', which guarantees that the message has not been changed, can be achieved by the citizen card. Consequently, it would enable citizens to conduct legally binding transactions on public self-service systems. In home banking and private commerce the problem of identification is well known and has been met with separate solutions. In the public sector the citizen card would have provided a universal solution.

A second hypothesis states that the citizen card could contribute to preserve *constitutional* democratic forms in the context of the 'information society'. This hypothesis is motivated by the possibility of using the citizen card as a security key. Utilising encryption technology, the card would make up a comprehensive security asset in electronic communication between authorities and citizens as well as among private citizens. Today, encryption technology can easily be downloaded from the Internet, but the citizen card would undoubtedly push its use forward and basically build up trust in the future ICT infrastructure. Hence, the citizen card could play an important part in the attempt to reformulate traditional rights and basic concerns like integrity, legal security, and equal opportunity. Guaranteeing these traditional concerns in a changed, technologised environment, could be seen as a way for the constitutional state to maintain its legitimacy.

As previously noted, beside the security key another use of the citizen card has been suggested. The card could be used as a tool of control by citizens; that is a 'little brother' function contrary to the Orwellian prediction by Moreno noted above. First, it could be used to encode personal data stored in public databanks, so that information could only be used with the consent of the owner of the data. Second, but not least, in this line of thought the citizen card was suggested to serve as a tool to access information registered about oneself in public databanks, or in public files available on the Internet.

Rather than an attempt to preserve traditional constitutional values this could be seen as a step to empower citizens digitally. In practice this could happen by reversing the flow and control of information in the relationship between state and citizens from top-down to bottom-up. Depending on how radical such a transformation of the polity would be, it could be in line with both a consumer and a cyberdemocracy model.

THE CITIZEN CARD AND THE STRATEGIES OF THE DIFFERENT ACTORS

As the discussion so far illustrates, the citizen card, its function and proper use have been the subject of considerable debate. Different participants in the formation of the Danish information society have explicitly or implicitly set up contesting strategies for the citizen card. Two main strategies have characterised the debate:

1   *An efficiency-oriented strategy* pursued by the Ministry of Interior and the National Association of Local Authorities in Denmark.
2   *A citizen-oriented strategy* supported for somewhat different reasons by the Danish Board of Technology, ICT experts and concerned citizens engaging in the public debate.

The first strategy has supported the multi-purpose ID card, and increasingly the client card as well. It has held that the citizen card should be mandatory, or at least replace cards held by large numbers of people, i.e. student cards and library cards, so that substantial administrative savings could be gained. In fact rationalisation has almost been treated as the sole goal of a citizen card. Arguments about improved service and security for citizens have frequently been used in public, but almost ignored in internal negotiations between authorities regarding the citizen card (Rosenkrands 1998).

Political, not to say ethical aspects, have to a large extent been left out of the agenda. Thus, it has been administrative solutions, especially the perspectives in a further development of the CPR system, which has been the driving force in this strategy. Citizenship, in this line of thought, is perceived very passively, as persons are either identified as 'numbers', that is data contained in public banks, or merely as recipients of public service.

The second strategy has strongly supported the security key but has also been in favour of the client card. Most proponents of this line have claimed that the citizen card should be offered to citizens on an optional basis. The Board of Technology and cyber enthusiasts, who themselves use Internet and e-mail regularly, have supported the idea of the citizen card as a universal security solution. Rationalisation and better use of public data have been rejected as legitimate motives with respect to the citizen card as well as self-service systems. In contrast the Board of Technology and its supporters have taken openness and integrity as their point of departure, concerning themselves with the question of how the citizen card could meet such democratic values. This implies a view on citizenship which stresses that the citizen should be an active participant in the technological infrastructure. In this perspective the citizen card is considered as both a preserver of basic rights and an extra tool to control the information flow to, from, and within the public administration.

CURRENT PERSPECTIVES FOR THE CITIZEN CARD

The current stalemate over the citizen card leaves the question as to whether the card will ever become reality unanswered. The interesting questions therefore now become which strategies will prevail in the long run, and which consequences this will have for Danish society in the 'information age'.

The bureaucracy did not get its multi-purpose ID because this type of card is generally considered illegitimate. However, as noted above, the government has promised to implement digital signature solutions as soon as possible. This means that self-service systems are likely to flourish and thus help to realise the vision of a 'paperless administration'. The citizen-oriented strategy will allegedly welcome this development as long as electronic services are voluntary and offer new opportunities for citizens. Even so, proponents of this strategy still point to the fact that general security in electronic communication could be enhanced by the citizen card. Also, the option that citizens could to some extent control the information flow to, from, and within the administration and protect personal data still lingers on. So, when 'gains' and 'losses' are counted, it looks like a preliminary victory to the supporters of the efficiency-oriented strategy.

All things considered, the development so far favours demo-elitist as well as consumerist concerns. Demo-elitist rationalities have been at the very core of Danish ICT policies for a number of years, and lately there has been a tendency of the demo-elitist view to adopt elements from a consumerist line of thought. For instance, self-service systems imply both administrative benefits through rationalisation as well as new forms of citizen service. However, both the presentation of the government's Info 2000 plan, as well as the intervention of the Board of Technology and concerned ICT experts have served to highlight the democratic implications of specific technological choices, and to repolitisise the debate on both the citizen card as well as the notion of the 'information society'. That this intervention also has had real political repercussions was seen in the compromise reached in 1996 on the citizen card as a client card (the card as a voluntary option including personal identification and encryption possibilities). However, the downfall of the compromise amply demonstrates that the counter-vailing bureaucratic (and political) forces are very reluctant to 'open up' public administration and to empower citizens.

Whether a new compromise is in the making is an open question. The current proposal for a legislation on digital signature is a much watered-down version of the original ideas on a citizen card, and basically meant to secure 'document authenticity' and 'document integrity' in dealings between private enterprises, the public sector and citizens. However, if a new compromise is to be realised, we will expect a development which simultanously strengthens a consumerist model, on the one hand, and a constitutional as well as a cyber-democratic model, on the other hand. This would be the case if for instance the efficiency of bureaucracy can be increased, while at the same time the rights and capabilities of citizens are renewed, or even expanded. The opposing strategies in the case of the citizen card indicate that 'trade-offs' between efficiency-oriented and citizen-oriented rationalities could result in an information society founded on a path-dependent pattern which includes both consumerist and cyberdemocratic values and concerns. The coexistence of such rationalities calls for new terms to describe the information society.

CONCLUSION: ANY SIGHT OF CYBERDEMOCRACY?

The history of the Danish citizen card shows that even though citizen-oriented concerns like integrity, legal security and openness have been treated carelessly by authorities, they are gradually finding their way to the ICT agenda. Once said to have the potential to become a tool for Big Brother, the chip card technology has just as much capacity to become a 'little brother' tool; that is a personal key by which citizens guard their integrity and monitor authorities.

The case of the Danish citizen card indicates that demo-elitist, consumerist and constitutionalist democratic models are likely to intermingle when it comes to specific ICT applications as well as forming a model for the information society. At the same time new democratic options are in sight. Cyberdemocracy (or neo-republicanism) may serve as a preliminary notion for these renewals in the polity of the information age.

However, neither cyberdemocracy nor neo-republicanism, as little as any of the other democratic models discussed in this chapter will be brought about by ICT per se. Rather, the shaping of the information society will depend on three main forces: the technological 'development', the historical, institutional and democratic setting of the society in question, and not least the strategies and discursive struggles in which politicians, bureaucrats and citizens engage.

Notes

1 The three basic models for the citizen card are analytical constructions. The models express different rationalities for the use of the card which has been derived from the public debate by the authors.

References

Board of Technology (1994) *Plastkort som borgerkort*, København: Teknologinævnet.
March, J. G. and Olsen, J. P. (1989) *Rediscovering Institutions*, New York: The Free Press.
——(1995) *Democratic Governance*, New York: The Free Press.
Ministry of Finance (1992) *Effektiv edb i staten*, København: Publikationscentralen.
Ministry of Research and Information Technology (1996) *Info-samfundet år 2000*, København: Schultz Grafisk A/S.
——(1994) *Info-samfundet for alle – den danske model*, København: Schultz Grafisk A/S.
Rosenkrands, J. (1998), *Fremskridt i sneglefart – demokratiske hensyn i IT-politikken 1992–1997*, København: COS Research report 1/98.
Stripp, S. (1995a) *Registre og borgerkort*, København: Teknologinævnet.
——(1995b), '*The Citizen Card – a little helper for privacy?*', unpublished, Teknologinævnet.

7 Relegitimating the democratic polity

The closed circuit television revolution in the UK

C. William R. Webster

INTRODUCTION

Debates about electronic democracy or teledemocracy usually focus on the direct and complex relationships between Information and Communication Technologies (ICTs) and democratic practice. Typically, and as the case studies in this volume illustrate, the focus is on new electronic and informational relationships between citizens and politicians, between citizens and government and amongst citizens themselves. The case study presented in this chapter explores the diffusion of Closed Circuit Television (CCTV)[1] surveillance cameras in public 'places'[2] across the UK. CCTV is distinct in two important ways from the other Technologically Mediated Innovations in Political Practice (TMIPP) put forward in this book. First, the focus of this chapter is CCTV, a specific 'policy tool' used to meet policy requirements and service objectives rather than a new technology designed to enhance political practice. It is a tool designed primarily to detect and deter crime and reduce the fear of crime (FOC)[3] and its direct input into political practice is not immediately obvious nor its primary goal. Nevertheless, as a policy tool provided by the democratic agencies of the state, CCTV is illustrative of the relationships between new technology and policy processes, processes which are at the heart of modern democratic practice. By examining a policy tool in its policy, political and democratic settings, the tool itself must be seen as a TMIPP. The second way in which this case study is distinct from those that precede it is because the nature and application of this particular technological tool has fundamental implications for the evolution of public spheres and civil society. Thus, CCTV is not just a policing tool for ensuring law and order but also a tool of citizen and societal control utilised by agencies of the state to suppress and control citizen behaviour. The extent of surveillance is therefore forging new citizen–state relations and fundamentally transforming democratic values and relationships in society.

The purpose of this chapter is to explore the changing relationships in the contemporary democratic polity which are resulting from the introduction and diffusion of new CCTV surveillance systems. The three key aims of this chapter are: to highlight the rapid uptake of CCTV in 'public places', to discuss this uptake in respect of the democratic models put forward in Chapters 1 and 2, and to highlight changes in relations which result from the introduction of CCTV, especially changes in relations between the institutions of democratic governance and the citizenry. In addressing these aims, the question is raised of whether the 'surveillance revolution' is accompanied by new emerging forms of democratic practice or whether CCTV is being used as a policy tool to relegitimate the existing 'constitutional' model of democracy.

THE UPTAKE OF CCTV

A 'surveillance revolution' has swept the UK in the 1990s as CCTV surveillance systems have been installed in many of the UK's towns and cities.[4] The uptake of CCTV surveillance systems in public places by local authorities and other public agencies can be considered 'revolutionary', since its uptake has been both rapid and widespread (Webster 1996). Not only have we seen an unprecedented speed of installation but also a remarkable diversity of implementation across a variety of 'public' places. In just a short space of time systems have been installed in town and city centres, in schools, hospitals, libraries, car parks, residential and rural areas. This is in addition to the numerous private surveillance systems installed in a wide variety of locations, including banks, shops, offices, garage forecourts, fast food outlets and business parks. The new Labour government has continued the stance of the previous Conservative government by supporting CCTV through political rhetoric, policy, operating guidance and financial assistance (through the Home Office and Scottish Office 'CCTV Challenge Competitions'). Home Office and Scottish Office statistics (Home Office 1995a, 1996, 1997, 1998; Scottish Office 1996a, 1997, 1998) show (Figure 4) that the government has encouraged the installation of CCTV across all regions of the UK and has contributed over £50 million to the installation of some 10,000 surveillance cameras (Home Office 1995b).

Part of the explanation for this 'surveillance revolution' is the belief that the

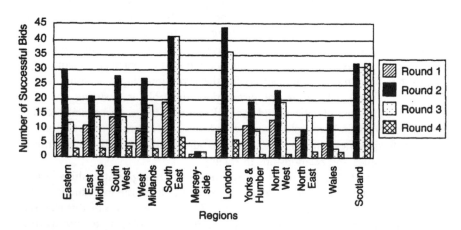

Figure 4 Successful bids in the CCTV challenge competition: number of schemes by region

cameras 'help prevent and detect crime ... [and] ... also deter criminals and reassure the public' (Home Office 1994: 3). CCTV has been promoted against this belief and marketed to the general public primarily as a 'state-of-the-art' technological tool to combat crime. The stated purpose of CCTV is (usually) to deter and detect crime and reduce the FOC.

Typically the systems are evaluated in reference to the levels of crime and FOC in surveyed areas. This is usually achieved via pre- and post-installation analysis of crime statistics and public attitude surveys. Figure 5 illustrates the dramatic reductions in recorded crime since the introduction of CCTV in Newcastle city centre (Brown 1995). Such evidence taken alone suggests the expansion of CCTV surveillance technology has met its primary goal of crime reduction.

The view that CCTV actually reduces crime has been widely and successfully disseminated across society and accordingly there is widespread support for CCTV amongst politicians, policy-makers and the general public. Scottish Office Home Affairs Minister Henry McLeish when announcing the results of the 1998–9 Scottish Office 'CCTV Challenge Competition' said; 'We are giving CCTVour strongest support because there can be no doubt that CCTVworks ... [and] ... most crucially for me, CCTV helps reduce the fear of crime on the streets' (McLeish 1998: 11). Consequently, the deterministic view that crime reduction is inevitable following CCTV installation has cascaded down into the general consciousness of the population. Public perception surveys, such as those conducted by the Home Office (Honess and Charman 1992; Brown 1995) and by prospective operators show clearly that the public views CCTV as a highly effective tool to reduce crime and the FOC. For example, a recent public perception survey in the Easterhouse district of Glasgow showed that 95 per cent of local residents were 'satisfied' or 'very satisfied' with the introduction of a CCTV system and 70 per cent felt that the installation of CCTV would 'improve' or 'greatly improve' the quality of life in their area (Ross and Hood 1998). The overwhelming support for CCTV is unquestionable and it is noticeable how little

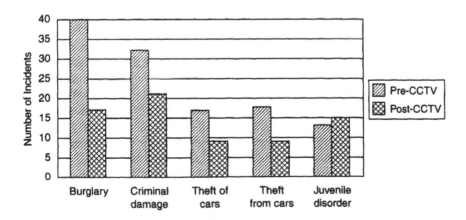

Figure 5 Average monthly incidents before and after the installation of CCTV in Newcastle

debate there has been across society on the use and impacts of such sophisticated surveillance systems. The belief that society needs these systems has overridden any dissenting voices who question their effectiveness and impacts.

It is important to appreciate that the diffusion of CCTV is much more than just about reducing crime and the FOC, it is also instrumental in ensuring societal order and deterring anti-social behaviour. Just as criminal activity is discouraged so too are general misdemeanours such as littering and loitering. Equally the managerial capability of the policing agencies is augmented through the application of CCTV. Greater resource flexibility, improved responsiveness to incidents as well as statistical improvements in 'clear up rates' demonstrate enhanced efficiency, effectiveness and value for money in service provision. CCTV has also been credited with revitalising the economic vitality of town centres by encouraging shoppers and tourists to use and visit local amenities (Graham et al. 1996). CCTV policy is clearly not simply about reducing crime but part of a wider debate on urban regeneration, public service provision and law and order policy.

Although CCTV has proven to be very popular, its introduction raises a number of important issues for democratic practices and relationships in the contemporary polity. These issues stem from questions raised over the ability of cameras to reduce crime and the as yet unknown impact they have on human behaviour and the citizen–state relationship (Webster 1998). The ability of CCTV to reduce crime, the premise on which it has been marketed, cannot be taken as fact. Doubts continue about whether CCTV can actually reduce crime and if it does, on the effects upon neighbouring areas as displacement occurs (Short and Ditton 1995; House of Lords 1998). Critics of CCTV argue its intro- duction is irreversibly altering the relationship between individuals and the state. For these critics CCTV is primarily a tool for maintaining social order in a 'big brother' surveillance society (see e.g. Davies 1995). It is a tool which impinges upon individual basic civil liberties and in particular individual rights to personal privacy and the right to go about daily lawful business unhindered by the state. If CCTV does not work as a crime reduction tool, if it has unknown implications for human behaviour and for relations between citizens and the state the question of why we are adopting CCTV surveillance technology so widely in society must be asked. Moreover, these issues raise serious questions about the extent of rationality and logic in democratic and policy processes, about the unequivocal support for CCTV and about the limited extent of the current public discourse on the use and impacts of its application (Webster 1996).

The diffusion of CCTV can be seen in the simplest terms as government delivering the services citizens want – reduced crime and improved safety. Citizens' desires have been realised through a high-profile solution based on ICTs and the (promised) technological capabilities of new surveillance technolo- gies. Clearly the application of new ICTs (CCTV) is inherently interlinked with the legitimacy and popularity of government, government policy and service provision.

CCTV AND DEMOCRATIC RELEGITIMATION

While the adoption of new CCTV surveillance technology is being utilised as a tool to combat crime and improve general policing, it also provides opportunities to reinforce the existing social order and power structures in society, including the relegitimation, reinvention or renewal of the democratic polity. The provision of CCTV serves as a pertinent illustration of the ability of democratic institutions to reflect popular opinion and to respond effectively to societal demands. In responding to citizens demands for reduced levels of crime and improved safety the democratic institutions of governance have been able to reassert their legitimacy and right to represent the interests of citizens, thereby providing evidence that government, at both the national and local level, can be re-popularised through the intensive application of ICTs. Such 'populist' democratic practices (Bellamy and Taylor 1998) and policy processes enable the democratic institutions of the state to be relegitimated as the focal point of the contemporary polity. The renewal of the democratic polity around a policy tool, albeit a new high-profile ICT intensive policy tool brings us to the fundamental questions which this book has endeavoured to address – are we seeing the emergence of new democratic practices based around new ICTs, and if so in what form is this democratic renewal taking? Is the traditional constitutional democratic model of democracy reasserting itself or is the 'chain of command' being reinvented in an amended form such as the demoelitist, neo-republican, consumer or cyber models discussed in this book? Is the uptake of CCTV illustrative of a highly managed top-down democratic process reinforcing the existing social order, or is it the result of a more consumerist bottom-up response to the demands of citizens?

Managing ICTs in the democratic process: the packaging of CCTV

One of the key features of this case study focuses on the successful packaging of CCTV policy and in particular, the shaping of policy through political communication and marketing strategies. The successful dissemination of the view that CCTV 'works' highlights the role of political discourse in shaping the public's perception of CCTV and consequently in generating public support for widespread citizen surveillance. Political communication in the shape of policy statements, political discourse, advertising and the use of 'sound-bites' has served to shape and set the CCTV policy agenda into a situation amenable to CCTV diffusion. The success of such political communication can be gauged by the extent of public support for CCTV. Its extent shows that the 'appreciative setting' (Vickers 1995) of society has adjusted so that the large-scale surveillance, monitoring and tracking of citizens in public places by the state is deemed on the whole to be acceptable and perhaps even desirable. A good example of policy packaging communicating positive messages about CCTV is the proliferation in the UK of television programmes such as 'Police Camera Action' and

'Eye-Spy' based almost exclusively on CCTV footage. These programmes serve not only to heighten public sensitivity to crime but also the cameras' ability to assist in the detection and prevention of crime, thereby reinforcing the belief that the cameras are needed and that they work.

Alongside these democratic practices designed to shape and influence public opinion and central also to the packaging of the technology has been the commoditisation of information (Bellamy and Taylor 1998) through the increased use of performance indicators and customer satisfaction surveys. Commoditised information in the form of market research, opinion polls and referenda to represent popular consent for policy and performance indicators to evaluate service delivery have become central to the strategic management of politics and the policy process. In the CCTV policy arena there has been a multitude of statistics showing citizen preferences (usually supporting proposed CCTV schemes) and the performance of systems (usually showing large reductions in criminal activity in surveyed areas). A requirement of the 'CCTV Challenge Competition' is that prospective operators show demand for cameras (usually achieved by surveying the public's perception about FOC and the desirability of CCTV in the locality) and that once installed they evaluate performance (usually achieved by measuring the (falling) levels of crime and the FOC). The commoditisation of information is central to political communication, evaluating service delivery, gauging citizens preferences and therefore legitimating the democratic process.

The centrality of packaging strategies signals a break with the traditional 'chain of command' constitutional model of democracy as parliamentary debate is no longer the main focus of the political nexus. Instead we are witnessing the evolution of a highly managed populist approach to democracy where packaging and marketing techniques are of central importance for gaining support for policy preferences and consequently legitimacy for the democratic institutions charged with representing citizens, policy-making and service delivery. The main form of political participation is consensus creation with the main political intermediary being the campaign institutions of the state. These are all features which fit well with the characteristics of the demo-elitist model which suggests the management of process by expert discourse and elites.

The consumerist model is similarly highly influenced by the notion of a 'managed democracy', but where the demo-elitist model suggests ICTs will be utilised to realise the top-down control of democratic expression, the consumerist democratic model assumes such expression is channelled and contained through the consumption nexus. The consumer democracy perspective argues that individual interests will only be protected if the individual has the means to protect them. Hence the provision of vast quantities of information about the performance of public services and the increased use of opinion polls and customer satisfaction surveys to gauge and express public opinion. The significance of new democratic consumerism lies in the fact that the consumption nexus is being asked to deliver more than just improvements in the efficiency and effectiveness of public services. It is significant in that it allies the need for improved service performance with a desire to make government responsive and accountable to popular influence. In this model the provision of CCTV would be seen as a direct response to citizens demands.

Citizens, civil society and surveillance

What then is the role for citizens in the highly managed democratic practices that I have described and what do such practices say about the nature of citizenship, civil society and discourse in the contemporary polity? It is clear that we are entering an era of widespread public surveillance, realised through the use of new ICTs, and in which new relationships between citizens and the state are being forged. The new citizen–state relationship is characterised by state surveillance of citizens and the passive acceptance of this situation as the norm. The extent of this surveillance has led some commentators to argue that the surveillance 'revolution' is actually the beginning of a 'surveillance society' (Davies 1995; Lyon 1994) where technological advances result in increased monitoring, tracking, surveillance and control of citizens. It is also clear that citizens willingly encourage the surveillance of their own movements in return for other perceived benefits, particularly personal safety and reduced crime. CCTV has been promoted as a straightforward trade-off whereby citizens surrender some of their privacy for safety. This suggests that civil rights are being downgraded at the expense of policy effectiveness as the dominant democratic value. Moreover, this indicates democratic renewal from the constitutional model to the demo-elitist model.

Although the diffusion of CCTV and public support for CCTV has been phenomenal, technological aspects of the technology used are shaping relations in civil society and between civil society and the policing agencies of the state. Central to these changing relations are the capabilities of ICT inherent in CCTV and the new capacity for surveillance and monitoring they allow. An intrinsic part of the increased surveillance of civil society are the new 'information flows' generated by the informatisation of service delivery. This is because the introduction of ICTs to improve service provision can only be realised if citizens concede large quantities of personal data about themselves and their behaviour to the 'informated' state. In the case of CCTV continuous live monitoring occurs and data is captured and stored for immediate response or for future reference.

The application of ICTs in political processes have for some time been seen as a means of control and surveillance (Gandy 1994; Lyon 1994; Davies 1995). The Foucaudian perspective would suggest that CCTV is a manifestation of a general expression of power, a new technological element of the disciplinary network designed to provide obedient individuals in society (Foucault 1977). Furthermore CCTV can be seen as reinforcing the administrative power of the state to penetrate and regulate the activities of citizens (Giddens 1985). A recent European Parliament report by the Scientific and Technological Options Assessment (STOA) unit (STOA 1998) categorises CCTV as a 'technology of political control' which can be used to enhance both policing and 'internal control'. This report warns against the 'immense power' of surveillance technology which means it can be used for both law enforcement and advanced state suppression. The report strongly recommends that the European Parliament develop appropriate transparent mechanisms for democratically accountable political control of CCTV so that its potential is not controlled by unaccountable elites. This report argues that the nature of CCTV surveillance technology reinforces certain democratic values. In particular, CCTV strengthens the 'protective state' whereby democratic elites have a paternalistic role in protecting citizens' rights and ensuring law and order. While this report shows European Parliament policy-makers are concerned about the use of CCTV, the extent of public debate and understanding about a technology which can clearly be seen as a tool to control citizens, it also suggests discourse has been shaped and manipulated through agenda-setting and information-shaping to ensure the acceptance of the desired policy tool.

The managed policy processes which surround the provision of CCTV imply limited public debate and discourse and a diminished conception of citizenship. Discourse across society has been stifled with debate limited to the achievements of the technology. Public debate on CCTV has been very limited with those opposing CCTV marginalised in the policy process. First, through a lack of consultation, and second, through the dissemination of the view that CCTV 'works' and that 'only those with something to hide have something to fear'. The result is that only criminals and civil liberties activists argue against CCTV. Civil liberties groups who might be expected to argue against CCTV on the grounds of diminishing individual rights to privacy and the extension of the 'big brother' state have been sidelined by the official policy of supporting the individual right to personal safety (see e.g. SCCL 1994).

The recent House of Lords Select Committee report on 'Digital Images' (House of Lords 1998) stresses the importance of ensuring public support and acceptance for CCTV. This report recognises that the continued diffusion of CCTV is dependent upon public acceptance of the technology and that currently 'public acceptance is based on a limited, and partly inaccurate knowledge of the functions and capabilities of CCTV systems' (House of Lords 1998: 4.8). The report goes on to argue that public acceptance based on limited awareness is fragile and reversible and therefore they recommend 'that the government give urgent consideration to introducing tighter control over any [CCTV] system . . . to meet the requirement of continued public support' (House of Lords 1998: 4.14). Clearly their concern is with the current state of public debate about CCTV and the continued management of public discourse to ensure continued acceptance and diffusion. In particular, they note the importance of the government's role in shaping and leading this discourse: 'we want to see public acceptance of surveillance . . . this is more likely to be the case if there is a wider public debate on the issues involved, and we consider that the government should provide such a debate' (House of Lords 1998: 4.22).

One possible explanation for the lack of public debate is offered by Sclove (1995) who argues that policy-making in the field of science and technology has traditionally been 'less' democratic and involves less public deliberation and discourse than other policy fields. This Sclove argues is primarily because of the technical nature of policy-making which excludes citizens from engaging in debate and consequently allows policy formulation to remain the domain of political elites.

Limitations in public debate arising from the domination of political discourse by government result in the erosion of traditional public 'spheres' (Habermas 1989). These public spheres, which allowed citizens to discuss political ideas, formulate political identity and express political will, are being diminished by private media, party politics and the government through their ability to set agendas and shape debate (Dahlgren and Sparks 1991). Discourse therefore is limited to vertical top-down monologue and horizontal dialogue is minimised. The 'crisis' of democracy for these authors is arising directly from the lack of public space to engage in political discourse.

The sophisticated use of political communication and marketing techniques to shape and limit discourse implies that policy-making is a top-down process where policy and discourse is determined by policy specialists. This perspective is consistent with the demoelitist model of democracy. It suggests the capabilities of new technologies are being utilised to serve the interests of the most powerful actors in the policy process and that the application of CCTV is being shaped by organisations diffusing the technology to reinforce existing power structures in the policy process and within society more widely. Policy formulation and negotiation occurs between policy experts and professionals within governance structures. Citizens are seen as passive recipients of policy as determined by political elites and policy specialists. Their main role in the policy process is to express preferences, which are then used to legitimate political decisions, policy action, political institutions and the policy process itself.

Similarly, the key role of the citizen in the public policy process in a consumer democracy is to express and register consumer preferences through market research techniques which are then used and exploited to shape public policy and the delivery of public services. Policy is shaped to meet the demands of citizens with the main focus being inclusivity in the policy process and not the legitimacy of the process itself, as in the demoelitist model. It is a model therefore which sees the individual as active, competent and rational in the making of choices and in the expression of preferences. It is a model therefore, which implies some degree of public discourse.

Although the policy process has the appearance of being a two-way process, limiting citizens' involvement to just the expression of a need for a service is a very limited manifestation of citizenship. The nature of the policy processes surrounding CCTV and the impact of the technology itself suggests an impoverished conception of citizenship. Citizens have a diminished role in the policy process, where traditionally they were involved in public debate and consultation their role is now limited to expressing preferences through market research techniques.

Reviewing the democratic models

The evidence presented here suggests that CCTV is a very populist solution to the problem of crime, a simple case of politicians giving the consumers of the service what they want. Questions raised about the ability of CCTV to reduce crime and the FOC, its impact on human behaviour, and the erosion of public discourse suggests that the policy process is highly managed. These questions imply that CCTV is a high-profile symbolic technological tool which does more to show politicians being responsive to citizens than in tackling the complex problems surrounding crime. In this perspective it does not matter that CCTV is an unproven technology or that it may have undesirable consequences for human activity, what is important is that the objective of political reflexivity is realised. This is achieved through a highly populist managed policy process where the desired view is disseminated and critics are minimised.

Although the highly managed nature of this case-study topic suggests that CCTV is illustrative of the demo-elitist model of democracy, this is only the case if public support for CCTV is the result, and has been generated through, the management of the political and policy process. The key question is whether the demand for CCTV is genuine and the result of a broad understanding of its technological capability or whether it has been manipulated and created by those with a vested interest in the diffusion of the technology. If the latter is the case, if CCTV is merely an initiative designed to relegitimate and renew the polity as a response to the 'democratic deficit', then the question is raised of whether the emerging recentred form of democracy is enabled by the capabilities of ICTs embedded in CCTV or whether CCTV is a neutral tool exploited in the relegitimation of institutions and institutional activity in the polity? Because surveillance technology can be used as a tool for political and social control and because its application is altering relations between citizens and the state, CCTV cannot be considered an apolitical technological tool. Consequently, the emergent forms of democracy must be intertwined with the diffusion of ICTs in the polity.

The final point which this chapter must address is which of the emergent models of democracy detailed in Chapters 1 and 2 are most consistent with the features and characteristics of this case study. Although none of the models are a perfect fit, democratic renewal in a highly managed and populist form places this study 'centre left' on the 'democratic continuum' (Figure 3). If CCTV diffusion is state-driven, the result of political steering and governance modes of service provision, then the demo-elitist model seems to describe the case study best. If, on the other hand, the widespread public support for CCTV is society-driven, the result of citizen demand, that is, it is based on a good understanding of the technology, then the study shifts along the democratic continuum towards the more deliberative neo-republican and consumerist models. The most likely scenario however, is that the case of CCTV falls somewhere between the models, because it is clear that the policy process is highly managed by elites, but also because societal support for CCTV is extensive and undeniable.

CONCLUSION

The rapid installation of CCTV surveillance cameras in public places across the UK is occurring in response to escalating levels (actual and perceived) of crime and the FOC, and the apparent ability of the cameras to help prevent and detect criminal activity. Their introduction is the result of both a demand by citizens for the right to personal and communal safety, and a desire by politicians and the democratic institutions of governance to demonstrate they are actively tackling the problems of crime, disorder and other anti-social behaviour.

Despite overwhelming demand for the consumption of CCTV, its adoption raises a number of important issues surrounding democratic relationships within the polity. In the absence of wide-ranging public debate, it becomes apparent that the packaging and marketing of CCTV has been instrumental in the shaping of favourable public opinion by projecting the need for greater surveillance. Such shaping of public opinion suggests the policy process is being manipulated through agenda-setting and information-shaping to (re)assert societal control, on the one hand, and democratic legitimacy and renewal, on the other. CCTV may therefore be seen to represent both the introduction of a symbolic high-profile technological tool in the 'fight against crime' and a highly managed populist public policy process in which satisfying citizens demands and expectations are central to the legitimisation of policy and the distribution of services.

The importance of policy packaging in the policy processes surrounding CCTV diffusion highlights two distinct features of the modern democratic process. First, that the management of political communication is taken to be one of the central processes in the democratic and policy process, and second, that a central role exists for the extensive use of marketing techniques and the collection and provision of large quantities of information. The provision of CCTV therefore offers quintessential evidence of democratic institutions exploiting the application of new technology to help renew their legitimacy and thereby re-establish their place at the centre of the democratic polity.

Notes

1 'CCTV' is widely used as a generic term to denote the use of video surveillance cameras and systems in public places where camera technology is linked in 'real-time' to a control room containing monitoring and storage equipment. A strict technological definition would be 'a system in which the circuit is closed and all the elements are directly connected' (Constant and Turnbull 1993: 1). However, such a definition is a bit misleading as the systems do not have to be closed and because they incorporate a number of technological elements beyond television, including cameras, infrastructure, monitors, recording/storage equipment and sophisticated computerised software.

2 When referring to public systems I mean those unique systems which survey 'public' spaces and are operated, promoted and financed (in whole or in part) by institutions in the public sector and in particular the democratic institutions of governance. Public spaces are those spaces to which citizens have free and unhindered access.

3 While the stated objectives of CCTV systems are usually to detect and deter crime and reduce the fear of crime (Home Office 1994; Scottish Office 1996b), it is equally the case that CCTV impacts upon other undesirable anti-social behaviour. While these

impacts may be seen as desirable they are not usually stated as the objective or purpose of CCTV.

4 A number of academics and commentators have noted the diffusion of CCTV systems in towns and cities across the UK (see e.g. Graham 1996; Graham et al. 1996; Fyfe and Bannister 1996; Brown 1995; Honess and Charman 1992). While the vast majority of the initial large-scale public schemes were located in towns and cities, diffusion has moved beyond metropolitan areas into a wide range of public spaces and places (Webster 1996).

References

Bellamy, C. and Taylor, J. (1998) *Governing in the Information Age*, London: Open University Press.

Brown, B. (1995) *CCTV in Town Centres: Three Case Studies*, Crime Detention and Prevention Series, Paper No. 68, London: Home Office Police Department.

Constant, M. and Turnbull, P. (1993) *The Principles and Practice of CCTV*, London: Paramount.

Dahlgren, P. and Sparks, C. (eds) (1991) *Communication and Citizenship: Journalism and the Public Sphere*, London: Routledge.

Davies, S. (1995) *Big Brother: Britain's Web of Surveillance and the New Technological Order*, Pan.

Foucault, M. (1977) *Discipline and Punish: The Birth of the Prison*, London: Allen Lane.

Fyfe, N. R. and Bannister, J. (1996) 'City watching: closed circuit television in public spaces', *Area* 28(1): 37–46.

Gandy, O. (1994) *The Panoptic Society*, Boulder, Colo.: Westview.

Giddens, A. (1985) *The Nation-State and Violence*, Cambridge: Polity Press.

Graham, S. (1996) 'CCTV – big brother or friendly eye in the sky?', *Town and Country Planning* 65(2): 57–60.

——Brooks, J. and Heery, D. (1996) 'Towns on television: closed circuit television surveillance in British towns and cities', *Local Government Studies* 22(3): 1–27.

Habermas, J. (1989) *The Structural Transformation of the Public Sphere*, Cambridge: Polity Press.

Home Office (1994) *Closed Circuit Television: Looking Out for You*, London: Home Office.

——(1995a) *Closed Circuit Television: Winners by Government Regional Offices*, London: Home Office.

——(1995b) *Preventing Crime into the Next Century: Michael Howard*, News Release, 22 November 1995, London: Home Office.

——(1996) *Closed Circuit Television Challenge Competition 1996/97: Successful Bids*, Home Office, London: Home Office.

——(1997) *Closed Circuit Television Challenge 3 Competition 1997/98: Successful Bids*, Crime Prevention Agency, London: Home Office.

——(1998) *Closed Circuit Television Challenge Competition 1998/99: List of Winners by Region*, Home Office Press Release, 17 June 1998, London: Home Office.

Honess, T. and Charman, E. (1992) *Closed Circuit Television in Public Places: Its Acceptability and Perceived Effectiveness*, Crime Prevention Unit Series, Paper No. 35, London: Home Office Police Department.

House of Lords (1998) *Digital Images as Evidence*, Select Committee on Science and Technology, Fifth Report, London: House of Lords.

Local Government Association (LGA) (1997) *Speaking for Communities: A MORI Survey of Public Attitudes to Local Government*, London: LGA.

Lyon, D. (1994) *The Electronic Eye: The Rise of the Surveillance Society*, Cambridge: Polity Press.

McLeish, H. (1998) 'Scottish CCTV Challenge Competition – 1998', *The Herald*, 28 February 1998: 11.

Ross, D. W. and Hood, J. (1998) 'Closed circuit television (CCTV) – the Easterhouse case study', in L. Montaheiro, B. Haigh, D. Morris and N. Hrovatin (eds) *Public and Private Sector Partnerships: Fostering Enterprise*, Sheffield: Sheffield Hallam University Press, pp. 497–516.

Scientific and Technological Options Assessment Unit (STOA) (1998) *An Appraisal of echnologies of Political Control (Working Document)*, European Parliament, Directorate General for Research, The STOA Programme, Luxembourg: European Parliament.

Sclove, R. (1995) *Democracy and Technology*, London: Guildford Press.

The Scottish Council for Civil Liberties (SCCL) (1994) *Civil Liberties and Video Cameras*, Briefing No. 2, Glasgow: SCCL.

Scottish Office (1996a) *Closed Circuit Television Challenge Competition 1996–97: Successful Applications*, Scottish Office: Crime Prevention Unit.

——(1996b) *CCTV in Scotland: A Framework for Action*, J4499 4/96, HMSO Scotland: Scottish Office.

——(1997) *Closed Circuit Television Challenge Competition 1997–98: Applications Recommended for Approval*, Scottish Office: Crime Prevention Unit.

——(1998) *Closed Circuit Television Challenge Competition 1998–99: Successful Applications*, Scottish Office: Crime Prevention Unit.

Short, E. and Ditton, J. (1995) 'Does CCTV affect crime?', *CCTV Today* 2(2): 10–12.

Vickers, G. (1995) *The Art of Judgement: A Study of Policy Making*, Advances in Public Administration Series, London: Sage.

Webster, C. W. R. (1996) 'Closed circuit television and governance: the eve of a surveillance age', *Information Infrastructure and Policy* 5(4): 253–263.

——(1998) 'Changing relationships between citizens and the state: the case of closed circuit television surveillance cameras', in I. Th. M. Snellen and W. B. H. J. van de Donk (eds) *Public Administration in an Information Age: A Handbook*, Informatization Developments and the Public Sector Series, No. 6, Amsterdam: IOS Press, pp. 79–96.

8 Electronic service delivery and the democratic relationships between government and its citizens

Stavros Zouridis and Victor Bekkers

INTRODUCTION

Contemporary Dutch public administration increasingly uses new information and communication technologies (ICTs) to support its service delivery (see Bekkers, Zouridis and Korsten 1998). As in many other European countries, Dutch municipalities experiment with one-stop shops. National government has also initiated new experiments (see, for an international comparison, Lips and Frissen 1997). For instance, the Student Loans Agency tries to optimise its accessibility by means of ICTs. Students are able to use the traditional paper forms to communicate with the agency, but they can also use their smartcards or the Internet.

In this chapter we analyse the use of ICTs for public service delivery. We also explore the democratic implications of electronic service delivery. It appears that though the emphasis on service delivery is inspired by a consumer model of democracy, the use of ICTs for service delivery promotes both a demo-elitist model of democracy and a consumerist democracy. Although the quality of public services can be improved with ICTs, its use may also cause a drift away from the constitutional model of democracy. This development may threaten some fundamental legal and democratic guarantees which were inherited from the constitutional model of democracy. These guarantees are rarely taken into account by the leading political coalitions.

POLITICAL AND ADMINISTRATIVE BACKGROUNDS OF AN INCREASED ATTENTION ON SERVICE DELIVERY IN THE NETHERLANDS

The attention on public service delivery is related to some general trends in Dutch public administration. Although it was partly inspired by the experiences in the United States and the United Kingdom, some of the political and administrative backgrounds of this development may be specific to the Netherlands. Two alleged 'crises' are seen as the main cause of the increased attention on public service delivery: (1) the so-called 'crisis' of the welfare state which had developed after World War II, and (2) the so-called 'crisis' of the constitutional democratic relationship between citizens and politics.

The gradual expansion of state intervention after World War II led to a welfare state in which citizens were nurtured from 'the cradle to the grave'. During the 1980s public administration increasingly experienced the imposition of spending limits due to government's attempts to reduce public expenditure. Slowly a consensus grew within the leading political coalitions that the welfare state as it had developed thus far should be transformed. For example, the leading political coalition believed that public administration should return to its 'core business'. By means of budget cuts, public administration was forced to reconsider its policy programs and its organisation. In the eyes of politicians budget cuts as such were not enough. Public administration should not only deliver less services, it also had to increase the efficiency with which these services were produced. The efficiency drive, which was not specific for the Netherlands but a general trend in Western Europe and the United States, has had several implications for public administration's service delivery.

First, public administration was increasingly conceptualised and managed as a business corporation (see e.g. Osborne and Gaebler 1992). Within this framework, a strong emphasis was laid on the service delivery aspect of public administration. Management within public administration would to a certain extent be similar to management in a business corporation. The new generation of public managers, which was partly inspired by the Anglo-American hype of 'new public management' (see Noordegraaf and Ringeling 1995), conceptualised public administration as a business which should be managed with businesslike techniques. Suddenly some of the classical government tasks (like policing) were defined as (public) services. And because these tasks became services, they had to be assessed by the criteria of quality, efficiency, and the satisfaction of clients. To meet these criteria, government agencies increasingly had to reorganise their structures and processes. For example, the functional orientation and organisation of public administration had to be replaced by an orientation based on citizens and their needs and preferences. In the past it was common that the workflow was taken as a starting point for the organisation of public service delivery. That proved 'inefficient' from a client's perspective: clients were confronted with an organisation they could not comprehend, with different departments and civil servants for a single service, and generally with slow and compartmentalised service delivery. Thus, organisations were and are still restructured to improve the coherence from the point of view of the citizens. The bureaucratic organisation is replaced by a more flexible and consumer-oriented organisation. The 'new' organisations also proved to be an answer to a second alleged 'crisis' which had been 'discovered' in the meantime: the alleged democratic deficit between citizens and institutionalised politics (see e.g. Tops et al. 1991; Van Praag, Jr 1993; Tops 1994; Van Gunsteren and Andeweg 1994).

Ever since the 1970s, when compulsory attendance was abolished, voter turnout in the Netherlands has been gradually decreasing both for the national and the municipal elections (Van Holsteyn and Niemöller 1995; Janssen and Korsten 1995). The municipal elections of 1990 produced an all-time low in turnout. In several municipalities less than 50 per cent voted. Many local politicians concluded that the legitimacy of local politics and city councils was endangered because of the voter turnout. Therefore, many municipalities started a process of political and administrative renewal which aimed to restore and improve citizen involvement (see Gilsing 1994; Tops and Depla 1994; Depla 1995). One of the programmes of this renewal process was to improve local service delivery. Politicians assumed that citizens were not satisfied with service delivery: service delivery by public administration was supposed to be slow and inefficient and, above all, very compartmentalised. By reorganising public administration, both the quality and the efficiency of public administration could be improved.

Thus, at the end of the 1980s two developments coincided. The new leading generation of public managers was committed to a more efficient, businesslike public administration. Service delivery should be the core of that new public administration. This generation of managers was partly inspired by the new public management (Osborne and Gaebler 1992). According to these managers, the 'crisis' of the welfare state should be dealt with by improving public service delivery and by creating a more lean and efficient public administration. This new generation of public managers was supported by the leading political coalition because improving service delivery was also one of the main programmes of the politicians. They believed that an improved public service delivery and a more efficient organisation of public administration would restore citizens' trust in (local) politics. As a result, the programmes of leading politicians and officials coincided around 1990. The 'discourse coalition' came into being because of the shared commitment to improve public service delivery. Both sides were strongly committed to a more efficient, businesslike public administration. Within that framework, which was technocratic to a certain extent, they were both attracted by the new (information and communication) technologies.

ICTs and the quality of public service delivery

The (leading) coalition of politicians and public managers with a preoccupation for improving public service delivery embraced the (new) possibilities of ICTs. Related to the quality and efficiency of public service delivery, the strategic potential of ICTs can be found in a number of aspects, such as speed or quality (see also Bellamy and Taylor 1998; Taylor et al. 1996). Whether this strategic potential of ICTs is realised, depends upon the specific ICT application in question.

First, services can be delivered more rapidly. The fact that it is possible to process and retrieve more information in less time increases the quality and efficiency of service delivery. The waiting time for clients in order to complete their transactions with civil servants can be reduced. The time it takes to handle cases may even be diminished, especially when it concerns routine cases. The speed of service delivery also increases when the civil servant who handles a specific case has real-time access to databases which are located in other units or organisations.

Second, ICTs can be used to increase public access to service agencies. Information kiosks facilitate better access to public services. People who want to retrieve government information are able to visit the web pages of an agency whenever they want. Citizens are also able to apply electronically for permits or benefits, even without leaving their homes. The increased access of service agencies can stimulate the openness of government (Zouridis and Frissen 1995a). Improved access to government information may also enhance the bureaucratic competences and skills of citizens (Scheepers 1991).

Third, new technologies are able to facilitate remote communication and transactions. Thus, new ways of communication and transaction have already been developed with the development of new ICTs. According to a recent research, in 1998 the Dutch people spent an amount of approximately 1.1 billion guilders (300 million English pounds) via the Internet. If electronic payments become more safe than they are at the moment, the electronic handling of transactions will probably increase even more. Network technology can also be used to increase the (remote) political participation of citizens. A digital political discussion on the Internet between elected representatives and citizens is one example, but future developments may also lead to new kinds of 'virtual participation' via virtual reality applications.

The use of ICTs for public service delivery may also be directed to an enhanced transparency of citizens. ICTs are sometimes used to register and process the needs and preferences of citizens. Data coupling and data mining techniques enable policy-makers to acquire a better insight into their clients' situations. This facilitates a better targeting of policy programmes and more tailor-made service delivery. Clients are not just seen from one aspect or one perspective, but are seen as a whole person: information which was collected for different purposes (tax, social security, population registration and so on) is combined and integrated (see also Lips and Frissen 1997). The starting point for service delivery thus becomes the clients' needs and preferences, instead of the needs of the bureaucracy and bureaucrats. This prospect attracted and still attracts both new public managers and the leading politicians.

The integration of public services and the destruction of the administrative walls between bureaucratic departments and government agencies is further stimulated by the communication potential of ICTs. ICTs can be used to encourage linkages and communication across organisational boundaries, both within and between organisations. By means of network technologies separate organisations are able to share their information. 'The network is the computer', according to the advertisements of SUN microsystems. Information-sharing means that the functional and geographic boundaries of units and organisations blur (see Frissen 1996). A client does not have to visit several counters anymore.

Although these strategic potentials relate to the use of ICTs for service delivery, they cannot be seen as given entities. The potential of ICTs to improve service delivery and to promote a more businesslike public administration (as it is described above) are not imposed by some universal and absolute technological characteristics. Although some of these potentials could be seen as inherent characteristics of the technology, they also reflect the design choices of leading (political) coalitions. How transparent should an organisation be for other organisations? Who has access to which information systems? Which data are combined with each other? And for which purposes are these data combined with each other? Which elements construe a profile of a citizen? Generally the use of ICTs for a more efficient public service delivery might become a value which serves the vested interests of some stakeholders, while other stakeholders see them as constraints (or even infringements) for their freedoms. Therefore, we have to acknowledge that ICTs are important resources in the hands of certain actors because they influence the access, distribution and exercise of power. But whose values and whose power are served by electronic service delivery? Do these values relate to a specific model of democracy? And which model(s) of democracy are promoted or stimulated by electronic service delivery? To answer these questions we first look at some examples of electronic service delivery. Then we analyse some of the administrative and political issues which arise regarding electronic service delivery. Both the description and the analysis provide some clues as to possible answers concerning questions regarding democracy and its (future) development.

SOME TYPICAL EXAMPLES OF ELECTRONIC SERVICE DELIVERY IN THE NETHERLANDS

In this section we describe some illustrations of the way in which Dutch public administration uses ICTs for service delivery. These illustrations relate to different types of technological applications. Therefore, the way they affect the democratic relationships between public administration and its citizens also differs. They seem to share a theoretical inspiration from the consumer model of democracy or sometimes they support a consumer or a demo-elitist model of democracy in practice. Although some of the applications do not directly concern the communication between citizens and public administration, they relate to the democratic (or consumer) relationships between public administration and its citizens.

Electronic handling of student scholarships (http://www.ibgroep.nl)

The Dutch Department of Education uses an information system to handle student scholarship applications. By means of this information system, service delivery in this realm has been improved substantially, for example by reducing the time which was necessary for the handling of the application. To apply for a scholarship, students fill in a form, which is processed automatically by an information system. When the information is registered, the system automatically checks whether the information is complete. Then the system automatically reviews the application by comparing the information of the student with the conditions which are stated by law: is this student entitled to a scholarship and what will be the amount of the scholarship? The system then draws up the decision and sends it to the student. If students are entitled to a grant, the system automatically transfers the amount of the scholarship on a monthly basis. The information system handles nearly all applications without human intervention. The bureaucratic discretion is almost completely absorbed by the information system. Even the clause that states that the situations in which strictly holding on to the act would be unreasonable is automatically implemented.

RINIS (International Routing Institute for Information Flows)

In the Dutch social security sector, a broker institute or clearing house has been established in order to rationalise the exchange of information between a large number of social security organisations. Policy programmes to detect fraud and abuse of social benefits have made those organisations more aware of the interdependencies with respect to the exchange of information between them. RINIS is a network with standardised data definitions and procedures which enable an agency to retrieve information (personal data) from other agencies. The RINIS institute functions as a broker or as a go-between. If one of the organisations which functions in the area of social security needs information on a specific client, it retrieves its information via RINIS. Because of the exchange of information, the necessary personal data only have to be retrieved once. In the past every organisation collected the personal data it needed, and therefore citizens had to pass the same information several times. One of the basic assumptions of the RINIS concept is the protection of the informational autonomy of the organisations which participate in the project. RINIS can therefore be defined as a means of procedural and technical integration which tries to rationalise the exchange of information between the back offices of the organisations involved.

The EZ-shop (http://info.minez.nl)

The EZ-shop is a project of the Dutch Department of Economic Affairs (Ministerie van Economische Zaken). It is a hypertext-application which can be accessed via the Internet. By means of this application the Department of Economic Affairs is able to inform the public and to distribute its information among its target groups. The EZ-shop offers summaries of policy documents which are disclosed through a system of key words. Users are able to order the policy documents electronically by filling in a digital form. On several subjects the department has constructed a digital dossier. Every dossier contains linkages to policy documents, press reports and other information on the subject. The information to which the dossiers refer is also electronically available via the pages of the EZ-shop.

The EZ-shop offers a digital subsidy guide for private enterprises. This guide contains the subsidy regulations for which the companies can apply. Information is supplied about the conditions under which a company is able to apply for a subsidy, where and when one can apply for certain subsidies, and how long an entrepreneur is entitled to receive a subsidy from the Department of Economic Affairs.

Digital discussions on the Internet (Department of the Interior)

Government agencies are able to use the Internet to communicate with citizens and to deliver their services. An example of a digital discussion on the Internet was the digital debate on the implications of ICTs for the openness of government and the supply of government information. We organised this debate for the Department of the Interior (Zouridis and Frissen 1995*b*), and evaluated its possibilities for interactive policy preparation and interactive evaluation of public policy. Everybody with an e-mail address was able to participate in the debate. One could participate actively by sending contributions, but the participants were also able to participate passively (by receiving the contributions). We first analysed the group of participants. The participants in the experiment were mostly men. Their age varied from relatively young to middle-aged (mostly from 20 to 50 years old). A lot of the participants were scientists and politicians, although a number of participants were mere citizens. A majority of the participants did not have an active contribution to the debate. As far as they became active, they usually reacted on the contributions of other participants. The experiment demonstrated that electronic mailing lists can be used effectively for the distribution and dissemination of government information. ICTs then contribute to the speed of dissemination and the interactive means of communication.

Matching digital databases

Dutch municipalities are free to give additional financial aid to citizens who find themselves in a social and economically deprived position. Research demonstrated that people who were to benefit from these funds did not benefit because they did not apply for financial aid. The effectiveness of the policy programme was therefore found to be very low. In several municipalities databases were coupled in order to get a better profile of the people who should apply for these additional funds. In addition to these profiles targeting strategies were developed to reach out to these people and to show them how to apply for additional financial aid. Thus, by means of ICTs, municipalities were able to increase the access of their citizens to the additional financial aid.

SOME ISSUES WITH REGARD TO ELECTRONIC SERVICE DELIVERY

Although the examples we have cited demonstrate that ICTs can be used to improve the quality of public services (the speed of service delivery, the remote communication between citizens and politics, and the transparency of both organisations and clients), they raise some issues regarding their democratic implications. These issues may provide clues with regard to the (hidden) agendas and leading coalitions, but also with regard to the democratic models that lay behind the design of ICTs. These issues also bring into question some of the assumptions concerning the consumer model of democracy and its contribution towards improved democratic relationships between citizens and public administration. We address five – related – legal, political, and administrative issues: (1) the informational privacy of citizens, (2) boundaries within and between organisations, (3) political and public accountability, (4) the automation of bias, and (5) citizenship in a consumer democracy.

Informational privacy: big brother and soft sister?

Electronic service delivery requires the collection of the citizens' personal data. The electronic handling of student scholarship applications demonstrates that this personal data is increasingly collected and processed by means of ICTs. For example, the collection of personal data can be 'outsourced' to the customer or it can be done by means of data coupling. With the possession of more personal data public administration is able to improve its services. Service delivery can then be developed towards more tailor-made services and government agencies are better able to take into account the individual needs and preferences of citizens. Thus, under the veil of service delivery public administration increases its possibilities to collect personal data. The examples demonstrate at least three new possibilities for collecting personal data. First, by means of data coupling and the integration of information systems government agencies are able to exchange their personal data. Second, public administration increasingly uses data mining techniques to generate new personal data. An analysis of databases provides insight in the preferences of citizens, but also in the relationship between their consumer profile, their political profile, and their satisfaction with service delivery. By means of profiling government is better able to anticipate the (future) behaviour of citizens. A third way to collect additional client information is created by recording the digital footprints of citizens. For example, when citizens or enterprises use the EZ-shop to retrieve government information they can be logged: which pages are retrieved, which key words are used by (which) citizens, which links are used by which types of consumers, and so on? Thus, the citizen's digital footprints can be recorded and analysed to process their search patterns and their fields of interest.

This development creates a new dilemma (see Frissen 1996): on the one hand, public administration is better able to serve its citizens; on the other hand, the informational privacy of citizens may be violated. Data coupling and the recording of the citizen's digital footprints are coins with two sides: public administration will become both 'big brother' (by surveilling its citizens) and 'soft sister' (by improving service delivery and tailor-made services) at the same time. Thus at the same time both a demo-elitist model of democracy ('big brother') and a consumer model of democracy ('soft sister') are supported by the use of ICTs.

Blurring or reifying organisational boundaries

Electronic communication and the sharing of information have a profound impact on the boundaries of government organisations. Very often scholars conclude that ICTs lead to fading organisational boundaries (e.g. Ashkenas, Ulrich, Jick and Kerr 1995; Martin 1996). Empirically this is just one of the changes which may occur. There are other possibilities. It is important to raise the issue of changing organisational boundaries because possible changes may have some important legal, political and administrative implications. If organisational boundaries are going to blur, what does this mean for public and political accountability? What does it mean for the ownership of information? And who is accountable for the accuracy and preciseness of information if ownership is dispersed among many different agencies? Before answering these questions, we have to look at some of the scenarios which give us an impression of the changing nature of organisational boundaries (for a complete summary of the scenarios, see Bekkers 1997).

As a consequence of the electronic integration of information systems the organisational boundaries may fade. For an illustration of this scenario we refer to the example of RINIS. Because of the exchange of information the boundaries between the participating organisations fade. Although the EZ-shop is also an example of fading organisational boundaries, it demonstrates that the degree of accessibility can be controlled. The second scenario can thus be referred to as a scenario of controlled transparency. In the last scenario organisations try to protect their boundaries by making them much harder to penetrate. Authorisation procedures, the establishment of firewalls, and the development of Intranets are just some examples of protection strategies. In the RINIS system the autonomy of the organisations is protected by the agreement that some organisations have a monopoly on certain data. Income information is the exclusive domain of the Tax and Customs Administration. Income information can be collected by other government organisations, but the only income information which is recognised as such is the information which carries the trade mark of the tax authorities. Thus, although sometimes ICTs may lead to a reinforcement of existing tasks and competences, the illustrations demonstrate that in other cases the tasks and competences of individual organisations become entangled.

Second, there are a range of issues concerning political and public accountability and the idea of a political centre ('politiek primaat'). The integration of information systems and databases may challenge traditional ideas of political and public accountability (Bekkers 1997). If the tasks of two or even more organisations become entangled, it is not always clear who is responsible for the execution of these tasks. The unity of command and a clear division of responsibilities are necessary conditions for effective public and political control as it is conceptualised in the constitutional model of democracy. Another point of interest is the idea of a political centre, an ingredient of the electoral chain of command and of the constitutional model of democracy. The idea of a political centre in society or in public administration may be challenged by the idea of virtual policy organisations of virtual policy sectors (Frissen 1996). The interconnectivity of systems and infrastructures is facilitated by network technology. Network technology is often assumed to lead to a horizontalisation of (power) relations in cyberspace. A horizontalisation of relations, which can be observed in the digital discussions on the Internet, undermines the idea of a political centre. The electoral chain of command and more generally the constitutional model of democracy are based on the assumption that there is one central, superordinated place in our society: a cockpit where the (democratic) decisions are made. In a virtual world there may be no such central point. And even if there is such a central point, it is by no means certain that it is a political centre as it is conceptualized in the constitutional model (Castells 1996).

Third, we have a range of issues concerning the citizen concept of public administration, in particular the automation of bias and quasi-transparency. Data in government databases reflects the way a leading coalition of policy-makers define the world. Kraemer and Dutton (1982: 193) speak of an 'automation of bias'. Information systems may be seen as indications of what an organisation or a leading coalition of stakeholders define as relevant. In this way information systems and the data definitions which lay behind them influence decision-making processes and how public administration approaches its citizens. Therefore, the idea of increased transparency has to be questioned. Should we not speak of quasi-transparency (Bekkers 1993)? First, computer technology favours hard, quantitative data. Qualitative aspects can hardly be incorporated in the system. Second, the leading coalition of stakeholders and systems designers within a policy field define the actual contents of a policy problem. If these problems address citizens, these citizens are hardly consulted in the design and use of information systems. Third, data coupling underlines the fact that there are many definitions of one and the same phenomenon. For instance, in Dutch higher education there are about twelve definitions of a student. Which definition wins if these databases are coupled? And which interests are served when a specific definition wins? The fact that the vested powers of stakeholders are mostly served by the automation of bias points in the direction of the demo-elitist model of democracy. ICTs automate the democratic control (by public administration) of (groups of) citizens or societal organisations (see Van de Donk 1997).

Citizenship in a consumer democracy

One of the political and administrative backgrounds for the emphasis on service delivery and efficiency had to do with the alleged 'crisis' in the democratic relationship between citizens and politics (the alleged democratic deficit in the electoral chain of command). According to politicians, citizens' trust in politics and administration would have decreased because of the low degree of efficiency of services and the compartmentalisation of government agencies. By restructuring public administration and introducing ICTs, citizens would get more involved in politics as it is defined in the constitutional model. Politicians assumed that an increasing satisfaction with service delivery would automatically lead to an increase in political involvement by citizens. Although research shows that citizens generally do not attribute the quality of public services to the efforts of politicians (see Tops et al. 1991), this remains a dominant belief within Dutch political discourse.

An active government which does not wait for citizens to apply for decisions (on allowances, grants and so on), could also have counterproductive effects from a democratic (especially neo republican) point of view. Because of the emphasis on service delivery, citizenship has been reduced to a consumer model. As consumers citizens do not have to take responsibility for their lives. Instead, they can wait for government to take the appropriate measures. Thus at the same time that citizens' trust is restored their political involvement decreases. Active citizenship (which is seen as the basis of a democratic society from a neo-republican perspective) is not necessary anymore because by means of ICTs public administration 'knows' the preferences and needs of its citizens. One of the goals of political and administrative renewal ('active citizenship') is thus frustrated by the way in which public administration collects and uses the personal data of its citizens.

CONCLUSION

ICTs increasingly support processes of public service delivery. In many ways they improve the quality and the efficiency of service delivery. Their design and their use for service delivery supports the framework which has been promoted by leading coalitions of politicians and (new) public managers. The new public management has focused the attention of Dutch public administration towards service delivery. Improving service delivery was seen as a remedy for both the alleged 'crisis' of the welfare state and the gap between citizens and politics. ICTs played a crucial role in the process of improving service delivery. By means of ICTs service delivery could better be geared to the needs and preferences of citizens while at the same time improving the efficiency of public administration, for example by redesigning the service delivery processes (see Taylor, Snellen and Zuurmond 1997). Therefore, electronic service delivery seems to meet the demands of both public managers and politicians. Partly these have been inspired by a consumer model of democracy. ICTs are meant to better serve the clients of public administration or to empower clients by making the organisation of service delivery more transparent. Although to a certain extent the consumer model of democracy may be valid, the issues we raise in this chapter demonstrate that the use of ICTs for public service delivery may threaten some fundamental aspects that have been inherited from the constitutional model of democracy (e.g. self-determination of citizens, their informational privacy, and their active citizenship).

Although electronic service delivery may have been inspired by a consumer model of democracy, in fact it also supports a demo-elitist model of democracy. The leading (political and administrative) coalitions may have been used to promote a consumer rhetoric to regain 'democratic' control over society. While being inspired by a consumer model of democracy, the design and use of ICTs for electronic service delivery thus may also cause a development towards a demo-elitist model of democracy. In particular, the 'demo' side of that model may be supported by ICTs which are designed and used for public service delivery. These ICTs offer public administration (and leading political coalitions) 'strategic guidance', as the examples of the digital discussions on the Internet and the EZ-shop demonstrate. The transparency of both bureaucratic elites and the 'people' contributes to an improved communication between 'elite' and 'demo': some of the examples strengthen the vertical flows of communication between government and its citizens. In a way, the electoral chain of command could well be electronically restored by using the 'informating capacity' or the reflexivity (Zuboff 1988) of ICTs for public service delivery.

However, the examples also demonstrate the emergence of a new kind of electoral chain based on a new way of organizing the 'input side' of the electoral chain of command. ICTs create direct relationships between consumers and bureaucracy. Therefore, they recentre democracy from the political nexus, 'a nexus formed mainly around parliamentary and electoral processes, onto a consumer nexus, a nexus formed largely around the consumption of public services' (see the chapter by Bellamy earlier in this book). We believe that the discussion in this chapter demonstrates that the consumer nexus raises some specific issues with regard to the legal guarantees inherited from the constitutional model. Although some of the guarantees can be institutionalised by new and modern means (e.g. the citizens charters), they explicitly need to be deliberated and discussed.

References

Ashkenas, R. et al. (1995) *The Boundaryless Organization: Breaking the Chains of Organizational Structure*, San Francisco.

Bekkers, V. J. J. M. (1993) *Nieuwe vormen van sturing en informatisering*, Delft.

——(1997) 'Een grenzeloze overheid? Over de betekenis van informatisering voor de verschuiving en/of vervaging van overheidsgrenzen – een theoretische verkenning', *Bestuurswetenschappen* No. 1: 27–42.

——Zouridis, S. and Korsten, A. F. A. (eds) (1998) 'Dienstverlening', *Bestuurskunde jrg.* 7 (3).

Bellamy, C. and Taylor, J. A. (1998) *Governing in the Information Age*, Buckingham.

Castells, M. (1996) *The Rise of the Network Society: The Information Age. Economy, Society and Culture*, 1, Oxford.

Depla, P. (1995) *Technologie en vernieuwing van de lokale democratie: vervolmaking of vermaatschappelijking*, Den Haag.

Donk, W. B. H. J. van de (1997) *De arena in schema: Een verkenning van de betekenis van informatisering voor beleid en politiek inzake de verdeling van middelen onder verzorgingshuizen*, Lelystad.

Dutton, W. H. et al. (1996) 'Innovation in public service delivery', in W. H. Dutton (ed.) *Information and Communication Technologies: Visions and Realities*, Oxford, pp. 265–282.

Frissen, P. H. A. (1996) *De virtuele staat. Politiek, bestuur, technologie: een postmodern verhaal*, Schoonhoven.

Gilsing, R. (1994) 'Lokale bestuurlijke vernieuwing in Nederland' *Acta Politica* 29: 3–37.

Gunsteren, H. van and Andeweg, R. (1994) *Het grote ongenoegen: over de kloof tussen burgers en politiek*, Haarlem.

Holsteyn, J. van and Niemöller, B. (eds) (1995) *De Nederlandse kiezer 1994*, Leiden.

Janssen, J. I. H. and Korsten A. F. A. (eds) (1995) *Gemeenteraden kiezen: Analyse van de gemeen-*

teraadsverkiezingen in Limburg en Nederland, Delft.

Kerckhove, D. de (1996) *Gekoppelde intelligentie: De opkomst van de WEB-maatschappij,* Den Haag.

Kraemer, K. L. and Dutton,W. H. (1982) 'The automation of bias', in J. N. Danziger, W. H. Dutton, R. Kling and K. L. Kraemer *Computer and Politics,* New York.

Lips, M. and Frissen P. H. A. (1997) *Wiring Government: Integrated Public Service Delivery through ICT,* Alphen aan den Rijn/Diegem.

Martin, J. (1996) *Cybercorp: The New Business Revolution,* New York.

Negroponte, N. (1996) *Being Digital,* London.

Noordegraaf, M. and Ringeling, A. B. (eds) (1995) *De ambtenaar als publiek ondernemer,* Bussum.

Osborne, D. and Gaebler, T. (1992) *Reinventing Government: How the Entrepreneurial Spirit is Transforming the Public Sector,* Reading, Mass.

Praag Jr, Ph. van (ed.) (1993), *Een stem verder: Het referendum in de lokale politiek,* Amsterdam.

Scheepers, A. W. A. (1991) *Informatisering en de bureaucratische competentie van de burger,* Tilburg.

Taylor, J. A., Snellen, I. Th. M. and Zuurmond, A. (eds) (1996) *Beyond BPR in Public Administration: Institutional Transformation in an Information Age,* Amsterdam.

Tops, P. W. (1994) *Moderne regenten: Over lokale democratie,* Amsterdam.

——and Depla, P. (1994) 'Vier jaar politieke en bestuurlijke vernieuwing in grote gemeenten': *Bestuurswetenschappen* 48: 120–134.

——et al. (1991) *Lokale democratie en bestuurlijke vernieuwing in Amsterdam, Den Haag, Utrecht, Eindhoven, Tilburg, Nijmegen en Zwolle,* Delft.

Zouridis, S. and Frissen, P. H. A. (1995a) *Openbaarheid van digitale informatie,* Tilburg.

——(1995b) *Digitale participatie: Verslag van een experimenteel digitaal debat over (de Wet) openbaarheid van bestuur,* Tilburg.

Zuboff, S. (1988) *In the Age of the Smart Machine: The Future of Work and Power,* Oxford.

9 Infocracy or infopolis?

Transparency, autonomy and democracy in an information age

Wim van de Donk

The thread of governance runs through all the web of social life in varying forms, in varying units.

(Charles Merriam, *Public and Private Government*, 1944)

INFORMATIZATION AND DEMOCRACY: A CONJOINT REAPPRAISAL

Over the last forty years, the capacity of computer discs has been multiplied about 600 times and the price of a one-megabyte memory chip has fallen from approximately £5,500 to £2. In the 1970s, the Arpanet consisted of lines that enabled the transfer of 56,000 bits per second. A few years after the beginning of the new millennium, we will have lines that transfer several hundred billions of bits per second (Levy 1997: 34–44).

As far as the meaning of these technological revolutions for the praxis of democratic governance is concerned, even a historical perspective (that normally discourages from an all too discontinuous interpretation of the implications of technological innovations) leads to quite conspicuous claims. Towards the end of the History of Government, in which Finer goes through some 5,000 years of empires, monarchies and states, the author almost subtly remarks: 'In terms of its 5,200 years duration, government began yesterday' (Finer 1997: 1624).

In the context of Finer's three-volume exposition on the history of government this somewhat remarkable sentence immediately follows the pages he devotes to the advent of modern information and communication technologies (ICTs) in the world of public administration. Summarising the significance of these technologies, he approvingly quotes Giddens:

> In an age increasingly invaded by electronic modes of the storage, collation and dissemination of information, the possibilities of accumulating information relevant to the practice of government are almost endless . . . .
> Control of information, within modern, pacified states with very rapid systems of communication, transportation, and sophisticated techniques of

sequestration, can be directly integrated with the supervision of conduct in such a way as to produce a high concentration of state power.

(Giddens 1987: 309)

The claim that ICTs facilitate a high concentration of state power might be a slightly provocative one in a time where many people seem to believe in 'cyberdemocracy'. The notion of the state developing into a Cyborg may be equally deviant in the specific context of this book on ICTs and democratic governance. After all, isn't democratisation supposed to be about sharing, dividing and separating power? As much as it is about giving the right to vote to every citizen, it is, indeed, about checks and balances and the institutionalisation of a certain form and degree of separation, not concentration, of powers.

Speaking about the political potentialities of ICTs, a further dissociation with Finer and Giddens looms up. As far as the meaning of ICTs for the existing pyramids of power is concerned, one is generally invited to do away with the related image of a strong Weberian hierarchy and to replace it with the more authentic one. Hierarchies as pyramids will most likely function as the Egyptian sepulchre again, as a definite and dusty burial pit of central power (e.g. Frissen 1998; Levy 1997). ICTs, and in particular the Internet, are associated with phenomena and processes that challenge any kind of lasting centralisation and concentration of power even more radically than democratisation. The future of central power in an information society is far from rosy. Informatization, it is claimed by comparison, 'facilitates' a movement towards further fragmentation, decentralisation and deterritorialisation of power.

In a more 'constructive' sense, informatization is associated with a resurgence and renewal of democracy. More specifically, informatization is expected to facilitate all kinds of (direct as well as participatory) *digital democracy* (e.g. van de Donk and Tops 1995), which at least potentially undermine the 'elitist' or pyramidal character of representative democracy. ICTs are, furthermore, said to contribute to the transparency of power, to favour interactive decision-making and the empowerment of citizens. As Bellamy rightly remarked earlier in this volume, these and other democratic potentials of ICTs are still, to a large extent, assumptions about the future shape of democracy in an information age. Whether or not the information society will be a (more) democratic society largely remains to be seen.

Depending on the model of democracy one is using as an appreciative scheme for the assessment of the impacts and implication of the use of different applications of ICTs in different kinds of democratic practices, the conclusion, of course, will be quite different. In this contribution, some concerns about the democratic nature of governance in an information society are discussed on the basis of an empirical inquiry into the implications of the use of information systems within governmental bureaucracies. Three points should be made in advance. First, I am looking into the implications for the democratic quality of the information society that are engendered by what cyberdemocrats united in organisations like the Citizens Internet Empowerment Coalition (CIEC) often consider as 'yesterday's technology': administrative information systems in governmental agencies. In my opinion, however, these (mainframe) systems are there to stay, and they will be, moreover, for the foreseeable time at least as important for the praxis of democratic governance as the more colourful Internet-related applications of ICTs (like governmental websites, virtual pressure groups and political news groups).

The use of the rapidly expanding intra-governmental communication networks as a means for successful integration of these systems, creates a situation where these systems are more and more embedded in larger information infrastructures, which means that these systems are becoming even more important than they were before (as 'stand alone systems'). Zuurmond is rightfully extending Richard Nolan's logic of ongoing intra-organisational standardisation and integration to the inter-organisational level (Zuurmond 1998). His 'Infocracy' is, indeed, to a large extent a virtual organisation that is displacing and expanding, in both an empirical and normative sense, its boundaries far beyond the traditional bureaucracy (Bekkers 1998; Killian and Wind 1997).

Second, I focus my contribution to this volume on the meaning of ICTs for democratic governance on what I consider to be the 'daily life of democracy': processes of policy-making and decision-making. In most models of democracy (as well as in ICT-related discussions on the future of democratic governance), attention is mainly (if not exclusively) focused on – and hence biased towards – what one can see as the higher features of democracy (e.g. institutions and formal processes like elections; voting systems, political parties, campaigning and so on). An assessment of the democratic quality of the information society cannot, however, be limited to the study of the impacts of the use of ICTs for the most conspicuous institutions, moments and actors of democratic life.

These policy-making processes are especially highlighted in what could be called a network model of democracy in which it is acknowledged that practices of democratic governance involve many actors that do not formally belong to the democratic system (like voluntary organisations and non-profit organisations that are active in the public domain). It is this model that I (and this is my third preliminary remark) want to take as my starting point for an assessment of the meaning of ICTs for democratic governance. Such a network or associational model of democracy (some prefer to call it the demo-elitist or neo-corporatist model of democracy) explicitly recognises the role of a broad variety of societal organisations in the (self) organisation of society. Like the other models, it is a mixture of a normative ideal type and an empirical description of (usually) Western European democracies. Recently it has been heralded as the model of the civil society, the model that is truly 'making democracy work' (Putnam 1993) or the model of strong democracy (Barber 1984). Thus, in this chapter I briefly outline some characteristics of such an approach to democracy. I focus in particular on the institutional prerequisites and principles that it contains for the (organisation of the) democratic quality of policy-making processes.

In the third section of this chapter I look into the way informatization is reinforcing some important capabilities of government. Finer's claim that government only began yesterday seems not as incredible as it might look at first sight (Finer 1997: 1642). ICTs are contributing to a degree of transparency and penetrability of (parts of) society that have never been reached before. This transparency and penetrability is not only relevant to individual citizens, but also many of the organisations and associations that are active on the public domain. As commercial organisations discovered some while ago governments' expanding databases are rich sources of policy information that can be obtained with all kinds of new tools (e.g. data mining and profiling techniques).

In my penultimate section I briefly discuss some results of research into the implications of the use of governmental information systems in the field of (redistributive) policy-making with regard to Dutch Nursing Homes. Although these results are confined to a rather restricted and specific policy arena, I believe that they contain some lessons that are relevant for the more general way in which information societies are going to find and implement the answers to Lasswell's famous question: who gets what, when and how? (Lasswell 1936).

In my final section I try to discern in a more general sense some (potential) threats and opportunities of the extended use of governmental information systems for the prerequisites and principles that are recognised in the network model of democracy.

A THOUSAND POINTS OF LIGHT: DEMOCRACY IN A CIVIL SOCIETY

In his 1988 presidential campaign, George Bush called upon voluntary organisations to play 'a critical role in solving the country's social problems' (see in Smith and Lipsky 1993: 4). Speaking about a 'thousand points of light', Bush echoed De Tocqueville's earlier analysis of the American society. In his well-known *De la Democratie en Amerique*, he was particularly enthusiastic about the role that many voluntary, private, non-profit associations and organisations played on the public domain. He considered this a particular strength of the American society, and, in particular, an effective protection against a possible concentration of power within the formal organisations of the state. Recently, again, Robert Putnam discovered the importance of these organisations for the (democratic) quality of society (Putnam 1993). Authors like Barber (1984, 1996), Etzioni (1973, 1988, 1996), Hirst (1996), Lindblom (1990), Dahl (1998), Scott (1998) and Whutnow (1991, 1995) have also stressed the importance of a set of strong players on the middle ground of society. These organisations are seen as pathways to participation (Berger and Neuhaus 1977; Smith and Lipsky 1993), said to be contributing to various forms of self-governance, pluricentric policy-making and coproduction. Furthermore, they are likely to enable societal learning and probing, thereby contributing to what Lindblom once described as the 'intelligence of democracy' (Lindblom 1965).

They are, indeed, considered as the institutional prerequisites of pluralism, 'civic culture' and civil society. Taken together, they form a kind of 'third sector' that is adding (to the other two coordination mechanisms, markets and hierarchies) a third, authentic and typical way of deciding upon and arranging the affairs of society. Streeck and Schmitter talk about different kinds of 'organizational concertation', that develop between mutually dependent actors in the form of sometimes 'highly complex formulae of party representation and informal deliberation' (Streeck and Schmitter 1991).

These general images of a 'societal' model of democracy, however, do conceal the extreme heterogeneity that characterises the field of 'societal, voluntary or non-profit organizations', to mention just a few names that we come across in the literature. Some of these organisations are clearly much more involved in democratic processes than others. Important differences can be found in the position they have and the role they play in the different societal sub- or policy sectors. These differences are not only explained by the typical issues, interests, goods and services that characterise a certain sector, but also by the national, historical and cultural institutional characteristics of the broader political system. In this respect it is not a surprise that in the Netherlands, nation of many religious minorities, the role of non-governmental, voluntary associations has traditionally been very important. Long before the state got involved, these organisations were active in all kinds of policy sectors that we nowadays consider as typical features of the welfare state. In the Netherlands, too, they have been incorporated into all kinds of policy networks, policy communities and issue networks that Bellamy discussed earlier in this volume in the context of the demo-elitist model of democracy. In the Netherlands, this model has become known as the model of 'wrinkling and arranging', that is, the 'Polder model' that has largely contributed to Holland's social and economic success (Visser and Hemerijck 1997; Hendriks and Toonen 1998).

Bellamy also pays attention to some less sunny sides of such a shadow state (e.g. Wolch 1990). These organisations as well as the policy networks they are embedded in can actually be(come) rather closed, and the organisations that form them can lose their societal legitimation. The implementation of policies that are decided upon can run aground as a consequence of the 'syrupiness' of the processes in these networks, or, as the Germans like to put it, in the 'Eigengezetzlichkeit der Vorstaatlichen Strukturen'.

The field is not only very heterogeneous, it is also a highly dynamic one. New organisations appear on the scene as fast as others disappear. Some have been transforming into state or market organisations. In the 1980s, notably, many non-profit, voluntary organisations were pushed or pulled (due to market ideology and/or as a consequence of eroding financial support from traditional members, inflation of their own capital and the cut-back of governmental subsidies) towards competition and the market. Some of them now consider their former 'memberships' and supporters mainly as clients as a result and have 'professionalised' both staff and management. Others have become entirely dependent on government subsidies.

Many authors expect these developments to fundamentally affect the typical role of these organisations, some of them even speak about a 'crisis' of the non-profit and voluntary sector, and doubt whether the 'third sector' will be able to survive the forces of 'etatization' and 'marketisation'. Although an infusion of government money has generally augmented the programmes of voluntary associations in those societies where such funds have been provided, the typical result has been greater competition among voluntary associations for scarce public funds and more explicit contractual relations requiring voluntary associations to pursue narrowly defined objectives. The norms legitimating these contractual relations derive from long standing assumptions about 'public accountability', 'When accountability becomes the dominant operation norm, voluntary associations become less clearly distinguishable fromgovernment agencies and for profit firms' (Whutnow 1991: 298; see also Dobkin Hall 1992; Douglas 1987; Salamon 1996; Salamon and Anheier 1996; Smith and Lipsky 1993).

Compared with the recent appreciation of non-statal organisations that especially support this idea or model of (societal) democracy (e.g. Fukuyama on the value of social capital and the role of trust), the scholarly attention for these organisations lags behind. Our knowledge about this sector is limited (if not for profit, then for what?). Typologies and theories that can be helpful to investigate (changes in) the way(s) they contribute to democratic governance are, as matter of fact, lacking. The third sector is, indeed, a miscellaneous sector, concealing a ragbag of organisations (Burt and Taylor 1998; Burger et al. 1997). A more thorough understanding of the very different kinds or organisations (environmental grass-roots organisations, associations that are responsible for the development and the maintenance of self-regulations (e.g. codes of practice), non-profit hospitals and their umbrella organisations) and the roles they play in the public domain is necessary for further empirical and theoretical understanding of the way informatization is threatening or encouraging them.

As a start, it would be possible to use a simple model of the policy process in order to create an initial typology. More than typologies which focus on size (big, small), age (traditional voluntary organisations or new grass-roots non-profits), staff (volunteers or professionals), focus (service delivery or interest representation) or sector (health care, environment, education), such a typology seems sensible for a systematic study into the question of if and how informatization (in the domain of public administration or within these organisations) is changing their role and function in the daily praxis of democratic governance. One could expect the results of such an investigation to reproduce not only the versatile and heterogeneous character of the field, but also reflect the ambiguous 'impacts' ICTs tend to have in a more general sense.

Intermediary, voluntary organisations fulfil functions in all stages that can be discerned – at least analytically – in a democratic policy-making process. Jenkins (1978) comes up with seven different stages:

- Initiation
- Information
- Consideration
- Decision

- Implementation
- Evaluation
- Termination.

Such a division may very well be perceived as a division of roles and tasks that have to be played and fulfilled in democratic governance. Like the formal institutions of a democratic system, societal organisations are sometimes occupied with just one or two of them, while others are involved more or less simultaneously in each of the stages. Some are mainly concerned with issue representation and agenda setting (like environmental organisations), others are particularly active in the field of delivering services and implementing policies (like welfare organisations, hospitals, museums and even symphony orchestras).

The specific rationale for the existence of this kind of non-statal organisation is as different as the actual activities they undertake. It is much easier to describe what they are not (non-profit, non-governmental organisations) than what they are, exactly. The rationale for the existence of these organisations is as multi-coloured (market failure, professionalisation, discretion or a need for or right to a specific (political, cultural, ethnic or religious) identity) as are their organisational and other qualities.

What they do share, however, is a certain degree of institutional singularity and autonomy (discretion, ability and capacity to define an own view of the world). In this perspective the stages mentioned above appear highly important. This is even so for organisations that are, de facto, completely dependent on governmental subsidies and working in the domain of implementation/execution.

It is precisely this singularity and autonomy that Lindblom recognised as an important institutional prerequisite for a pluralist and 'intelligent democracy' in which a variety of actors are able to contribute to continuous 'learning' and 'probing' (Lindblom 1990). In order to attain (maintain) acceptable levels of probing, it is, according to Lindblom, important to watch that: 'significant inequalities in opportunity to probe – for example, inequalities of education, availability of information or available time – do not reduce the number of probers and quality of probing' (Lindblom 1990: 232). This concern for learning, pluralism and an 'open society' is a constant anti-synoptic strand in his work, following Polybius, Polanyi and Popper. Safeguarding a certain degree of openness in and variety of relatively independent information powers (and, indeed, information domains) is highly important for both theory and practice of democracy. A separation of the most important information powers is a crucial element of the doctrine that is safeguarding the democratic nature of public administration in an information age. When public administration is integrating and disciplining its internal information domains, and using them as a platform for successful control of society (and external information domains), these doctrines might be in need of a reassessment (e.g. De Mulder in van de Donk and Snellen 1998).

HIGHWAY OR RAILWAY? WHAT IS THE INFORMATION INFRASTRUCTURE FOR THE INFORMATION SOCIETY?

It is interesting to see that the advent of (inter)sectoral information systems facilitate the trend to interconnect the information bases that are used in the different stages of a policy cycle. In many domains, these databases are filled almost automatically and constantly with the data that are produced in all kinds of administrative transaction systems (e.g. in the field of social security, social allowances, health care, insurance). In policy areas where the extended use of information systems has started at the level of implementation/operations, the inclination is strong to collect and analyse the 'informated' data of these processes at higher levels of aggregation, thus facilitating a more or less continuous feedback in the form of monitoring and management information. Powell (1987) has rightly spoken of an audit explosion in this respect.

These information systems are more or less tightly embedded in planning and control systems (or systems for 'quality management') that are expected to inspire and inform evaluations and monitoring efforts. The ongoing integration and standardisation of data and information (information management) is as important as the technologically induced push towards a greater interactivity and accessibility in the use of that information.

Integration and standardisation: both developments now transcend existing organisational borders. In the Netherlands at least, the 'coupling' of databases is a dynamic process which not only concerns the technical level of intra- and inter-organisational integration of (administrative) databases, but also regards the 'hyperlinks' that are established between different laws. In several policy domains, 'information policies' have developed that more or less make compulsory actor's (statal and non-statal) use of unique data definitions and universal identifiers. This holy mission for standardisation (and integration) is ubiquitous: in the field of social security, health care, land information, tax administration (on incomes as well as properties). Those who strongly believe in the value of high-quality customer service, one-stop shops and efficiency are most easily seduced by the new optima that ICTs enable. Frissen (1998) has justly observed that Big Brother is often represented by his Soft Sister (for instance in the field of Geographic Information Systems, that seem to regenerate political and administrative ambitions regarding (integrally) coordinated public policy-making and are therefore leaving the domain of electric wires and sewerage systems and moving into the domain of all kinds of social data). These applications also renew the practical importance of space and territory, in a time that seems to be dominated by visions of 'de-territorialisation' and virtualisation. According to some authors, informatization predominantly facilitates 'postmodern' trends such as these. I think that Antony Giddens is also right when he suggests that informatization is actually reinforcing the (hyper)modernisation of our societies. This process is, indeed, fuelled by the increased transparency and higher degrees of penetrability and surveillance of (at least some parts of) society.

Giddens (1987) has identified the expanded capabilities for direct and indirect surveillance as one of the major forces of (hyper)modernisation: 'Surveillance refers to the supervision of the activities of subject populations to the political sphere – although its importance as a basis of administrative power is by no means confined to that sphere. Supervision may be direct . . . But more characteristically it is indirect and based upon the control of information' (Giddens 1990: 59). The capacities for such a surveillance, according to Giddens, are especially reinforced by two conditions: the accumulation of 'coded information' and the ability to use forms of direct surveillance. These conditions are especially favoured by the development of abilities and possibilities for supervision on (combinations of) societal or organisational domains, the development of supervision and control as a special function in administrations and organisations, the development of incentives and sanctions in these domains and the development of an ideology and symbols that support the development of (systems and acceptation of) surveillance (Giddens 1987: 14, see also in Dandeker 1980).

Those who are not distracted by the colourful (but harmless) websites that ministries and municipalities use to present themselves on their 'national information infrastructures' are able to see that still far and away the most money and effort is put into the development of information policies, systems and infrastructures. These systems are changing, at great pace, the way governments are organised and do business (see e.g. the discussion in Bellamy and Taylor 1998; Snellen and van de Donk 1998). Following the paths of technological developments, huge and extensive data communication networks are installed. These governmental networks (which most often do not allow the colourful and 'anarchistic' use by individual 'netizens' or 'virtual communities') are installed to connect all kinds of statal organisations in order to support them in bringing their individual as well as common activities to higher degrees of perfection. The metaphor of an electronic highway is much less adequate here than the metaphor of a highly regulated and controlled railroad system.

As we know from empirical research by Killian, Wind, and also Davenport, the design of these systems is often inspired by a kind of utopian model of political information, most often guided by technocratic ideals (or is it logic?) of a full information union. This full information union ('Informationsverbund') is, however, a terminal station that is not easily entered. The development of these information infrastructures most often stop at levels that do not demand or require such a full and complete consensus on data definitions (like a kind of technical level of a resource union or a level that only facilitates the smoothness of inter-organisational communication and work processes) (see Killian and Wind 1997, 1998; Davenport et al. 1992). Nevertheless, in some policy sectors, the ideals of the information union are served time and again by the willingness to reform and reorganise. And every new generation of the technology seems to help realising it, and the use of communication technologies has largely 'facilitated' steps in this direction.

We do not know, yet, the impacts these new infrastructures will have on the (localisation, allocation, separation and distribution) of (information) powers.

These impacts are likely to be different in each policy sector. However, some early results from empirical studies into the way these kinds of information infrastructures do change the power relationships between governments and non-governmental organisations, do allow for some concerns about the future of this particular 'model' of democracy. Although the societal organisations that show up in the particular study I briefly present in the next section are far from representative for the highly miscellaneous set of 'societal actors' that are, one way or another, involved in the processes of democratic governance, I think that at least some of the lessons that can be drawn from this study do transcend the particularities of it.

INFORMATIZATION: AUTONOMY, TRANSPARENCY, HIERARCHY

In the Netherlands the care for elderly people in nursing homes (of which there are about 1,500) is organised by private, non-profit organisations (most of the time foundations). Almost all are related to a certain ideological, cultural or religious group in society. In the 1960s and 1970s, these nursing homes were entitled to receive financial support from the state to cover the greater part of their operating costs. During the 1980s, some of the Dutch regional governments that became responsible for the (re)distribution of subsidies developed sophisticated information systems. A comparative study of the (re)distributive policy-making process in these governments and in governments that did not use information systems reveals that in the former these processes showed a clear reinforcement of techno-rationalistic characteristics (van de Donk 1997). More zealous policies and clearly non-incremental policy goals were formulated and attained, even in situations where existing research would suggest a more incremental pattern of policy-making (e.g. in situations of moderate growth). Policy proposals in informated governments were more refined and anticipating and based on systematic analysis of the data the homes had to submit in order to get the subsidy. These data, or to be more specific, the computer software, helped to produce a set of viable alternatives that met the goals set within the specified set of boundary conditions, and on the basis of systematic and continuous feedback.

Agenda-setting and actual decision-making, formerly a joint process between representatives of the field (individual foundations and their different (Protestant, Catholic, etc.) umbrella organisations) and civil servants and politicians became, for the most important and crucial part, a solo act of civil servants. Also the implementation stage was less susceptible to 'political manoeuvring' by the actors involved. Civil servants or politicians who formerly had to negotiate with the nursing homes and their umbrella organisations and had to give in to all kinds of pressures and claims could simply announce their policies. In other words policies were 'applied' algorithmically, not 'negotiated'.

The 'information environment' of political decision-makers became more and more dominated by index numbers and quantitative indicators, statistical computations and so on.

These indicators, more than other kinds of qualitative information (formerly much more important in the decision-making processes about the annual budgets) also 'suggested' all kinds of anticipatory and detailed policy interventions. Electronic networks shoved aside the importance of the former social networks. Government computing clearly reduced the possibilities for other actors to set and influence the policy agenda. Governments relied on their statutory powers to fill their databases with (detailed) data that contributed to the comparability and the transparency of the organisations in the field. New information requirements were formulated again and again to improve transparency, accountability and particularly, comparability, aggregability, analysability and reliability of the data. Although some of the founders of investment information systems, they did not have the means (financially, and most important, formally) to come up with the bureaucracy and to catch up on the backlog in analytical competencies they were facing. On the contrary, for a definition of the situation (important for discussions about the (re)allocation of money, policies regarding up or downscaling of the organisation of care and so on) they became more and more dependent on the information that was produced by statist spreadsheets. Albeit formed in splendid isolation, the proposals and interventions of informated governments were, even when they were unfavourable to a large group of homes, most often seen as more authoritative.

The enhanced 'rationality' of the processes and outcomes as a consequence of informatization could be explained by the profound changes that informatization has engendered in the institutional configuration of the policy arena. These arenas were, as a consequence of informatization, transformed in 'hierarchies'. Informatization at the same time reinforced the power of the bureaucratic apparatus and weakened the position of the private actors in the field (foundations that administered one or more nursing homes and their umbrella organisations). The power of the bureaucratic apparatus was reinforced by the radically improved capacities to analyse, anticipate, construct and present the data in such a manner that their interests were optimised at the expense of those of the other players. In most informated governments, bureaucrats and politicians formed a dominant and stable coalition that successfully exploited the radically increased transparency of the field. The formerly somewhat closed 'information domains' that supported a certain degree of autonomy were opened up at great pace.

This transparency weakened both the autonomy and the strategic competences of the individual foundations and associations that governed one or more nursing homes and, especially, that of their umbrella organisations. The latter were becoming more and more powerless because they were deprived of their capacities (as well as opportunities) to define a common interest that could be the basis of a strategy to oppose the policy proposals (earlier consensus appeared to be most often founded on a certain ignorance of the exact consequences of the proposals for each of their members). For example, in a situation where the governmental proposals for a (re)distribution of subsidies illustrated a more or less accidental but very detailed case for about half of the allied foundations to profit from the proposition, and that the others would go downhill, these umbrella organisations were forced to make only very general, non-committal statements. Informatization in the domain of the governmental bureaucracies put them in an awkward position. The formal statutory position to collect data enabled the state to realise a head start with regard to the initiation, analysis, consideration, implementation and evaluation of policies in this field.

WILL THE INFORMATION SOCIETY BE A CIVIL SOCIETY?

'The central paradox of democracy – that the people are sovereign but many: there is no one will of the people but several, sometimes contradictory will. It is probably for this reason that a healthy voluntary sector is characteristic of a democracy' (Douglas 1987: 47). One of the crucial questions regarding the possibilities for democratic governance in an information society is, in my opinion, the question as to whether 'the increasing capability for new flexibilities in the patterning of human connectivity' that Bellamy mentions in her introductory chapter will indeed give rise to a trend towards a further pluralisation in the democratic polity.

Although nursing homes and their umbrella organisations are not the most exciting part of the democratic polity, the relationships between them and the state bureaucracy is more or less representative of other parts and sectors of the democratic polity of the welfare state. The same appears to be true for the way in which informatization in state bureaucracies (starting at the operational levels of execution and implementation of, for instance, re-distributive policy-making) has contributed to the transformations with regard to these relationships. A reinforcement of the position of statal actors *vis-à-vis* the actors in the policy field can also be found in other domains of policy-making (e.g. Bekkers 1998; Zuurmond 1998).

Although I can agree with the assumption that 'The characteristics from the electronic reality of systems, databases and networks that can be derived from the Internet anarchism, self regulation, fragmentation virtualisation, decentralisation and self referentiality are conflicting with the institutional characteristics of politics and administration: order, regulation, coherence, centralisation, territoriality and intervention' (Frissen 1996: 256), the empirical study I have presented here shows that it is not reasonable to expect that this conflict will be always and everywhere won by the characteristics of the technology. The complex processes of intermediation between the two sets of characteristics can, indeed, have many and even opposite outcomes in different domains of the democratic polity.

That an increased transparency and penetrability can be, technically, more easily organised reciprocally does not by definition mean that it will be organised in such a manner. On the contrary, for important parts of the democratic polity informatization seems to perpetuate, reinforce and firm up the modernistic characteristics of politics and administration that Frissen mentioned. ICTs contribute to a strengthening of bureaucracies which are transformed at great pace in highly successful infocracies. The coupling of databases and the integration of information management is fuelled by a new plan for the role of the state. The era of bureaucracy bashing is over – there seems to be a change in attitude everywhere in Europe. And as the *Economist* of 26 September 1997, dramatically depicted through its cover design the 'invisible hand' is, in fact, a glove, stuffed with information systems.

As we have learned from the case presented above, the infocratic scenario is a possible model for the future of democratic governance. It is certainly so for important parts of the daily life of democracy in some of the important policy sectors in Western democracies. A certain degree of pluralism and mutual adjustment between statal and societal actors has characterised many of these democracies.

Informatization and infocratization are undermining, at least potentially (and, clearly, in some sectors more than in others), much of the institutional variety and institutional prerequisites of the 'societal model of democracy', which have been particularly important in policy domains of the welfare 'state'. Many of the values that inspired this model are currently recognised in the network model of policy-making. Coproduction and modes of pluricentric policy-making that imply a modest role of state bureaucracies have proven to be much more effective in many fields of society because they respect more than the central rule approach the notion of an 'intelligent democracy' in which capabilities and responsibilities are divided among many actors that are part of the democratic polity.

Will informatization threaten the production relationships that underlie forms of coproduction and interactive policy-making? Mutual adjustment is, indeed, leading to other forms of social configurations than the one that seems to be engendered by informatization in public administration. That is, in spite of all the optimistic images of a chaotic, versatile and fragmented Internet scenario (which may be more adequate for other sectors or parts of the polity), the infocratic configuration is appropriate for at least some of the most important parts of the democratic polity. That configuration is characterised by highly central, unicentric and unilateral exercises of power (and discipline). Informatization might very well threaten the social pluralism and the intelligence of democracy as it was understood by Braybrooke and Lindblom. An infocratization of policy networks is endangering the institutional prerequisites for such an intelligence. The presence of myriad quasi-autonomous groups, a certain level of fragmentation and a pluralistic distribution of information and power are indispensable conditions for a democratic polity (Braybrooke and Lindblom 1963: 244). Whether informatization will continue to respect these conditions in other policy domains remains to be seen, as does the extent to which the information society will be a civil society.

References

Almond, G. A. and Verba, S. (1963) *The Civic Culture*, Princeton: Princeton University Press.

Anheier, H. K. and Seibel, W. (1990) *The Third Sector: Comparative Studies of Nonprofit*

Organizations, Berlin: Walter de Gruyter.

Aquina, H. (1988) 'PGO's in the Netherlands', in C. Hood and G. F. Schuppert (eds) *Delivering Public Services in Western Europe: Sharing Western European Experience of ParaGovernment Organization*, London: Sage, pp. 94–107.

Barber, B. R. (1984) *Strong Democracy: Participatory Politics for a New Age*, Berkeley: University of California Press.

——(1996) 'Three challenges to reinventing democracy', in P. Hirst and S. Khilnani (eds) *Reinventing Democracy*, Cambridge: The Political Quarterly.

Bekkers, V. J. J. M. (1998) 'Wiring public organizations and changing organizational jurisdictions', in I. Th. M. Snellen and W. B. H. J. van de Donk (eds) *Public Administration in an Information Age: A Handbook*, Amsterdam/Berlin/Oxford/Tokyo/Washington: IOS Press, pp. 57–74.

Bellamy, C. and Taylor, J. A. (1998) *Governing in the Information Age*, Buckingham: Open University Press.

Berger, P. L. and Neuhaus, R. J. (1977) *To Empower People: The Role of Mediating Structures in Public Policy*, Washington, DC: American Enterprise Institute.

Braybrooke, D. and Lindblom, Ch. E. (1963) *A Strategy of Decision*, New York: The Free Press.

Burger, A., Dekker, P., van der Ploeg, T. J. and van Veen, W. (1997) *Defining the Nonprofit Sector: The Netherlands*, Working Paper no. 23 in the series of the Comparative Nonprofit Sector Project of the Johns Hopkins University.

Burt, E. and Taylor, J. A. (1998) *The Voluntary Sector in the Information Age: Mapping the Terrain*, Paper for the Virtual Society? Programme, Manchester, 16 March 1998.

Cohen, S. (1985) *Visions of Social Control: Crime, Punishment and Classification*, Cambridge: Polity Press.

Dahl, R. A. (1982) *Dilemma's of Pluralist Democracy*, New Haven: Yale University Press.

——(1998) *On Democracy*, New Haven: Yale University Press.

Dandeker, Chr. (1980) *Surveillance, Power and Modernity: Bureaucracy and Discipline from 1700 to the Present Day*, New York: St Martin's Press.

Davenport, Th. H., Eccles, R. G. and Prusak, L. (1992) 'Information politics', *Sloan Management Review*, pp. 53–56.

Dobkin Hall, P. (1992) *Inventing the Nonprofit Sector and Other Essays on Philanthropy, Voluntarism and Nonprofit Organizations*, Baltimore: Johns Hopkins University Press.

——Donk, van de and Snellen, I. Th. M. (1998), 'Towards a theory of public administration in an information age', in I. Th. M. Snellen and W. B. H. J. van de Donk (eds) *Public Administration in an Information Age: A Handbook*, Amsterdam/Berlin/Oxford/Tokyo/Washington: IOS Press.

Donk, W. B. H. J. van de (1997) *De Arena in Schema: Een verkenning van de betekenis van informatisering voor beleid en politiek inzake de verdeling van middelen onder verzorgingshuizen* [A scheme in the Arena: An exploration of the impacts of informatization for policy and politics in the field of re-distributive policymaking for nursing homes], Lelystad: Konkijklijke Vermande.

——(1998) 'De Staat als Databaas? Over registreren en disciplineren: de Infocratie als digitaal panopticon' [The state as Databoss? About registrations and discipline: the Infocracy as a digital panopticon], in F. B. van der Meer and A. B. Ringeling (eds) *Bestuurskunde en Praktijk. Liber Amicorum voor prof. mr. dr. I. Th. M. Snellen*, Alphen aan den Rijn: Samsom.

——and van de Tops, P. W. (1995) 'Orwell or Athens? Informatization and the future of democracy', in W. B. H. J. van de Donk, I. Th. M. Snellen, P. W. Tops (eds), *Orwell in*

Athens: A Perspective on Informatization and Democracy, Amsterdam/Oxford/Tokyo, Washington, DC: IOS Press, pp. 13–32.

Douglas, J. (1987) 'Political theories of nonprofit organization', in W. W. Powell (ed) *The Nonprofit Sector: A Research Handbook*, New Haven: Yale University Press, pp. 43–54.

Eisenberg, P. (1997) 'A crisis in the nonprofit sector', *National Civic Review*, 86 (4): 331–341.

Estelle, J. (ed) (1989) *The Nonprofit Sector in International Perspective: Studies in Comparative Culture and Policy*, New York: Oxford University Press.

Etzioni, A. (1973) 'The third sector and domestic missions', *Public Administration Review* 33 (July/August): 314–323.

——(1988) *The Moral Dimension: Towards a New Economics*, New York: Free Press.

—— (1996) 'A moderate communitarian proposal', *Political Theory* 24 (2): 155–171.

Finer, S. E. (1997) *The History of Government, 3. Empires, Monarchies and the Modern State*, Oxford: Oxford University Press.

Frank, R. G. and Salkever, D. S. (1994) 'Nonprofit organizations in the health sector', *Journal of Economic Perspectives* 8 (4): 129–144.

Frissen, P. H. A. (1998), 'Public administration in cyberspace', in I. Th. M. Snellen and W. B. H. J. van de Donk (eds) *Public Administration in an Information Age: A Handbook*, Amsterdam/Berlin/Oxford/Tokyo/Washington: IOS Press, pp. 33–46.

Giddens, A. (1987) *The Nation State and Violence*, Berkeley: University of California Press.

——(1990) *The Consequences of Modernity*, Cambridge: Polity Press.

Gidron, B. et al. (1991) *Government and the Third Sector: Emerging Relationships in Welfare States*, San Francisco: Jossey Bass.

Gladden, E. N. (1972) *A History of Public Administration, 2. From the Eleventh Century to the Present Day*, London: Frank Cass.

Hendriks, F. and Toonen, Th. A. J. (eds) (1998) *Schikken en Plooien: De stroperige staat bij nader inzien*, Assen: Van Gorcum.

Hirst, P. Q. (1996) 'Democracy and civil society', in P. Q. Hirst and S. Khilnani (eds) *Reinventing Democracy*, Cambridge: The Political Quarterly, pp. 97–116.

Hodgkinson, A. A. and Lyman, R. W. (1989) *The Future of the Nonprofit Sector*, San Francisco: Jossey-Bass.

Jenkins, W. I. (1987) *Policy Analysis: A Political and Organisational Perspective*, London: Martin Robinson.

Killian, W. and Wind, M. (1997) *Verwaltung und Vernetzun: Technische Integration bei organisatorische Vielfalt am Beispiel von Agrar- und Umweltverwaltungen*, Opladen: Leske & Budrich.

——(1998) 'Changes in interorganizational coordination and cooperation', in I. Th. M. Snellen and W. B. H. J. van de Donk (eds) *Public Administration in an Information Age: A Handbook*, Amsterdam/Berlin/Oxford/Tokyo/Washington: IOS Press, pp. 273–291.

Lasswell, H. (1936) *Politics: Who Gets What, When, How?* New York: Peter Smith.

Levy, P. (1997) *Cyberculture*, Paris: Odile Jacob.

Lindblom, Ch. E. (1965) *The Intelligence of Democracy: Decision Making Through Mutual Adjustment*, New York: Free Press.

——(1979) 'Still muddling, not yet through', *Public Administration Review* 39: 517–526.

——(1990) *Inquiry and Change: The Troubled Attempt to Understand and Shape Society*, New Haven/London: Yale University Press.

Pearton, M. (1982) *The Knowledgeable State: War, Diplomacy and Technology since 1930*, Hutchinson.

Pettigrew, A. M. (1972) 'Information control as a power resource', *Sociology*, pp. 187–204.

Powell, W. W. (ed.)(1987) *The Non-Profit Sector: A Research Handbook*, New Haven: Yale University Press.

Power, M. (1997) 'The audit explosion', in G. Mulgan (ed) *Life after Politics: New Thinking for the Twenty-First Century*, London: Fontana Press.

Putnam, R. D. (1993) *Making Democracy Work: Civic Traditions in Modern Italy*, Princeton: Princeton University Press.

Salamon, L. M. (1996) 'The crisis of the nonprofit sector and the challenge of renewal', *National Civic Review* 86 (4): 3–16.

——and Anheier, H. K. (1996) *The Emerging Nonprofit Sector: An Overview*, Manchester: Manchester University Press.

Scott, J. C. (1998) *Seeing like a State: How certain schemes to improve the Human Condition have failed*, New Haven/London: Yale University Press.

Snellen, I. Th. M. and van de Donk, W. B. H. J. (eds) (1998) *Public Administration in an Information Age: A Handbook*, Amsterdam/Berlin/Oxford/Tokyo/Washington: IOS Press.

Smith, S. R. and Lipsky, M. (1993) *Non Profits for Hire: The Welfare State in the Age of Contracting*, Cambridge: Cambridge University Press.

Visser, J. and Hemerijck, A. C. (1997) *A Dutch Miracle: Job Growth, Welfare Reform and Corporatism in the Netherlands*, Amsterdam: Amsterdam University Press.

Streeck, W. and Schmitter, Ph. C. (1991) 'Community, market, state and associations? The prospective contribution of interest governance to social order' in J. G. Thompson, J. Francis, R. Levaĉic and J. Mitchell (eds) *Markets, Hierarchies and Networks: The Coordination of Social Life*, London: Sage.

Whutnow, R. (1991) 'Tocqueville's question reconsidered: voluntarism and public discourse in advanced industrial societies', in R. Whutnow (ed) *Between States and Markets: The Voluntary Sector in Comparative Perspective*, Princeton: Princeton University Press.

——(1995) 'Between the state and the market: voluntarism and the differerence it makes', in A. Etzioni (ed.) *Rights and the Common Good. The Communautarian Perspective*, New York: St Martin's Press, pp. 209–221.

Wolch, J. (1990) *The Shadow State: Government and Voluntary Sector in Transition*, New York: Foundation Sector.

Zuurmond, A. (1998) 'From bureaucracy to infocracy: are democratic institutions lagging behind?', in I. Th. M. Snellen and W. B. H. J. van de Donk (eds) *Public Administration in an Information Age: A Handbook*, Amsterdam/Berlin/Oxford/Tokyo/Washington: IOS Press, pp. 259–272.

10 Virtual communities

New public spheres on the internet?

Kees Schalken

INTRODUCTION

There is always one wonderful story when we consider the consequences of Information and Communication Technologies (ICT) for democracy: the Santa Monica Public Electronic Network (PEN). Not only is the PEN one of the few well-described examples of how technology had a measurable effect on democracy, it is also one of those examples that demonstrate that there is a potential in new ICTs for enhancing citizen participation and therefore contributing to emerging models of democracy like the neo-republican model (inspired by Barber's 'strong democracy') or maybe even a new and unknown cyberdemocracy (Poster 1995).

Although the rise of the Internet generated a lot of talk about new forms of direct and deliberative democracy, not many examples can be found around the world that prove that these new models are storming the roads of democracy. On the contrary, in this chapter, on the basis of Dutch experiences with government homepages on the Internet, I will argue that consumer democracy and demo-elitist democracy are the models most often promoted through the introduction of ICT in democratic processes. Homepages and similar experiments mainly focus on the broadcasting of information and public service delivery. Those experiments on the Internet that try to go further to enhance citizen's participation are often conducted from an add-on strategy that emphasises an instrumentalist and incrementalist approach to traditional and existing institutions and processes. Also, these experiments appear to be very rarely successful in addressing the general public. Does this mean that we have to adjust our expectations about the potential for ICT to enhance more participative models of electronic democracy? Not quite yet I would argue. In the dynamics and the success of this global information and communications network, there is something that might be harvested for the benefits of democracy. Not large schemes and blueprints such as were the basis of success of the Internet, but grass-roots movements, economy of exchange and cooperation. A peculiar mix of hackers, techies, innovators, producers and eventually the general public was the driving force of these network's success.

The emergence of the Internet can best be characterised as the uncontrolled expansion of an amorphous infrastructure of information and communication networks which combined might create a global public sphere. Using the dynamics of the net, people gather in a large variety of electronic environments, called virtual communities. In these communities people gather to meet, socialise, fight, discuss politics, organise, play or fall in love. When, about twenty years ago, Marshall McLuhan described the development of new media as the emergence of a Global Village he missed only one letter. Not one Global Village but an innumerable number of Global *Villages* populate the Internet. When discussing the potential of the Internet and the global villages that are thriving therein for promoting democratic purposes, the public sphere might provide us with a better starting point than the early experiments of governments on the Internet. The idea of the public sphere, first described in a historical narrative by Habermas as the coffee and tea houses in the pre-industrial society, but later by others (e.g. Dahlgren 1995) applied to more modern media providers like public radio and television broadcasting, museums and public libraries, will be explored as a framework that might provide some hand and footholds when considering the question as to what the democratic potential of the Internet might be. But first I return to that modern tale of Santa Monica. A tale that, as usual, contains not only the Light but also the Dark side of the Force.

A MODERN TALE OF DEMOCRACY: THE SANTA MONICA PUBLIC ELECTRONIC NETWORK (PEN)

The history of the Public Electronic Network in Santa Monica (pen.ci.santa-monica-ca.us) has grown to be a classic parable of electronic democracy. Started in the late 1980s, the network received a lot of attention in discussions throughout the 1990s about the contribution and meaning of new ICTs and community networks to contemporary democracy. The lack of new and even strong examples of how community networks enhanced participation of certain deprivileged groups in society kept the PEN in the spotlights and prevented it from losing its actuality.

The Light side of the Force

The city of Santa Monica, California opened the PEN on 21 February 1989. Within two weeks, over 500 residents had signed up to the free system (McKeown 1991). At the end of 1991 almost 4,000 of the total of 96,000 inhabitants of the city of Santa Monica were registered as users and in total they contacted the network about 125,000 times. The development of the PEN is quite non-typical from the community networks we know nowadays. First, PEN was one of the first community systems supported by a local government. Other local systems that already existed were operated by local universities, volunteer organisations or libraries and Chambers of Commerce. The system began with a request from a city council member asking to research whether Santa Monica could provide computer access to a small group of his constituents. The question was directed to Ken Phillips, then director of Santa Monica's Information Systems department, who came to the conclusion that this system should not be limited to a bunch of buddies of one councilman (van Tassel 1994). A citizens' survey showed that Santa Monicans wanted such a system to be open to all residents. The results of the survey worked as a guide for the further development and design of PEN. Phillips managed to get sponsorship in the form of hardware from manufacturer Hewlett Packard and software from Metasystems software (Beamish 1995). Thus PEN was born from a governmental initiative, supported by commercial computer companies.

A second anomaly of the PEN is that it initially did not have any gateways to the Internet, so it was strictly oriented on the local community. Free access to the community network was provided for the complete population of Santa Monica. Citizens in possession of a Personal Computer and a modem could dial into the system for free. To enlarge the accessibility of the system for the complete citizenry, nineteen public terminals were installed in public spaces like the library, schools, recreation centres, senior citizen centres and other locations. Remarkably no less than 20 to 25 per cent of the PEN usage came from these public terminals (McKeown 1991) and this is what gave the PEN quite a leverage in the Santa Monica local community. Any resident could register with the city's Information Systems Department and get a user ID and password. At login, users saw a Main Menu and choose from options including City Hall, Community Centre, electronic mail and current events. The content of the PEN was quite diverse, containing many sources of information, such as crime figures, the catalogue of the library and data on the housing market. Through electronic mail, users could address questions or worries to the local municipality.

In reality the PEN grew beyond all that into a citizen to citizen phenomenon, with a culture of its own (McKeown 1991). The Santa Monica residents discovered that a community network can support purposeful political action. A diverse group of community members and some homeless residents organised themselves electronically using PEN. The most appealing result of this on-line organisation was the so-called SHWASHLOCK project. SHWASHLOCK is an acronym for SHowers, WASHers and LOCKers. An estimated 200 homeless people found their way to the public access terminals on the PEN and told users that these three items were most needed for them to find work and get off the streets. Santa Monica residents have always been frustrated over the 2,000 homeless people who subsist in makeshift shelters in the city parks and on the beaches, so the problem was recognised as a major local issue.

The PEN became the focal point for public expression about this issue (van Tassel 1994). The strength of PEN was that it gave an unprecedented possibility for the homeless people of Santa Monica not only to address city government, but moreover, to reach out to the local residents and express their opinions. This way they could let others know that their basic need to get off the streets was jobs, but they could not present an employable appearance without being able to shower, wash their clothing and store their belongings. It was difficult for homeless people to express their opinions to local government even on PEN, but they were able to join forces with the local citizenry who had easier access to governmental resources. Together the homeless people and representatives of the Santa Monica residents formed an action group and launched the SWASHLOCK programme. This group combined on-line discussions and actions with face to face meetings among each other and the municipality. The road to agreement on the SWASHLOCK project was not without constraints, since local social service providers expressed unease over the threat that the new group would be competing with them for scarce social service dollars (Wittig 1991).

As with every policy issue, many other players were involved. In this relatively small example there were no less than six stakeholder groups, the homeless residents, the on-line PEN Action Group, the social service agencies, various businesses, the City council, and other residents of Santa Monica (Schuler 1996). The solution was found by cooperating with existing agencies rather than starting new ones. In July 1990 the Santa Monica city council responded to the PEN Action Group's formal proposal and allocated $150,000 to install lockers and showers under the Santa Monica pier and agreed to open public showers elsewhere at 6:00 a. m. (Rheingold 1993: 269). A locker manufacturer agreed to provide 30 lockers for seven months without charge.

The Santa Monica SHWASHLOCK case demonstrates that using on-line resources for community organising can work. Not so much the direct connection the homeless people had to the local municipality, but the leverage the system gave them towards the local community was the key to success. The SWASHLOCK case is not the only example of Santa Monica residents using the PEN for local policy issues. In 1990 a proposal to keep a part of the Santa Monica beach public, against building a luxury hotel and restaurant was passed into law. Support for the proposal was for a large part gathered using the PEN system.

Thus the PEN and the SWASHLOCK project in particular have become well described and evaluated examples of the potential community networks contain to empower citizen groups for action and therefore enhance local democracy. Research by the University of Southern California's Annenberg School in 1990 surprisingly showed that the use of PEN is not related to traditional socio-economic characteristics that predicted computer usage in past research. Age, income and education are unrelated to frequency of PEN use, and only education is strongly related to adoption. This indicates that the potential for adoption of new communication networks is widespread throughout the community. The feeling was strong that: 'PEN has created a new breed of political activist – one that feels liberated by the convenience of computer communication. People who have never had the time or patience to play telephone tag with city officials, write letters or sit through interminable public hearings can now participate in local government' (Yarnall 1989: 30).

Alas, the parable of the PEN did not end in 1990, and the future demonstrated that there is an unexpected *Dark side* to the Force and this has subsequently tempered the high expectations and enthusiasm that PEN awoke in the early 1990s.

The Dark side of the Force

In 1993 a more thorough evaluation of the first four years of the PEN was conducted (Schmitz, Pillips and Rogers 1993) and though the research states that PEN has met most of its initial six objectives, other figures shade the parable of success of the PEN. Contrary to earlier studies which ascertained that the potential for computer networks like PEN were not related to social background, the evaluation report states that PEN users differ significantly from typical Santa Monicans, in income, gender and education. Sixty per cent of the people who use PEN most, describe themselves as very interested in politics and PEN users were more active (than the average city resident) in each of seven types of local political activity, ranging from attending city council meetings to contacting city officials (van Tassel 1994).

The research also demonstrates that discussions and talks on the PEN were mainly dominated by a small group of residents (referred to as a 'net bozo take over'). In 1991, more than 3,000 people were signed up for PEN, but only 500–600 logged on each month and most never added any comments to the discussions (Varley 1991). Next to this a small group of the regular visitors wielded a weapon that appeared to be destructive to discussions on the system. This phenomenon, well known among contemporary netizens, but relatively new in that time, was called flaming, a very direct, aggressive approach among participants of discussions towards each other. System administrators had hoped that, given the fact that most PEN participants live within two miles or less of each other, flamers would be dissuaded. The opposite proved true, and many discussions on the PEN ended in violent personal flames of mockery. The flames and mockery found a special victim in the female population on the PEN. Some males on PEN (young adolescents) began writing public sexual scenarios in which various PEN women were subjected to domination and other degrading behaviour (McKeown 1991).

The flaming and abusive sexual approach to women on the PEN confronted the system administrators with a problem. Since it was a public system they had to be very careful not to infringe on the right of free speech of the users. Thus the symptom was tolerated until the small group of dissidents were clearly chasing people off the system, among whom were many women and public representatives who rightfully resented the seemingly irrational personal attacks. The system administrators were only partly successful by issuing a posting limit for users that would not allow them to post more than a certain number of postings in a discussion group every week. This measure appeared to be too restrictive in certain serious discussions and was not appreciated by more regular users. The approach of the women who were frequently intimidated by young men appeared to be more successful. They created a group called PENFEMMES and refused to slink away from the attacks, but joined together on-line and face to face. They chose to systematically ignore their attackers, and vowed to start more woman-related discussions on PEN. According to some reports this action has made PEN a more interesting and female friendly environment.

The moral of the tale: questions, expectations and lessons to be learned from PEN

The research on the social and political one-sidedness of the user population of the PEN and the reports of abusive behaviour of a small group of users who managed to dominate discussions threw a dirty stain on the reputation of the PEN. Questions were raised about the architecture and design of the PEN; was it sufficiently utilised to support discussions or was it on the contrary decreasing a sense of community and cutting off, rather than enhancing public discussion of important current topics? Also the nature of electronic discussion was questioned and the effectiveness of on-line moderators or the establishment of moderated groups thoroughly discussed. Analysis indicated that PEN did not bring a whole new set of participants to the political process, nevertheless some individuals became involved in local politics and public affairs who might not otherwise participate (Docter and Dutton 1998).

Finally the question arose as to whether there is a true potential in computer networks to provide a long-lasting leverage for certain disempowered groups in a community, or was the Public Electronic Network in Santa Monica a special case of a one-off, coincidental, meeting of a specific selection of people (homeless and housed residents of a relatively small town) that could only learn about the nature of each other's existence, not by meeting face to face, but by using a computer network?

These questions concerning the democratic potential of the PEN is particularly pertinent because there are very few examples of equally strong and striking political action being taken through the use of community networks. PEN is the one example that suggests that new forms of democracy may be emerging that have a strong emphasis on the empowerment and participation of citizens. Santa Monica's Public Electronic Network thus became an example of either the neo-republican or in some measure even the cyberdemocratic model of democracy discussed earlier in this book. Even in a limited way PEN is proof that the realization of those models is not only theoretically possible. However, as the saying goes: one swallow does not make a summer. If PEN turns out to be a lone flower in the desert and its achievements coincidental it does not provide a strong case for cyberdemocracy. Therefore we need to leave the tale behind and take some time for a reality check.

REALITY CHECK: DUTCH GOVERNMENTS ON-LINE

Though some Dutch local governments are very active in experimenting with new forms of democracy on the Internet (bringing databases on-line, trying to enhance citizens' participation by initiating on-line public debate), the overall image is a less progressive one. In research on 160 Dutch municipalities that had some kind of presence on the Internet it was concluded that 8 municipalities provided citizens with limited interactive use as e-mail, in 12 municipalities the homepage gave the opportunity for citizens to voice their opinion and in only 7 municipalities was discussion about public affairs allowed (VB-Advies 1997). The huge majority of the municipalities use the Internet for purposes that are already provided by traditional media: news and information. Only 8 per cent of the municipalities make the most of the interactive possibilities of the net and even then in most cases only on an experimental basis. But even when the interactive possibilities are exploited and the Internet is used in an effort to actually enhance citizens participation, results are often very disappointing. In a recent report by the Ministry of Internal Affairs an overview was given of the initiatives of electronic citizens consultation that have been held since 1995. The conclusion was that although expectations were often not very high, in not any of the cases can success be noted. In all cases participation, the quality of discussion and relevance for policy ends were considered low or very low (Dutch Ministry of Internal Affairs 1998).

The image that is presented here is not new. Modernisation of processes of political decision-making and administrative institutions with aid of new kinds of technology has always been conducted via an add-on strategy (Laudon 1984). Building on existing institutions, procedures and habits, technology might have some influence, but a radical change is hardly ever observed, especially not in the short term. Information and communications technology has mainly been introduced in local democracy as a tool to enhance and improve existing institutions. To provide better service delivery, better and more information from different partners of municipalities inputted into the policy process. Technology is mainly used for gathering, processing and manipulation of growing amounts of information (Depla 1995). Thus it is mainly the model of a consumer democracy that comes into our minds when reviewing the initiatives of Dutch governments on the Internet. A consumer democracy that also contains elements from the demo-elitist model, with citizens viewed mainly as a source of information that can be exploited whenever the policy need arises.

International research seems to confirm this Dutch image of governments being very prudent when using new technologies for democratic purposes. Pratchett (1998) discovered a bias towards service delivery, away from other roles in modern polity. And Horrocks and Hambley (1998) found much the same results as those reported above in their own research into UK local government websites. Governments and political parties are very reserved to fully explore the possibilities of a new medium like the Internet, as long as they are not certain about the effect it will have on their daily routines. There are three main reasons for this conclusion. In the first place it seems that even new media are bound by the laws of incrementalism: when institutions have to implement change, they are automatically liable to build on existing organisations and institutions. Second, governments and political parties have a strong tendency towards controlling their environment. The Internet's dynamics are often contrary to that tendency. Conducting business on the Internet often automatically means handing over control. The last reason is an organisational aspect. Most experiments are organised from the standing organisations of bureaucracy that often have a systemic bias towards efficiency and service delivery, not democracy or citizens' participation.

Governments' natural tendencies towards incrementalism, control and efficiency make it hard to explore the real democratic potential of the Internet. Governments and political parties hardly dare to take any risks when implementing new media, especially when things are at stake. The call for examples on new means of democracy initiated by the Internet is rather loud but the actual proof is hardly ever found on the Internet, except maybe from some exceptional experiments that are as well known as the Minnesota E-democracy project and the previously mentioned PEN. Examples of new structures or organisations that empowered citizens in the spirit of the Internet are rarely found at the level of government or political parties. Even closely organised and monitored debates rarely ever result in measurable effects. This does not automatically mean that the democratic potential of the Internet is limited. The instrumental and institutional bias of governments might block a true exploration of the democratic potential that is contained within the Internet. For example, during the National Dutch elections in 1998, all political parties had their own websites, and most parties offered the possibility to discuss policy issues there. These discussion parts of the website failed to attract enough people to initiate a reasonable public debate (with the minor exception of the Socialist Party where at least some discussion was generated). This did not mean that no discussion on national politics occurred on the Internet or that citizens show a lack of interest for public debate. In the case of the Dutch National elections we just had to look elsewhere on the Internet. For instance on the public medium called the USENET, there is a news group called 'nl.politiek' (nl.politics). In the three weeks preceding the Dutch National Elections that news group generated the huge amount of 2,700 postings in a large range of subjects. But these news groups are considered to be too chaotic and non-serious to be of use for policy ends.

Nl.politics is not the only example of a lively discussion group, many more examples can be found outside governmental institutions in the way either minority groups or local communities are successful in applying the Internet for their own purposes. In contrast to governments they seem to be able to exploit the dynamics of the Internet and turn it to their advantage. Their efforts seem more closely connected to those emerging forms of democracy mentioned above, in particular the neo-republican, and perhaps even the cyberdemocracy model.

On the Internet, group dynamics are quite strong. Except from the solitary web surfer whose main goal is to gather information, most Internet users have an incessant inclination to meet others and gather around in virtual meeting places, engaging in a group dynamics that have also been described as virtual communities (Rheingold 1993). Because the concept of virtual communities has mostly been described as casuistic and in an empirical way and has hardly had any theoretical elaboration, it is sometimes easily set aside as slippery or inconcrete. This approach is rejected here, since it neglects the omnipresent group dynamics that is the most powerful driving force of the success of Internet.

Communication, discussion and the forming of virtual identities do not take place in isolation, but in an ongoing process of interaction with others. Virtual communities are the places where people meet people and are therefore essential in shaping the conditions for interaction. The theoretical elaboration of this new idea is an assignment for future research, but for the purpose of this article it will suffice to explore the nature of virtual communities and derive a typology from existing empirical and descriptive material.

THE NATURE OF VIRTUAL COMMUNITIES

Virtual communities are as diverse as the Internet itself. The diversity of the Internet is not only a technical but also a social diversity. The Internet is a huge jumble of technical protocols like for example Telnet, e-mail, FTP, IRC, USENET, Gopher, World Wide Web, RealAudio, Shockwave, ICQ, etc. It would not serve the purpose of this chapter to even start to describe them all. Many of these protocols are given a manageable graphical interface by software programs like Internet browsers (Netscape, Explorer) or news readers. These technical facilities have a limited independent meaning. Only by the creative and inventive use of these protocols by Internet users, can new environments emerge where people gather together. As, for example, in USENET news groups, mailing lists, discussion fora, homepages, chat groups, Multi User Dimensions (MUDs), FreeNets and Community Networks. However, it does not end with the different sorts of environments that make use of a variety of technical protocols and software programs, also they enclose a large amount of subjects. Classifications and hierarchies on the Internet are mainly based on people's interests, backgrounds, and hobbies but also geographical classifications remain a very popular entity in the virtual world (demonstrated by the large number of 'community networks' on the Internet).

To elaborate on the diversity of these environments on the Internet, we can use the example of the USENET, a technical protocol in which a huge number of users constructed about 100,000 newsgroups with the same amount of subjects. Many newsgroups are sleeping and lack real traffic, but some of them contain over 200 postings every day. Subjects in the newsgroups vary from animals, religion, politics, Star Trek and sex to, of course, technology itself. Not all newsgroups have the same regime when it comes to behaviour, etiquette or rules. Some newsgroups are totally free, and none really takes offence of what happens in it. Other groups, who usually have a group of frequent visitors, have a set of rules agreed upon by the participants. Those rules are known as netiquette and are often described in a file called the FAQ (Frequently Asked Questions). In those groups, new users will often be pointed to the netiquette when they step out of line. On the other side of the continuum between chaos and order, there are the moderated newsgroups. In those groups someone will be appointed as moderator and act as chairman for the group. There are different forms of moderation, but in most cases the moderator will decide on the structure of discussions in the newsgroups and sometimes even disallow certain contributions to be made.

The image of the USENET also describes and applies to large groups of other applications on the Internet, thus it is not difficult to conclude that diversity on the Internet is overwhelming. On IRC, on MUDs, on ICQ – not to mention the World Wide Web – one can find virtual environments like on USENET, in different shapes, with different subjects, different sets of rules and different atmospheres. These virtual environments are not the same as virtual communities, but knowing that they provide a parlour for the on-line communities, it is clear that it is difficult to give an unambiguous definition of what they are.

> People in virtual communities use words on screens to exchange pleasantries and argue, engage in intellectual discourse, conduct commerce, exchange knowledge, share emotional support, make plans, brainstorm, gossip, feud, fall in love, find friends and lose them, play games, flirt, create a little high art and a lot of idle talk. People in virtual communities do just about everything people do in real life, but we leave our bodies behind. You can't kiss anybody and nobody can punch you in the nose, but a lot can happen within those boundaries.
>
> (Rheingold 1994)

Rheingold's description of virtual communities comes from the pre-graphical Internet era, and although most environments are still text-based, in advanced graphical environments, new virtual communities are emerging (for example in the clans that team up in the 'shoot 'em up' multi-user game *Quake*). In his book Rheingold never defines exactly when to speak of a virtual community but they all seem to share the next characteristics: they consist of a group of people that gather on-line, have a common history, a common goal (even if that goal is just being together) and a common set of rules that is (sometimes silently) agreed upon.

An on-line gathering of people . . .

The groups of people that gather in virtual communities can be very diverse and either be stable or fluctuate over time. In most virtual communities there is a rather tight group of core users that know each other by name and habits. Next to the core group there is often a more loose group that is more fluid and changes a lot in composition. Many virtual communities contain a large group of people that are known as 'lurkers', users that are not really active but prefer to read along (or watch/listen along in more advanced environments) with the ongoing events without actually joining or commenting. Getting accepted by the core group is usually considered an achievement and is in some communities even formalised in a hierarchy of levels. Thus in virtual communities we often find a social stratification that resembles that of real communities (in Internet slang this is referred to as *irl*). Social networks, hierarchies and politics play an important role in both types of communities. Many other characteristics distinguish virtual communities from the irl dimension. In many virtual communities the identity a user takes is not set. Either you can stay anonymous or choose an avatar, an alternative identity that is a representation of yourself that is known to others. People can create their own physical, social and cultural identity. The so-called gender bending (men performing as women and women performing as men) is a quite well-known phenomenon on the Internet. Also the identities of Internet users are not necessarily unilateral. Many users are known to play with multiple identities in several virtual environments. A very strong example of virtual communities where people play with identities are MUDs.

> Text-based MUDs are a new form of collaboratively written literature. MUD players are MUD authors, the creators as well as consumers of media content. In this, participating in a MUD has much in common with script-writing, performance art, street theatre, improvisational theatre – or even commedia dell'arte. But MUDs are something else as well – MUDs are dramatic examples of how computer mediated communication can serve as a place for the construction and reconstruction of identity.
>
> (Turkle 1995)

The fact that people switch identities is not new. In daily life people change their attitude and behaviour on their way from home to work and vice versa. Participating in a group in an anonymous or alternate identity is a rather new and unique quality of virtual communities. This anonymity can sometimes create an open atmosphere in which users are enabled to simply open up their feelings and express their opinions without fearing the consequences. But also this is the main cause of users losing the sense of responsibility towards their actions and get entangled in the violent flame wars that can get quite vicious and personal. Because of that, not all virtual communities will allow anonymity or participation under an alternate identity, and it is required that you provide the organisers with name and address data.

Activities of virtual communities are conducted on-line, but in some cases virtual communities are strengthened because the virtuality is combined with real life meetings. A lot of virtual communities have annual gatherings and picnics where people meet the faces behind the screens.

With a common history . . .

Some virtual communities exist for quite a while on the Internet (some of the most lively MUDs are over eight years old, and ancient on-line communities like the Well (which celebrated their tenth anniversary in 1998) cherish their history. History, customs and rites play an important role in virtual communities. Often these are fixed in help files or in a specific file called the Frequently Asked Questions (FAQ). This FAQ is written and updated by the active members of the virtual community and serves as a guide for new users. Originally, FAQs were born out of purposes of efficiency, so older users would not have to keep answering the same questions to new users (which can be quite destructive in communities that have a high influx). The FAQs outgrew the purpose of introduction to new users and now often serve as a document of community memory. FAQs will usually tell you about the purpose and history of the community, who the community leaders are, what codes of conduct or rules are present and so on. Help files and FAQs play an important role in the continuity of virtual communities. Even when the group of core users totally vanishes out of sight, its history and customs are preserved in the FAQ.

A common set of rules . . .

Next to the history and customs, rules play an important role within virtual communities. Not a single virtual community on the Internet seems to be able to survive without at least some agreement about how to engage each other in either discussion, role play, chat or combat. On the USENET, there are some groups that could be considered chaotic and existing in a vacuum that do not allow any kind of rules. In most cases those environments lack continuity and are usually aggressive in nature. That does not mean that aggressive environments will lack rules. On the contrary, even in the most violent graphical game such as environments like QUAKE, in which the sole purpose of a participating character is to kill, maim and slaughter other characters, over time groups of people will form (so-called clans) that will try to gain superiority and enforce their rules or ideas of sportsmanship on other players (like it is considered unsportslike to relentlessly kill new players that enter the game without equipment). The rules of a virtual community are formulated and reformulated in history by those in charge. In most cases they will be written down in FAQs, help files or even in user agreements that have to be read and signed before entering the community. Most Community Networks that provide users with an alternate e-mail address or homepage (for example the Digital City of Amsterdam, Hotmail or Geocities), are very strict in those user agreements because of the issue of (legal) accountability for the actions of users. The enforcement of the rules is conducted in many ways. The rules can be enforced by either the organisers of the community, an appointed law group or even be left to a software program. On many IRC chat channels one can find a robot that does not only serve drinks to customers, but will also kick people off that have a habit of spamming (filling other peoples screens with the same lines of text). The punishment for breaking the rules can be diverse too. In most cases a warning system will be in use, but on repeated warnings people can lose certain rights, be put in jail, erased (the removal of a character) or even be banished from the community completely. On banishment, the existing character is not only erased, but the opportunity to return to the virtual community under an alternate identity is denied. Rule systems are often copied on the Internet. When a new virtual community comes into existence, many references are made towards other existing communities, and FAQs or user agreements are easily copied. That is why on the sliding scale between absolute chaos and strict law and order, we find many familiar types of rules systems. It gives users the opportunity to find and choose that environment they feel comfortable with. This does not always mean that in virtual communities it is easy to use the exit option as is sometimes suggested. Once a member of a virtual community establishes a certain position in the hierarchy, it will be all but easy to give that position up, and move on to the next community.

And a common goal

The common goal for virtual communities is not a very strict characteristic. Though some virtual communities strive for very idealistic goals like the empowerment of handicapped people or the search for a cure for AIDS, in many cases the common goal consists of no more than simple socialising, chatting or playing. Many activities within a virtual community are directed towards obtaining the set goals but for some communities the initial goals have been left behind, and they are mainly focused on their own continuation. In the history of the Internet, many virtual communities have grown and flourished on a base of economy of exchange and trust. For example, most MUDs have large groups of creators (wizards) that invest a lot of their valuable time in creating a playing environment for players, without getting any physical pay. The fact that many virtual communities are dependent on the good intentions of large groups of volunteers has always been a strength in the history of the Internet, but for the future, when these groups have to tread into competition with growing numbers of commercial institutions, this may well appear to be one of the weaknesses.

On the Internet many virtual communities with many characteristics thrive. Some are focused and strictly organised, others are seemingly purposeless, chaotic and free. We can call them virtual communities when they start having a common history and a common set of rules which is agreed upon. Everywhere on the Internet where people gather frequently such virtual communities arise. Even in the most violent environments, where the circumstances do not seem fit for social communications, people seem be drawn to the formation of communities. Two examples of such virtual communities are the Digital City of Amsterdam and the so-called Webgrrls.

The Digital City of Amsterdam

The Amsterdam Digital City (www.dds.nl) does not stand on its own. The initiators of the Digital City were inspired by the FreeNets in the United States and Canada. The FreeNets were the first example of so-called community networks, an on-line community with a geographical base: a town, county or region. The first FreeNet was founded in Cleveland in 1985, now one of the biggest community networks in the world with about 12,000 logins a day (over 6 million user sessions a year).

The Digital City of Amsterdam was funded in 1994, and with its 60,000 inhabitants, now it is considered a successful example of the way community networks can be organised. Community networks like the FreeNets and the Amsterdam Digital City are arranged and administered mainly by representatives of social organisations who get together and gather information about local community and raise the capital to acquire the necessary equipment to connect to the Internet. On community networks not only is information made available, but also new means of communication are being created. Access to the Digital City is free. Inhabitants of the virtual community can call in on a modem, though many inhabitants already possess Internet access.

In Amsterdam the free services contain electronic mail, discussion groups, newsgroups and limited access to the World Wide Web (the homepages of many special-interest groups, local organisations, including local government are accessible in the Digital City). Thus, the Digital City can serve as a boost for the social structure of the real city. Some considerations on the individualisation of society point out the fact that traditional meeting places (the public sphere?) appear to lose their function in present city life. The Digital City is a new (virtual) junction where citizens, social organisations and governments meet. Community networks like the Digital City of Amsterdam create new ways of interaction between politicians, civil servants and citizens and they are breathing new life into the formation of communities of citizens. However, this does not imply that community networks like the Digital City do not transcend their own communities. Through national or international networks contacts are made with all locations in the world. Thus, the Digital City of Amsterdam has many elements in it, that might give it the title 'public sphere'. The goal and ideology of the administrators of the Digital City tends strongly towards the empowerment of citizens (providing them with access and the possibility to be part of the network of the future). Also the intrusion of commercial interests and (local) governments is treated very carefully by the administration of the Digital City and usually frowned upon by the inhabitants.

The Webgrrls

The Webgrrls (www.webgrrls.com) (pronounce webgirls) is an international organisation for women that both meets on-line and in the real world. The history of the Webgrrls started on-line with one individual (Liza Sherman aka Cyber-grrl) who got interested in the possibilities the Internet offered for empowering women. In 1995 she founded the first chapter of the Webgrrls in New York City, with a homepage combined with real life social gatherings. Nowadays, chapters are forming in cities all around the world to provide a forum for women to exchange information, give job and business leads, learn about new technologies, mentor, intern, train, etc. On the one hand, the Webgrrls organisation is a group of equally minded women who use the net for social interaction, but on the other hand its goal is to educate and stimulate women to use new media for their own purposes. The Webgrrls Bizsite is specially set up to support women who try to make a business on the Internet. Special events and courses are organised to teach the ways of the Internet and the World Wide Web:

We also hold events to show girls how to use the Internet and the World Wide Web. We reach out to community groups that work with girls and bring them to a computer cafe called 'Cyberfelds'. Each girl is teamed up with a Webgrrl so they learn about the Internet from a woman who loves computers. Not only do they gain confidence from being exposed to technology in a friendly way, they have a woman mentor, someone to look up to and someone who shows them that computers aren't just for the boys.

(Introduction for the New York Webgrrls)

The Webgrrls fill a need that proves to be very successful all over the world. Local chapters are forming every day. The New York chapter, for example, has over 2,500 participants in the network. Not all activities of the Webgrrls can be analysed as being part of a public sphere, but the Webgrrls are an example about how special interest groups successfully utilise the new ways of interaction provided by the Internet by exploiting its characteristics.

THE INTERNET AS A PUBLIC SPHERE FOR DEMOCRACY

The Webgrrls and the Digital City of Amsterdam are only two of the many examples of very strong and sustainable communities that exist on the Internet. They are successful in gathering people around a certain subject or goal and organising participation in certain projects or special interest groups. The Internet is still growing rapidly and we can safely say that more and more people will gather in on-line communities in the future. But it is not easy to consider the implications these virtual communities will have for democracy and democratic purposes. One approach could be to review them as a new public sphere, a new environment in which democracy will be a self-evident element. Some of the virtual communities could (partly) provide local communities or special interest groups with a public sphere in which they conduct their rights as citizens. If we follow this line of argument the virtual communities on the Internet would strengthen a neo-republican conception of democracy by enhancing citizen's participation and introducing new forms of public debate and discussion in political and administrative processes.

The public sphere and the way it functions for democracy was first theorised by Habermas in 1962 and has been much discussed since then. The theory is well over three decades old, yet it continues to inspire thinking about media and democracy. Often it has been argued that modern mass media, like radio, newspapers and television (especially the public broadcasting services) could (or even should) be the nearest thing to an achieved public sphere in contemporary society (Dahlgren 1995). Habermas's concept of the public sphere appears both as a normative ideal to be strived for and as a manifestation of actual historical circumstances in early bourgeois Europe. Habermas defines some very explicit assumptions and conditions under which the public sphere can fulfil its function for democracy. One assumption is that of rational debate. The public rational debate in the public sphere was supposed to transform 'voluntas' into a ratio that in the public competition of private arguments came into being as the consensus about what is practically necessary in the interest of all (Habermas 1989). In other words, public opinion will almost naturally derive from rational debate in the public sphere. In this assumption about rational debate, another leading principle of the public sphere is defined: publicity. Publicity had a three-way effect. First, the public sphere itself had to be public. Every person had to be able to be a member of the public sphere and join the deliberations. It was true that in the historic public sphere only property-owning private people were admitted to a public engaged in critical debate, for their autonomy was rooted in the sphere of commodity exchange and hence was joined to the interest in its preservation as a private sphere (free from economic power), but in the leading economic theory of that time, everyone had equal chances for the acquisition of property. That in practice this was untrue, due to the fact that it was the interests of commodity owners that was fixed in the early industrial constitutions, does not mean that the public sphere had a theoretically non-elitist basis. Second, debate within the public sphere had to be public in a way that it had to be freed from the intrusion of commercial and government power. A debate among people could never be pure if those people were not able to speak in ultimate freedom. A third meaning of publicness in the public sphere refers to government institutions itself. Public opinion needed the publicity of government and parliamentary deliberations to keep itself informed of state business. Bentham conceived of parliament's public deliberations as nothing but a part of the public deliberations of the public in general.

The notion of a public sphere generally suggests an arena of free and public debate. Without adopting or even discussing Habermas's ideas of a rational debate leading to public opinion that can serve as vital inputs for democratic processes, one can safely state that without a vibrant public sphere democracy is flawed at the least. If the virtual communities on the Internet could be defined as a public sphere, in the sense that they generate new opportunities for citizens' participation and public debate, away from government and away from commercial interests, it could strongly contribute to the neo-republican form of democracy. The plurality, diversity and complexity of the communities populating the Internet, make it hard to speak of a unitary public sphere for democracy. Habermas's public sphere could be localised in tea and coffee houses. Virtual communities have no physical location and are sometimes even spread out on numerous computer systems over the world. Physical location and geographic borders are insignificant and sometimes even unknown in most virtual communities. For members of virtual communities the choice of participation is not only independent from geographical backgrounds, conceptions of time and place, but also independent from the physical or even psychological identity. This creates new dynamics in which interaction is made up by avatars or virtual identities – flaming, gender bending on one side, but strongly conditioned by rule systems, habits and traditions on the other.

The group dynamics of the Internet make it difficult to conceptualise a unitary public sphere from which public opinion will arise that is furthermore connected to structures of public decision-making. The use of the network technology of the Internet has changed the nature of contemporary community. Only those communities that combine their virtuality with the locality of a city, state or country (for example the many Community Networks) on the Internet have the potential to strengthen the neo-republican idea of democracy.

Communities that follow the physical geography of existing governments are in a vast minority on the Internet. Pluriformity, diversity, virtuality and functionality are the main organisational concepts of the others. It is not at all certain whether the virtual communities are intrinsically more open or democratic than existing democratic communities. However, this does not mean that those communities do not contain any potential for democracy. Many of the interactions in those communities will have a public status, although this publicness will be difficult to connect or even understand in and through existing democratic institutions, as will accepted ideas of government or state. Virtual communities will therefore mostly contribute to the new and unknown concept of cyberdemocracy. What cyberdemocracy will look like is still hard to imagine, but a small seed of understanding might be hidden in the virtual communities on the Internet.

Notes

1 The paper had one additional author: Donald Paschal, a homeless resident. His account is typical for the amount of leverage and empowerment the PEN provided for certain individuals: 'I am homeless. If you knew me, it might come as a shock to you, as it does to me. I did not start out this way. This is not a career choice we make when planning our lives in high school. We without shelter are looked on with disdain, fear, loathing, pity and hatred. This difference makes normal contact with other humans almost impossible. Not only might we be dirty or perhaps smell bad, we are different. In the minds of many, people who are different must be avoided. This is why Santa Monica's PEN system is so special to me. No one on PEN knew that I was homeless until I told them. After I told them, I was still treated like a human being. To me, the most remarkable thing about the PEN community is that a city council member and a pauper can coexist, albeit not always in perfect harmony, but on an equal basis. I have met, become friends with, or perhaps adversaries with, people I would otherwise not know of, even if I were homed' (cited in J. van Tassel 1994).

References

Beamish, A. (1995) *Communities On Line: Community Based Computer Networks*, Department of Urban Studies and Planning, Massachusetts Institute of Technology. http://sap.mit.edu/anneb/cn-thesis.

Dahlgren, P. (1995) *Television and the Public Sphere: Citizenship, Democracy and the Media*, London: Sage.

Depla, P. (1995) *Technologie en de Vernieuwing van de Lokale Democratie, Ver Vol making of Vermaatscappelijking*, Amsterdam: Vuga.

Doctor, S. and Dutton, W. H. (1998) 'The first amendment online: Santa Monica's public electronic network', in R. Tsagarousianou, D. Tambini and C. Bryan (eds) *Cyber democracy, Technology, Cities and Civic Networks*, London: Routledge.

Dutton, W. H. and Guthrie, K. (1991) 'An ecology of games: the political construction of Santa Monica's electronic network', in *Informatization and the Public Sector* 1 279–301.

Guthrie, K. Kendall and Dutton, W. H. (1992) 'The politics of citizen access technology: the development of public information utilities in four cities', *Policy Studies Journal* 20: 574–597.

Habermas, J. (1989) *Structural Transformation of the Public Sphere*, Cambridge: Polity Press.

Holub, R. C. (1991) *Juergen Habermas: Critic in the Public Sphere*, London: Routledge .

Horrocks, I. and Hambley, N. (1998) 'The "Webbing" of British local government', *Public Money and Management* 18 (2): 39–44.

Laudon, K. C. (1994) 'The possibilities for participation in the democratic process: telecommunications, computers and democracy', in K. W. Grewlich and F. H. Pedersen (eds) *Power and Participation in an Information Society*, Brussels: European Commission.

McKeown, K. (1991) 'Social norms and implications of Santa Monica's PEN (Public Electronic Network)', presentation delivered at the 99th annual Convention of the American Psychological Association (1991) http://www.mckeown.net/PENaddress.html

McLean, I. (1989) *Democracy and New Technology*, Cambridge: Polity Press.

Ministry of Internal Affairs (1998) Ministerie van Binnenlandse Zaken, Elektronische Burger Consultatie, eerste ervaringen, Den Haag.

Poster, M. (1995) Cyberdemocracy: Internet and the Public Sphere, University of California. Article can be found at: http://www.hnet.uci.edu/mposter/writings/democ.html.

Pratchett, L. (1998) unpublished doctoral thesis, DeMonfort University, Leicester, UK.

——(1998) 'Technological bias in an information age: ICT policy making in local government', in I. Th. M. Snellen and W. B. H. J. van de Donk (eds) *Public Administration in an Information Age*, Amsterdam: IOS Press.

Rash, W. (1997) *Politics on the Net: Wiring the Political Process*, New York: Freeman.

Rheingold, H. (1993) *The Virtual Community: Homesteading on the Electronic Frontier*, New York: Addison-Wesley.

Ryan, M. P. (1992) 'Gender and public access: women's politics in nineteenth-century America', in C. Calhoun, (ed.) *Habermas and the Public Sphere*, London: MIT Press.

Schalken, C. A. T. and Tops, P. W. (1994) *The Digital City: A Study into the Backgrounds and Opinions of its Residents*, paper presented at the Canada Community Networks conference, Ottawa. http://cwis.kub.nl/~frw/people/schalken/dceng.htm.

Schuler, D. (1996) *New Community Networks: Wired for a Change*, New York: ACM Press.

Stefik, M. (1996) *Internet Dreams, Archetypes, Myths and Metaphors*, London: MIT Press.

Tassel, J. van. (1994) 'Yackety Yak, Do Talk Back! PEN, the nation's first publicly funded electronic network, makes a difference in Santa Monica', in *Wired Magazine* 2.01.

Turkle, S. (1995) *Life on the Screen: Identity in the Age of the Internet*, New York: Simon & Schuster.

Varley, P. (1991) 'Electronic Democracy', in *Technology Review* 94: 42–51.

VB-Advies Groep B. V. (1997) *Teledemocratie, een onderzoek naar Internet en de lokale democratie*, Den Haag: VB-Advies.

Wittig, M. (1991) 'Electronic City Hall', *Whole Earth Review* 71 (Summer): 24–27.

Yarnall, L. (1989) 'The new improved government input device', in *CIO* 20–29.

Part III

Conclusion

11 New technology and democratic renewal

The evidence assessed

Pieter Tops, Ivan Horrocks and Jens Hoff

In writing this book we set ourselves the task of exploring the relationship between new forms of information and communication technology (ICT) and the current restructuring and redefinition of many of the fundamental relations within the political systems of Western European countries. Our basic claim was – and is – that ICTs play an important role in this process, while at the same time becoming an integral feature of the 'new' models of democracy now emerging. Our analytical strategy was to construct a number of different models of democracy which were not to be understood as 'ideal types' but rather, as Bellamy states in Chapter 2, grounded in a set of rival discourses connecting notions of citizenship and democratic values and procedures to technological change.

We are aware, of course, that what we have presented is not a full-fledged comparative study of all relations within the polities of a great number of European countries, and that our results therefore should be seen as indicating tendencies rather than presenting conclusive evidence. Thus, what we present are cases from a limited number of countries – the Netherlands, United Kingdom and Denmark – dealing with only three of the relationships within the polities; between citizens and political parties, citizens and administration and between citizens themselves. Only in one category – political parties – are the cases strictly comparative. The remainder of the case studies vary from country to country. Nevertheless, we think it possible and acceptable to generalise to some extent from the cases. First, because the countries we are dealing with are normally considered to be among the more 'advanced' European countries when it comes to the development and use of ICT in political and governmental organisations. Other countries can therefore be expected to 'copy', or are already copying, some of the technologically mediated innovations in political practices (TMIPPs) that we analyse in this volume. Second, because the multitude and variation of cases in this volume bear similarities to the 'most different case design'. Although we have used this case design somewhat coincidentally the results arrived at in most of the case studies are strikingly similar. Thus, even though there are small variations between cases the overwhelming conclusion points towards the dominance of what we have labelled the demo-elitist model, allied closely with the consumer model of democracy. However, the case studies also indicate clearly that this dominance does not go uncontested. Exponents of the neo-republican and cyberdemocracy models are also in evidence, and several of our cases illustrate conflicts over the ways in which ICT applications should be developed as well as the democratically ambiguous uses of ICT.

Another point of contention of which we are acutely aware is the question as to whether we are being tautological in the application of the models. That is, are the results we are arriving at determined by our methodology? Our argument against such a claim is that we see the models as strictly heuristic devices which are only meant to provide a starting point for capturing the discourses from within which TMIPPs develop. We therefore expected, and indeed have seen, that the models may not be as internally coherent as the term 'model' may suggest. To us such 'openness' is a strength rather than a weakness because it has enabled us to use the models to expose the conflicts and competing interpretations of democracy of the different actors. This is in line with our interpretation of the models as discourses – 'never closed entities and never fully constituted' (see Chapter 1).

In this, penultimate, chapter we summarise our analyses of the role ICTs play in the restructuring and redefinition of relations within the polities of the countries in question. As we have already noted, the relationships we explore are between: (a) citizens and political parties, (b) citizens and administration, and (c) citizens themselves. In the final chapter we move on to present some reflections on the models of democracy used throughout this book.

The relationships between citizens and political parties

In the three case studies from Denmark, the United Kingdom and the Netherlands the authors analyse the changing relationships between voters and political parties and the impact that ICTs have on these relationships. The chapters start with a general recognition of a profound alteration in the position of political parties. The classical mass parties as described by Duverger are in decline. They have been replaced by more professional and managerial organisations, which have been incorporated in the state system and are more detached from civil society than they used to be. Scholars speak of the development of catch-all parties, cartel parties, modern cadre parties or professional electoral associations. As Smith notes, the evidence in favour of party decline is convincing, but that evidence relates specifically to the mass party archetype, not the concept of party per se. Parties still have a paramount role in political systems: they are central in generating candidates, in fighting elections and in determining the character of a country's government.

The directions in which political parties evolve is still mixed and inconclusive. But there is no doubt that in the modernisation processes that parties are involved in ICTs play a certain role. These innovations concern the relationship between parties and voters and the internal organisation of the parties, i.e. the relation between party elites and party members and between party members themselves. Concrete examples of TMIPPs are the growing use and importance of websites by political parties, the application of bulletin board systems (BBS) and other communication networks, and the use of all kinds of data applications to support and stimulate effective election campaigns. In addition, there are a limited number of examples of non-partisan initiatives, such as the so-called voter compasses in the Netherlands, that nonetheless are important for the relation between citizens and political parties.

Strategies

A striking and common result of the analyses of the different countries is that political parties appear to have entered the world of new technology without any predefined or explicit strategy concerning the ways in which the use of new technology might effect democracy. Similarly the possible electoral effects of new technologically mediated practices fail to register, although there are a few exceptions, as we shall see later. Whereas predefined strategies are rare in our studies, it is possible, as Lofgren notes, to identify intrinsic considerations. In the main, parties consider their website as a means to secure symbolic values for the organisation (see the Danish case). In other words, it is important for parties to be seen to be engaging with the Internet and exploiting its capabilities in a confident manner. This contributes to the public's perception of the party as up to date and relevant. The most important reason for developing a site is, therefore, indirectly electoral – to demonstrate that the party is modern and keeps up with technology. And the fact that some other parties already have a homepage often acts as the catalyst for other parties to set one up.

The highly symbolic meaning of the development of the majority of websites does not imply that they are unimportant, however. After all, the 'management of meaning' is an important part of politics. Nevertheless, in terms of a party's direct electoral strategies websites are rather unimportant, although once again there are some exceptions. The advanced website of the (rather small) Socialist Party in the Netherlands aimed at potential voters such as school-going youths, students and young intellectuals who would otherwise be more difficult to contact is one such example. Another is the use of websites to inform nationals overseas of the possibility of voting at 'home'. For parties which anticipate a lot of support from these expatriate residents this seems to be a rational strategy and the fact that the Internet is used all over the world makes it an ideal medium for such a purpose. The Dutch Conservative Liberals and the British Labour and Conservative parties have all used their websites for this purpose.

In general, however, we can conclude that websites have not been very important for elections and election results – the examples above being possible exceptions. In fact the opposite is a more accurate statement: that elections are important for the introduction and development of websites. In Denmark, the United Kingdom and the Netherlands elections have been a stimulus for parties to develop websites. As we have already noted, this has to do with the symbolic significance of websites, but also because elections create windows of opportunity – for instance, for party members who believe in the democratic and organisational importance and possibilities of the new media. Nevertheless, the raised profile of website development could also be problematic, creating tensions within the party, as the example of the Dutch PvdA demonstrates. This conflict was a clash between party activists who saw the Internet as an instrument to renew and enhance party democracy and party professionals who primarily recognised the websites as a (symbolic) instrument in modern election campaigning. The fact that the party professionals won the conflict is symptomatic of the use of websites by parties in the countries in which we have carried out case studies.

In Denmark the main objective behind the development of websites has been to produce attractive 'shop windows' to present fairly standard party information to the electorate and party members. Danish parties' use of websites have until now neither embodied new interactive features nor challenged established forms of party organisation. The findings for the UK tend to suggest that the Web is not being used by parties to facilitate any significant increase in intra-party discussion, debate or 'democracy'. While the parties recognise the interactive opportunities the Web offers, they consider its capacity for downward dissemination of information to be of greater importance. The Web is generally used as a top-down communication device to present information straight to voters, avoiding the distorting effect of the traditional media. In the case of the Netherlands the conclusion is that party sites are predominantly (highly symbolic) campaign instruments, primarily used to inform the electorate about party information, and not to design new interactive forms of party or voter democracy.

The evidence from the case studies taken together leads us to some fairly straightforward general conclusions. First, if there exists a deliberate strategy behind the development of websites, then it is mainly inspired by the search for new information channels between politicians and the electorate controlled by party elites. Any examples of this new media creating new democratic platforms in and around parties, such as the bulletin boards in Denmark and the discussion platforms used by some Dutch parties, are largely piecemeal.

Second, many sites reflect the image the party has of itself. This was particularly visible in the Netherlands, where the PvdA presents itself on the Web as a modern people's party, the SP as an activist party and GroenLinks as a grassroots party. The same applies to the Social Democratic party (a classic West European social democratic party) and the Socialist People's Party (a leftist party, more settled in a grass-roots organisational style) in Denmark. Third, in the development of TMIPPs we also see reflections of the specific political party systems in the respective countries. For instance, the use of websites to provide information about marginal constituencies, and the use of desktop publishing systems which when linked to electoral databases have proved to be formidable campaigning tools in the UK, is a typical feature of the British majority system. After all, voter targeting in marginal constituencies is a logical thing to do under such an electoral system. On the other hand, it is no coincidence that an innovation like the voter compasses flourishes in the Netherlands. The Dutch party system consists of a rather large number of minority parties, among which the ideological or programmatic differences are sometimes hard to discern. The 'despairing' floating voter can then be assisted in making a choice by using the voter compasses. However, in the development and use of voter compasses one embraces a specific view of politics and political processes.

Models

In general, the analyses suggest that TMIPPs in the relationship between citizens and political parties are mainly inspired by, or can be understood in terms of a conformation of the demo-elitist model of democracy. However, there are elements of other models which are present to a greater or lesser extent. It is worthwhile to review these briefly, case by case, as they provide some indication of the existence and tensions between the different strategies and discourses at play here.

In Denmark we find overwhelming evidence of strategies which reinforce the trend toward professional party organisations. Top-down dissemination of information prevails, although there is evidence of the emergence of some new channels for communication between party members. The net.Dialog BBS operated by the Social Democrats, and Hotlips system operated by the Socialist People's Party are the examples. However, the former is populated by a small group of members – 'the old guard' as Lofgren refers to them. And there is no evidence of cross-contact with the party elite via the BBS. The latter is more open and includes both contributions from members and leadership, as might be expected of a system run by a party with a commitment to the grass-roots membership and a participatory, open, organisation. These are, however, exceptions which prove the rule – that the strategies and discourse at play here clearly promote the demo-elitist model, although there is evidence of relatively weak neo-republican tendencies in some political parties.

Smith's conclusion on developments among British political parties is unambiguous – the utilisation of TMIPPs is entirely consistent with strategies which promote both the demo-elitist and consumer model of democracy. Thus, ICTs are used to enhance top-down control of democratic expression and the anticipation and detection of public (voter) opinion. We are provided with numerous examples of the effects of this dual strategy: membership recruitment was a low priority, voter recruitment was not; the potential for 'upward' communication (from party members, for example) was valued far less than 'downward' communication of information to voters, and so on. Furthermore, Smith detects no evidence 'of party use of the Internet supporting the idea of the Internet as a new public sphere'. What is perhaps more surprising is the lack of evidence to suggest that British parties are using new ICTs to promote organisational renewal. Instead, Smith concludes that the emergent relationships around parties which ICTs can facilitate 'are those based upon campaigning; specifically, improving and developing forms of campaigning which make very little recourse to the role and initiative of a mass membership'.

Finally, comparative analysis of the case studies exposes two distinct differences between developments in Britain and the Netherlands and Denmark. The first, and perhaps most obvious, is the extent to which a consumerist discourse has come to dominate the British political landscape. This is further evidenced by Webster in his chapter on CCTV. The second is the total lack of any evidence of strategies which we might consider as promoting any type of political practice which we can associate with our neo-republican model.

At a general level there appears to be little doubt that the use of TMIPPs by Dutch political parties point us in the direction of the demo-elitist model. That is, party websites are primarily 'inspired by the search for new communication channels between politicians and the electorate'. While this may well be the case the fact that several political parties in the Netherlands have adopted ICT applications which allow interaction between members, and/or between members and party leaderships clearly indicates the existence of strategies which support elements of neo-republicanism. However, in most cases these strategies appear lightweight, and may even be more accidental than planned. Another important feature of the existence of a neo-republican bent within Dutch political practice is the potential for conflict this creates between supporters of the different strategies and democratic discourses. This is graphically illustrated by the conflict in the PvdA between party professionals and party volunteers over the modernisation of the party's website at the beginning of the 1998 election campaign. The standpoint of the party professionals equates to a demo-elitist view of democracy while that of the volunteers comes closer to a neo-republican view. Tops et al. conclude that although the professionals managed to win the conflict, the incident demonstrates that there are always counter forces active in a party which have to be dealt with.

A further dimension is brought to the Dutch case study through the development of voter compasses. These can be interpreted in two different ways. The first – preferred by those who developed the voter compasses – is that they enable voters to receive information on party platforms in a new and attractive way. From this perspective, a voter compass can be seen as a new instrument which fills the vertical relationship between politicians and voters in a demo-elitist model. But a second interpretation is possible. The use of voter compasses can also be interpreted as a development towards a form of consumer democracy, where voters shop on the electoral market. A voter compass gives voters information on which platform will best serve their needs and interests. The casting of a vote is not seen as an activity resulting from political discussions or from ideological ties, but as the aggregation of a certain number of pre-existing consumer preferences.

Relationships between citizens and administration

The relationship between citizens and administration concerns all kinds of service delivery processes, as our case studies amply demonstrate. Hoff and Rosenkrands study the discussions on the citizen card in Denmark and the different forms that it took. Webster gives us an overview of the introduction in the UK of closed circuit television systems (CCTV), which he describes as a specific policy tool used to meet policy requirements and service objectives. Zouridis and Bekkers present a handful of TMIPP configurations in the Netherlands, among which are electronic handling systems for student scholarships, and an information shop at the Department of Economic Affairs. Finally, van de Donk analyses the development of administrative information systems in government agencies and third sector organisations.

What all these TMIPPs have in common is that at the outset they seem to be relatively 'harmless'. They are designed to make government service delivery more effective or more 'customer oriented'. In this respect they would seem to do no more than respond to a general demand from citizens for government institutions to be cost-effective and efficient. However, there is more to it than that. In so doing the relationships between government and citizens are defined in a specific manner and reflect different views and images of democracy. These relationships are thus at the centre of modern democratic practices.

Strategies

As already noted strategies for introducing ICTs in governmental and bureaucratic processes are frequently legitimised in terms of the three E's – the economy, efficiency and effectiveness of service delivery. Usually the citizen, or the 'customer' of government, and their wishes and preferences, are promoted as the driving force for these developments. Zouridis and Bekkers put this development in a historical perspective. In the 1980s, they suggest, two general developments coincided, at least in the Netherlands, but probably also in other countries. A generation of 'new public managers' was committed to a more efficient, businesslike public administration in which service delivery should be the core of public administration. This new generation of public managers was supported by leading political coalitions who believed that improved public service delivery and a more efficient organisation of public administration would enhance citizens' trust in politics. As a result, around 1990 the programmes of leading politicians and officials coincided. This 'discourse coalition' came into being because of the shared commitment to improve public service delivery and a certain belief in the 'transformative' potential of new ICTs.

In the citizen card debate in Denmark Hoff and Rosenkrands identify two main strategies. One of these is strongly efficiency oriented and is supported by government departments who want to increase the steering capacity of bureaucracy. This pursuit of efficiency, enhanced and shaped by new ICTs is not neutral, however, but is connected to specific definitions of policy-making and the context and relationships in which this takes place. This tendency is formulated most radically in the contribution of van de Donk. In his study of nursing homes in the Netherlands he concludes that those institutions that did use information systems showed a clear reinforcement of techno-rationalistic characteristics. Policy proposals in informated governments were more refined and predictive and were based on systematic analysis of the data the homes had to submit in order to get government funding. The 'information environment' of decision-makers became more and more dominated by index numbers and quantitative indicators, statistical computations and so on. These indicators also stimulated all kinds of anticipatory and detailed policy interventions. In short, the desire to realise more efficient government performance, together with the design of new information systems often provokes a kind of 'techno-utopian' discourse which is guided by the technocratic ideals of rational decision-making. As van de Donk concludes, this discourse contributes to a strengthening of bureaucracies, which are transformed at great pace into highly successful 'infocracies'.

Webster points to a totally different effect of technologically mediated improvements of governmental service delivery in his chapter on CCTV. The introduction of CCTV in the UK appears to be a (successful) response to citizens demands for reduced levels of crime and improved safety. However, in reacting to this demand the democratic institutions of governance have been able to reassert their legitimacy and right to represent the interests of citizens. Furthermore, it also appears that citizens were willing to encourage the surveillance of their own movements in return for other perceived benefits, particularly personal safety and reduced crime. In the dominant political discourse CCTV has been promoted as a straightforward trade-off whereby citizens surrender some of their privacy for safety. This highlights the role of political discourse in shaping the public's perception of CCTV and consequently in generating public support for widespread citizen surveillance.

Zouridis and Bekkers point to a comparable dilemma – on the one hand, through the use of ICTs, public administration is better able to serve its citizens, on the other, the informational privacy of citizens may be violated. Data coupling and the recording of the citizen's digital footprints are two sides of the same coin. Thus, public administration becomes both 'big brother' (through surveillance technologies) and 'soft sister' (by improving service delivery and the tailoring of services). This is an illustration of the fundamentally ambiguous character of ICT discussed on a number of occasions in the early chapters of this book.

Models

The question which logically arises from the review and discussion so far, and which we now need to consider, is how do these developments equate to the models of democracy that we use in this volume? In their analysis of the discussion of the citizen card in Denmark, Hoff and Rosenkrands suggest that demo-elitist rationalities have been dominant so far. However, they expect future developments to take a different path – one that strengthens consumerist tendencies, on the one hand, and the constitutional and cyberdemocratic tendencies, on the other. This would be the case if, for instance, the efficiency of bureaucracy can be increased, while at the same time the rights and capabilities of citizens are renewed, or even expanded. An important condition is that the democratic implications of specific technological choices are repolitisised, as they argue was the case with the intervention of the Danish Board of Technology into the citizen card debate.

Webster comes to the conclusion that in the UK CCTV strengthens the 'protective state', whereby democratic elites have a paternalistic role in protecting citizens rights and ensuring law and order. The sophisticated use of political communication and marketing techniques to shape and limit discourse implies that policy-making is a top-down process where policy and discourse is determined by policy specialists. This perspective is consistent with the demo-elitist model of democracy. This, however, is not the whole story. Webster also notes that CCTV diffusion is not only state-driven, but might also be 'society-driven', i.e. the result of citizen demands. This fits with the model of consumer democracy. Webster concludes that the case of CCTV falls somewhere between the models, because it is clear that the policy process is highly managed by elites, but also because societal support for CCTV is extensive and undeniable.

In their chapter on electronic service delivery in the Netherlands, Zouridis and Bekkers conclude that developments have partly been inspired by a consumer model of democracy: they were meant to better serve the clients of public administration or to empower clients by making the organisation of service delivery more transparent. Although electronic service delivery may have been inspired by a consumer model of democracy, it is clear that features of the demo-elitist model are as important. The leading (political and administrative) coalitions have used a consumer rhetoric to regain 'democratic' control over society. Zouridis and Bekkers point in particular to the possibility that the use of ICTs for public service delivery may threaten some fundamental principles inherited from the constitutional model of democracy (e.g. self-determination of citizens, their informational privacy, and their active citizenship).

The relations between citizens themselves

It is usually considered to be of great importance to the democratic polity that there exists a relatively autonomous public sphere in which citizens can organise themselves free from interference or control by the state. 'Civil society', as it is often called, is a necessary precondition for a vital and healthy democracy. What does the rise of new technologies and the strategies and discourses in which they are embedded mean for the position of this civil society? Two case studies address this question, but they provide rather different answers.

Weakening civil society

Van de Donk analyses the impact of the use of information systems on the autonomous position of societal actors in a Dutch policy sector. His conclusion is that agenda setting and actual decision-making, formerly a joint process between societal and governmental organisations, has become in large measure a solo act of civil servants. For example, the implementation stage has become less susceptible to 'political manoeuvring' by the actors involved. Civil servants or politicians who formerly had to negotiate with the nursing homes and their umbrella organisations and had to give in to all kinds of pressures and claims can simply announce their policies. According to van de Donk these policies have been 'applied' algorithmically, not 'negotiated'.

Van de Donk goes on to conclude that TMIPPs lead to profound changes in the institutional configuration of policy arenas. These are transformed into 'hierarchies'. At the same time informatization reinforces the power of the bureaucratic apparatus and weakens the position of the private actors in the field. Van de Donk describes this as a process of 'infocratization', which is undermining, at least potentially, much of the institutional variety and prerequisites of a 'societal model of democracy'. This infocracy can be interpreted as a radicalisation or even a pathology of certain characteristics of the demo-elitist model. That is, the strong control and management of society by technocratically oriented political and bureaucratic elites.

Strengthening civil society

Schalken presents us with a radically different view of the relation between TMIPPs and the self-organisation of citizens through his analysis of 'virtual communities' on the Internet. A virtual community is a group of people that gather on-line, have a common history, a common goal (even if that goal is just being together) and a common set of rules that are (sometimes implicitly) agreed upon. He discusses successful (Webgrlls, Digital City of Amsterdam) and less successful (PEN) examples of virtual communities. These Schalken presents as public spheres which generate new opportunities for citizen participation and public debate, away from government and away from commercial interests. At the same time they create new forms of paternalism as they reflect specific views on the role and behaviour of citizens. In this sense they contribute to the development of neo-republican (and communitarian) conceptions of democracy.

However, for members of virtual communities the choice of participation is relatively independent from geographical backgrounds, conceptions of time and place, and even from physical and psychological identities. This sometimes creates new dynamics in which interaction is made up by avatars or virtual identities – flaming and gender bending on the one side, strongly conditioned by rule systems, habits and traditions on the other.

Schalken notes that it is not at all certain whether virtual communities are intrinsically more open or democratic than 'existing' democratic communities. Many of the interactions in these communities have a public status, although this publicness is difficult to connect or even understand in and through existing democratic institutions. Nevertheless, it would appear that virtual communities may contribute to the development of new cyberdemocratic models of democracy, although the exact form and nature of such models remains open to interpretation.

Summary

In Figure 6 we summarise the way in which the typical ICT applications, dominant political issues and dominant democratic ambiguities are articulated within our four models of democracy.[1] This demonstrates clearly that certain ICT applications align themselves with specific models of democracy. However, even though this illustrates that the processes of institutionalisation (closure) are well advanced in the majority of cases, there is clear evidence to suggest that a considerable degree of 'interpretative flexibility' still exists. In terms of the dominant political issues these strongly reflect the underlying democratic values of these models. We find the same tightly coupled relationship in respect to democratic ambiguities (although this surely also reflects the typical ICT applications for each model). One of the most interesting examples of the later is the tension in the demo-elitist model between loose and tight control. Thus, in trying to predict and then direct the behaviour of citizens, governments and political parties increasingly become hostage to the vagaries of public opinion. This, in turn, drives further efforts to refine control mechanisms. Elites and citizens are, therefore, consciously or unconsciously connected in an ongoing dialectic of reinforcing and undermining control mechanisms.

Notes

1 We reserve the term TMIPP to describe the way in which ICT applications connect with all other elements of our models. Our aim being to place ICT applications in specific political and democratic contexts.

	Consumer	Demo-elitist	Neo-republican	Cyberdemocratic
View on citizenship	(neo) liberal	(pluralist) liberal	Republican/ social democratic	Communitarian/radical democratic
Dominant democratic value	Freedom of choice	Effectiveness	Deliberation and participation	Community, accept of diversity
Political nexus	'moment of truth' (producer/consumer relation)	Expert discourse	Public sphere, media	Electronic discussion (Internet)
Central form of political participation	Choice of public services (exit)	Consensus creation, lobbying	Public debate, associations	Virtual debate, virtual and real actions
Main political intermediary	Service declarations, consumption data	Negotiation and campaign institutions	Meetings, hearings (real and virtual)	Electronic networks, electronic communities
Dominant procedural norm	Development of capabilities (rights)	Development of adaptive political system	Development of identities, development of adaptive political system	Development of identities, development of capabilities (competences)
Typical ICT application	Voter compasses, CCTV, websites, citizen cards, databases	Websites, BBSs, 'direct mail', information systems, voter compasses	Geographically located and moderated discussion groups (e.g. PEN, DCA)	Self-organised 'geographically dislocated' discussion groups (e.g. DCA, Webgrrls)
Dominant political issues	Data security, privacy, service delivery	Relegitimation and reorientation of governance institutions, packaging, management and marketing of political communication	Increasing participation, improving the quality of political discussions	Increasing political reflexivity competences and autonomy
Dominant democratic ambiguities	'big brother' and 'soft sister'	Tight and loose control	New public spheres and new forms of paternalism	Atomisation/ fragmentation and communality/ 'new networks'

Figure 6 Emerging models of democracy for the information age (2): applications, issues and ambiguities

12 Reflections on the models of democracy: cyberdemocracy?

Ivan Horrocks, Jens Hoff and Pieter Tops

As we emphasised in the previous chapter, the majority of authors primarily associate the TMIPP developments they describe with our demo-elitist model. However, strong elements of the consumer model of democracy also feature and appear to be intertwined with those of the demo-elitist model. The reasons for this 'duality' lie in the common features of both models which Bellamy discusses in Chapter 2. That is, the notion of a 'managed democracy' is common to both. Of course, in the case of consumer democracy democratic expression is assumed to be channelled through, and contained within, the consumption nexus, whereas top-down control of democratic expression is a clear feature of the demo-elitist model.

As well as sharing almost equal positions of prominence in our analysis there are other areas of common ground between the two models. As Webster makes clear in Chapter 7, one of the most important is the centrality of packaging and marketing techniques for gaining support for policy preferences and thus 'legitimacy for the democratic institutions charged with representing citizens, policy-making and service delivery'.

Having exposed the models and features which are common across our cases it is as important to identify differences. Of particular significance is the fact that there are clearly two different variants of 'new democratic consumerism' (to use Webster's phrase). As we might expect each reflects underlying societal conventions, values, and assumptions concerning democracy and citizenship. For example, within the continental European version – a 'soft' consumerism – citizenship is more narrowly defined than under the constitutional model, but there is still room for, and recognition of, the importance of citizen participation in decision-making processes. The case studies by Hoff and Rosenkrands and Zouridis and Bekkers illustrate this clearly. The second model of consumer democracy applies to Britain, and Webster's chapter illustrates the features of 'hard' consumerism well. Here citizenship is diminished substantially – the role rapidly being reduced to selective participation in ongoing market research exercises.

The changing nature of citizenship in the information society is further complicated, however, when we factor in the features of the demo-elitist model of democracy. As with the 'new democratic consumerism' there appears to be a distinct difference in the extent and depth to which demo-elitism has begun to penetrate democratic practice in Britain and our other case study countries. In Britain the extent to which packaging and marketing have come to dominate the political process signals a clear break with the traditional 'chain of command' of the constitutional model. We could argue that when combined with the consumerist trends already noted the result is that citizenship is not simply diminished but impoverished.

The diminution of the importance and role of citizens in the polity is not the only result of the emergence and growing primacy of the consumerist and demo-elitist models of democracy. As van de Donk illustrates in his case study of third sector (intermediary) organisations the role and survival of a considerable number of non-state actors appears to be under threat, unless they too can reinvent themselves in a way which 'fits' with the managed, consumerist democracies which seem set to take us into the twenty-first century. Furthermore, van de Donk's work also illustrates that 'steering' and control are no longer centrally located but instead spring from an increased attention to, and strengthening of, vertical flows of information and communication between often disparate governance institutions (elites) and other actors within the polity. This substantially reduces the autonomous role of a wide variety of societal organisations in the (self) organisation of society and therefore transforms a network, or associational, model of democracy into a truly elitist one. In other words, it affords primacy to the 'elitist' dimensions of the model at the expense of the 'demo' dimensions, such as, responsiveness, accountability and the openness of governance institutions.

One final point concerning interpretations of our models needs to be made before we move on to bring this conclusion to a close. This concerns the claim made in Chapter 2 that neo-republicanism draws heavily on communitarian ideas. It is important to recognise that this is in conflict with other current interpretations of neo-republicanism, such as that found in *Citizenship and Community* (Oldfield 1990). A reading of the case studies seems to suggest that communitarianism may more appropriately be associated with a certain form of cyberdemocracy based on the rather traditional grass-roots type of political activity which emphasises the value of strong community and with a strong anti-establishment and 'anti-state' component. This contrasts with another interpretation of cyberdemocracy which is more radical democratic in orientation, stressing reflexivity, competence building, and the acceptance of a 'mixed economy' of social welfare provision.

We conclude this book by returning to our fundamental research question: are the types of ICTs that we now see being introduced into the polities of Western Europe meant to restore or reinvent the electoral chain of command, or are they part of new political practices which indicate the emergence of new models of democracy? On the evidence produced in this volume it appears conclusive that the strategies and discourses employed by various actors to reinvent, religitimate and/or renew the democratic polity result in a steady, definite and discernible move away from the constitutional model. Demo-elitist, and, to a lesser extent, consumer models are in the ascent.

However, this is only a part of the story. As the discussion in Chapter 10 clearly illustrates there are examples of TMIPPs (PEN, the Digital City of Amsterdam, Webgrrls) which carry with them political implications. What remains as an open question is what impact and/or relationship these have on traditional, earthbound, policy processes and policy-makers/elites. Judging by the case studies presented in this book the answer appears to be little, if any, at the state or regional government level, and little, or none, in terms of mainstream political parties. On the basis of this finding it would be logical to suggest that cyberdemocracy in its present form(s) is superfluous to the operation of late modern democracy in our case-study countries and probably in the rest of Europe as well.

Unfortunately, or fortunately, (depending on one's point of view) we have a sneaking suspicion that this interpretation may be awry. It may be the case that we are so tied to mainstream definitions of (geographical) public spheres and the features of such phenomena that we are blind to the emergent virtual activities which allow people to discuss political ideas, develop political identities and express political will in new (and under-researched) ways. Furthermore, our methodological approach – which has been rather top-down in orientation – may not have been open enough to the importance of the development of citizen identities, which, in turn, imply new forms of reflexivity and new (political) competences.

The scenario which emerges then, is of a 'two-tier democracy': a 'big' democracy, concerned with policy and decision-making at a national and international level, dominated by practices associated with demo-elitist and consumer democracy. And a 'small' democracy where 'ordinary' citizens try to make a difference in terms of the quality of their everyday life. The main democratic problem of today seems to be that these two types of democracy are disconnected. This feature of present-day democracy is clearly illustrated by the increasing detachment of intermediary organisations (political parties, voluntary associations, interest organizations, etc.) from their members and/or 'ordinary people' caused by the ongoing professionalisation and integration of such organisations into elite networks, as van de Donk's case study demonstrates. This development has predominantly been interpreted negatively as a 'colonialization of the lifeworld' (Habermas) or an 'erosion of social capital' (Putnam). What seems more important and more interesting, however, is the exploration of the emergence of new citizen roles (identities) *vis-à-vis* both political-representative institutions and public administration, and the new roles being created for organisations in their relationship with the state. As we hope our analysis clearly indicates an exploration of the role of ICTs in this reshaping of the democratic polity is indispensable.

Index

Milton Keynes UK
Ingram Content Group UK Ltd.
UKHW031531071024
449327UK00005B/131